ISBN 978-1-5276-3067-3
PIBN 10140711

1 MONTH OF
FREE
READING

at

www.ForgottenBooks.com

By purchasing this book you are eligible for one month membership to ForgottenBooks.com, giving you unlimited access to our entire collection of over 700,000 titles via our web site and mobile apps.

To claim your free month visit:

www.forgottenbooks.com/free140711

PRAESIDI SOCIISQUE HARVARDIANIS

τροφεῖα

PREFACE.

———•◦•———

THIS book is the result of nearly four years of travel and study in the countries and colonies of which it treats. I have described and discussed no place that I did not visit, and in every one I remained long enough, and was fortunate enough in learning the views and experiences of the local authorities and best-informed residents, to make sure at any rate that I was not misled into mere hasty impressions. If I appear to present some of my conclusions with excessive confidence, this fault is to be explained, and I trust excused, first, by my conviction of the importance to Great Britain of the issues involved, and second, by my faith in the accuracy and wisdom of my many informants.

The Far East presents itself to the attentive traveller under two aspects. It is the last Wonderland of the World; and it is also the seed-bed of a multitude of new political issues. I have endeavoured to reflect in these pages this twofold quality of my subject. Therefore the record of mere travel is interwoven with that of investigation: the incidents and the adventures of the *hour are mingled with the factors and the statistics of the permanent problems. By this means I have hoped to reproduce upon the reader's mind something of the effect of the Far East upon my own. It is a picture which is destined, either in bright colours or in sombre, to become increasingly familiar to him in the future.*

I find myself wholly unable to acknowledge here even a small part of the help and hospitality I received, and I can only express this general but deep obligation. To Sir Robert Hart, Bart., however, first of all; to Sir Cecil Clementi Smith, ex-Governor of the Straits Settlement; to Sir G. William Des Voeux, formerly Governor of Hongkong; and to Mr. F. A. Swettenham, C.M.G., British Resident of Perak, I have to offer my special thanks. To my friend Mr. R. L. Morant, whose knowledge of Siam is more intimate than that of any foreigner living, and who at the time of my stay in Bangkok was governor of the late Crown Prince and tutor to the Royal children, I have to acknowledge great indebtedness. I need hardly add that these gentlemen must not be forcibly connected with any of my opinions. Mr. J. Scott Keltie, Assistant Secretary of the Royal Geographical Society, the Librarian of the Colonial Office, and the Librarian of the Royal Statistical Society, have been good enough to give me valuable technical assistance.

In a few instances I have reproduced here, with considerable alterations, parts of contributions to the daily and periodical Press, chiefly descriptions of places written on the spot. The greater part of the illustrations are from my own photographs; one or two are by that excellent photographer A. Fong, of Hongkong, one or two by Mr. Chit, and one by Mr. Loftus, both of Bangkok. The maps, which present certain geographical facts not—so far as I know—to be found in conjunction elsewhere, have been drawn under my own supervision.

H. N.

LONDON, *December* 31, 1894.

CONTENTS.

PORTUGAL IN THE FAR EAST.

CHINA.

KOREA.

JAPAN.

SIAM.

MALAYA.

CONCLUSION.

LIST OF ILLUSTRATIONS.

MAPS.

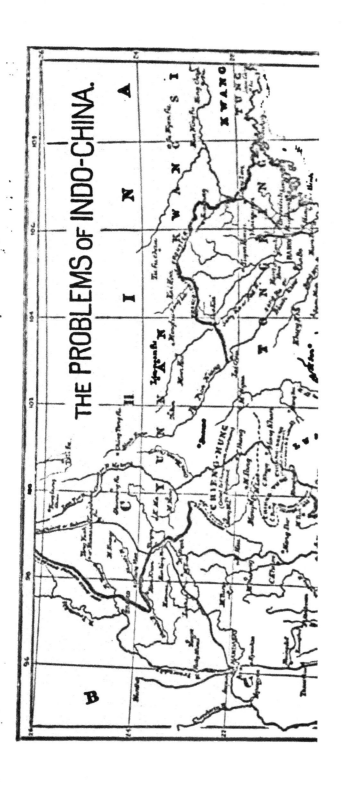

THE PROBLEMS OF INDO-CHINA.

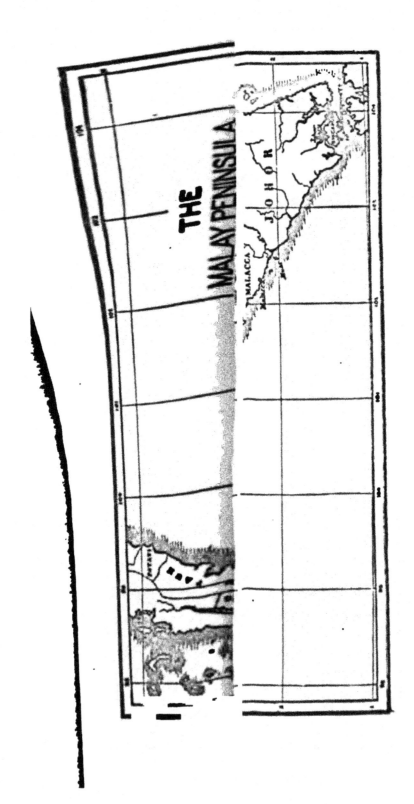

THE
MALAY PENINSULA

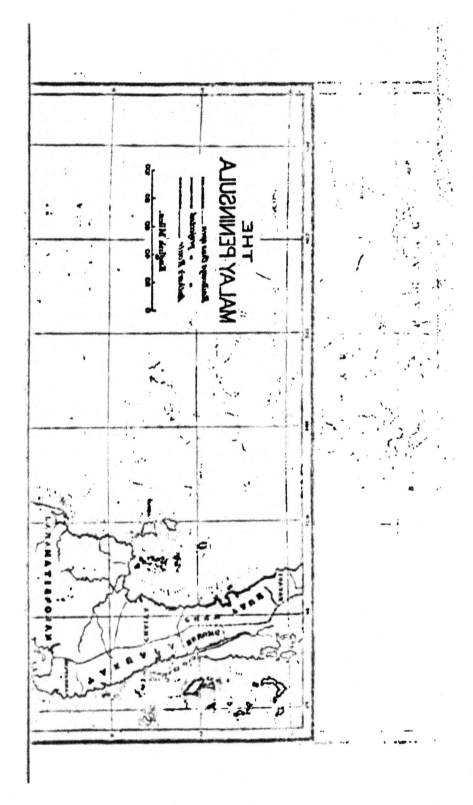

THE
MALAY PENINSULA

THE BRITISH EMPIRE IN THE FAR EAST.

CHAPTER I.

OUTPOSTS OF EMPIRE: SHANGHAI AND HONGKONG.

A N Englishman writing an account of the Far East finds himself in a dilemma at the outset. If he follows his natural inclination to describe at length the British Colonies there, their astonishing history, their race-problems, their commercial achievements, and their exhibition of the colonising genius of his race; and especially if he yields to the temptation to dwell upon their extraordinary picturesqueness, he lays himself open to the just criticism that these are matters already familiar to every one of his readers. On the other hand, if he takes this familiarity for granted, and omits them from his survey, the brightest colour is lacking from the picture and the most potent factor from the problem. This would obviously be the greater evil, and therefore in my own case, risking the reproach, I propose to touch upon the external aspects of the British Colonies in the Far East just enough to convey some notion of the physical conditions and surroundings under which our countrymen there live and labour, and to write at somewhat greater length of a few vital matters which do not present themselves on the surface. One thing, at any rate, can never be told too often or impressed too strongly, namely, that our Far Eastern Colonies are not mere outlying units, each with a sentimental and commercial connection with Great Britain, but bone of the bone of the Empire, and flesh of its flesh.

Among the many surprises of a journey in the Far East, one of the greatest is certainly the first sight of Shanghai.

I was writing below as we steamed up the Hwang-pu river, and did not come on the deck of the *Hae-an* till five minutes before she anchored. Then I could hardly believe my eyes. There lay a magnificent European city surrounding a broad and crowded river. True, the magnificence is only skin-deep, so to speak, all the architectural beauty and solidity of Shanghai being spread out along the river; but I am speaking of the first sight of Shanghai, and in this respect it is superior to New York, far ahead of San Francisco, and almost as imposing for the moment as Liverpool itself. A broad and beautifully kept boulevard, called of course "The Bund," runs round the river, with a row of well-grown trees and a broad grass-plat at the water's edge, and this Bund is lined on the other side from one end to the other with mercantile buildings second to none of their kind in the world—the "hongs" of the great firms, and the banks; the fine edifices of the Masonic Hall and the Shanghai Club; and the magnificent new quarters of the Imperial Customs Service. At the upper end of the Bund a large patch of green shows the Public Garden, where the band plays on summer evenings. At night all Shanghai is bright with the electric light, and its telegraph poles remind you of Chicago—I believe I counted nearly a hundred wires on one pole opposite the Club. And the needed touch of colour is added to the scene as you look at it from on deck, by the gay flags of the mail steamers and the Consular bunting floating over the town.

The first sight of Shanghai, moreover, is only its first surprise. As I was rolling away to the hotel the 'ricksha coolie turned on to the right-hand side of the road. Instantly a familiar figure stepped off the sidewalk and shook a warning finger, and the coolie swung back again to the left side. It was a policeman—no semi-Europeanised Mongolian, languidly performing a half-understood duty, but the genuine home article, helmet, blue suit, silver buttons, regulation boots, truncheon and all—just "bobby." And his uplifted finger turned the traffic to the left in Shanghai precisely as it does in front of the Mansion House. A hundred yards further on there was a flash of scarlet in the sun, and there stood a second astonishing figure—a six-foot copper-coloured Sikh, topped by a huge red turban, and clad also in blue and armed with the same truncheon, striding solemnly by on his beat. Then came the Chinese policeman, with his little saucer hat of red bamboo and his white gaiters, swinging a diminutive staff—a reduced and rather comical replica of his big English and Indian comrades. Then as we crossed the bridge into the French Concession there appeared the *sergent de ville*, absolutely the same as you see him in the Place de l'Opéra—peaked cap, waxed moustache, baggy red trousers, sabre, and revolver. And beyond him again was the Frenchified Chinese policeman. In fact, Shanghai is guarded municipally by no fewer than six distinct species of policemen—English, Sikh, Anglo-Chinese, French, Franco - Chinese, and the long-legged mounted Sikhs on sturdy white ponies, who clank their sabres around the outskirts of the town, and carry terror into the turbulent Chinese quarters.

Shanghai, like so much of the Empire, was originally *spolia opima*. It was captured from the Chinese on June 19, 1842, and opened to foreign trade in November, 1843. It is in the middle of the coast-line of China, in the south-east corner of the province of Kiang-su, at the junction of the rivers Hwang-pu and Woosung (or Soochow Creek), twelve miles above the point where these flow together into the estuary of the Yangtsze. Shanghai is thus practically at the mouth of the great waterway of China, and it is the chief outlet and distributing centre for the huge northern and central provinces. It has been called the " commercial metropolis of China," since so large a percentage of the total foreign trade of China passes through it. The native city, which has about 125,000 inhabitants, and lies behind the foreign city, was an important emporium of trade for centuries. Its walls, which are three miles and a half in circumference, were built in the sixteenth century to keep off an earlier Japanese invasion. The French obtained a grant of their present Settlement in return for services rendered in driving out the rebels in 1853. Shanghai has been the scene of a good deal of warfare. In 1853 the native city was captured by the rebels, who held it for seventeen months. In 1861, the Taiping rebels, after capturing Soochow in the previous year, advanced upon Shanghai, but were driven back by British and Indian regiments, aided by French marines. It was at this time that "Chinese Gordon" appeared upon the scene. The Imperial authorities, at their wits' end, allowed an American adventurer to enlist a number of more or less disreputable foreigners, and with their aid to raise and drill a horde of natives. These passed under the command of another American name Burgevine, who finally deserted to the rebels. The Imperialists were thus left with a mutinous and almost uncontrollable band of their own people to deal with, little more dangerous than the rebels themselves. It was these that Major Gordon, R.E., was allowed to discipline and lead against the Taipings, as the self-christened "Ever-Victorious Army," and it was no doubt owing to his extraordinary prowess that the Imperial authority was re-established. Opinions differ among students of Chinese history as to whether it would not have been better for China had the Taipings succeeded. I came upon many curious reminiscences of General Gordon up and down the coast of China. He was a man of remarkable virtues and of no less remarkable weaknesses, and the stories of him which survive in the Far East would make very interesting reading. I do not give them, however, because public opinion seems to have determined that this many-sided man shall be known under one aspect only of his life—that of hero. I will only say that there is correspondence of his still in existence in China, some of which I have read, which should in the interests of history be published. His opinions of the Viceroy Li Hung-chang, whom he greatly respected and whom he had once spent some time in trying to shoot with his own hand, were of a particularly striking character. The original regulations under which Shanghai is governed were drawn up by the British Consul in 1845. These were amended in 1854 by an agreement between the Consul and the inhabitants; and in 1863 the American Settlement was amalgamated with the British. A number of vain efforts have been made to induce the French to join this, but although much smaller both in area, population, and trade it has declined to do so, and remains under the "Réglement d'Organisation Municipale de la Concession Francaise" of 1862. The other two nationalities have not yet succeeded in agreeing with the diplomatic authorities for the revision of the "Council for the Foreign Community of Shanghai North of the Yang-king-pang" of 1870.

Modern Shanghai is thus divided, like ancient Gaul, into three parts: the English settlement, the American settlement, called Hongkew, and the much smaller French "Concession." Three creeks divide these communities from each other— Yang-king-pang, Soochow Creek, and Defence Creek between the English settlement and China. One wide thoroughfare, called "the Maloo," runs through Shanghai out past the race-course and the Horse-Bazaar into the country, and along this in the afternoon there is a stream of ponies and smart carriages and pedestrians and bicyclists. It is the Rotten Row of Shanghai, leading to the Bubbling Well, and the one country drive the community possesses. But in truth there is not much "country" about it, the environs of Shanghai being flat and ugly—the nearest hill being nineteen miles away, and covered with grave-mounds as thickly as the battlefields round Gravelotte.

Shanghai dubbed itself long ago the "Model Settlement." Then a noble English globe-trotter came along, and afterwards described it in the House of Lords as " a sink of corruption." Thereupon a witty Consul suggested that in future it should be known as the "Model Sink." For my own part I should not grudge it the first title, for it is one of the best governed places municipally—at any rate, so far as the Anglo-American quarters are concerned—that I have ever known. The French, as I have said, live apart under their own Municipal Council, presided over, and even dismissed at pleasure, by their own Consul. The English and American elected Municipal Council consists of nine members, with an elected chairman at its head. And a short stay in Shanghai is sufficient to show how satisfactorily this works. The roads are perfect, the traffic is kept· under admirable direction and control, the streets are quiet and orderly, and even the coolies are forbidden to push their great wheelbarrows through the foreign settlement with ungreased wheels. The third surprise of Shanghai does not dawn upon you immediately. It is a Republic—a community of nations, self-governed and practically independent, for it snaps its fingers politely at the Chinese authorities or discusses any matter with them upon equal terms, and it does not hesitate to differ pointedly in opinion from its own Consuls when it regards their action as unwise or their interference as unwarranted. Over the Chinese within its borders the Municipal Council has, however, no jurisdiction. In the "Maloo" there is a magistrate's Yamôn, and there the famous "Mixed Court" sits every morning, consisting of the Chinese magistrate and one of the foreign Consuls in turn. All natives charged with offences against foreigners or foreign law are dealt with there, petty criminals being punished in the municipal prison or the chain-gang, serious offenders, or refugees from Chinese law, being sent into the native city. The Chinese magistrate in the Mixed Court is, of course, a figure-head, chiefly useful, so far as I could see, in lecturing the prisoners while the foreigner made up his mind what punishment to award. In criminal cases the Mixed Court works fairly well, but in civil suits it gives rise to numerous and bitter complaints. The population of Shanghai on December 31, 1891, was estimated at 4,956 foreigners (British, 1,759; Japanese, 751; Portuguese, 542; French, 332; American, 450; Spanish, 245; German, 330), and Chinese, 175,000.

The Republic of Shanghai has its own army, of course, composed of volunteer infantry, 159 strong; artillery, with 4 guns and 45 men; and a smart but diminutive troop of 38 light horse. It has also volunteer fire-brigades, and no fewer than seven distinct postal systems of different nationalities. An amusing fact in connection with the artillery—amusing chiefly to any one who appreciates the red-tape which binds the military authorities at home, is that the latter presented the Shanghai volunteers with four excellent field-guns, and send out an annual allowance of ammunition. No doubt they believe that Shanghai is a British colony, whereas the fun lies in the fact that it is simply some land leased in perpetuity from the Emperor of China, and that it is always possible—it may be the case to-day for all I know—that a majority of those serving the guns are non-British subjects. But this is only for the joke's sake. The volunteers get great praise from the official inspector each year, and they may be called upon to protect British lives and property at any moment. So the War Office did a wise thing after all, in spite of the fact that the volunteers are a " politically anomalous " body

The social life of Shanghai is the natural outgrowth of its Republican institutions. It is democratic, and characterised by a tolerant good-fellowship. Upon this point a well-known lady was kind enough to set me right. "In Shanghai," she explained, "everybody is equal. In Hongkong everybody is not equal. There are those of us who call at Government House, and those who do not." After so lucid an analysis it was impossible to err. All male Shanghai meets in the Club—one of the most comfortable and complete in the world—before tiffin and before dinner, to exchange news, make up dinner-parties, and do business—all three with equal zest. And the hospitality of Shanghai is another surprise. You might as well attempt to give your shadow the slip as to escape from the gratuitous good cheer of the Model Settlement. As for sport, on the whole Shanghai is ahead of the rest of the East. It has its charming country club, its races twice a year, its regatta, when the Chinese authorities stop all the native traffic on the river, its polo, its two cricket clubs, its base-ball, and its shooting parties in house-boats up the Yangtsze and to the hills twenty miles away. And on Saturday afternoons if you walk out to the Bubbling Well about four o'clock you can see the finish of the paper hunt and a dozen well-mounted and scrupulously-dressed jockeys come riding in to the finish and taking a rather bad fence and ditch which has been carefully prepared with the object of receiving half of them in the sight of their fair friends. Finally, there are the hounds and their master. And what matter if a slanderous tradition does fret their fair fame, to the effect that once upon a time, discarding the deceptive aniseed-bag, a fox was imported from Japan, and that the end of that hunting-day was that one-half the pack ran into an unlucky chow-dog and broke him up, and the other half chased a Chinese boy for his life, while the master stood upon a grave-mound winding his horn to a deserted landscape ?

The trade of Shanghai may be roughly divided under five heads: imports—cotton piece-goods, metals, and kerosene oil; exports—tea and silk. The tea trade, as elsewhere in China, has fallen off grievously of late, owing to the gradual fall in quality, and the competition of Ceylon and Indian teas. Foreign tea-men have made efforts of every kind to induce Chinese growers to improve their processes of preparation, but without much result. It is chiefly in the English market, however, that the trade has suffered. Improvement in quality (says the Commissioner of Customs) is an absolute necessity, but " China can never hope to produce a tea which will compare with Indian according to the only standard which now seems to be applicable in England —the standard of strength, the capacity to colour, to a certain point of darkness, so many gallons of water to each pound of tea." It seems as unlikely that the Chinese will learn to improve their qualities as that we shall learn how to know good tea from bad, and how to " make " it when we have secured it. To every

Eastern tea-drinker the tea served at the best houses in England would be a horror. Nobody who has not travelled in the East, and arrived, after a day's tramp through a malarious and steaming jungle, at some poor Chinaman's shanty, and thankfully drunk a dozen cups of the beverage freely offered, can know how delicious and invigorating even the most modest tea can be. The same cause has already produced a standstill and will soon produce a reduction in the Chinese silk trade. Chinese silk would be as good as any in the world if it were properly prepared, but it is now used only to add to other kinds; whereas Japanese silk, because prepared with Western methods and conscientious intelligence, has increased its output tenfold since Japan began to sell it to foreigners. This is the old, old story of China, and it will probably never be altered until foreigners contrive—or their governments for them—to exert authority in the Celestial Kingdom, as well as to tender advice and drive bargains. The figures of Shanghai trade are, of course, a striking testimony to the preponderance of British interests and enterprise. In 1893 the number of ships entered and cleared, both under steam and sail, was 6,317, with a total tonnage of 6,529,870. Of these, 3,092 were British, and their tonnage 3,664,175. Or, to exhibit the comparative insignificance of the shipping of all other foreign nations, out of the above grand totals British and Chinese ships together numbered no fewer than 4,721, with a tonnage of no less than 5,280,310. The total foreign trade of Shanghai for 1893 was 139,268,000 Haikwan taels,* of which Great Britain, Hongkong, and India stand for 80,826,000, or over 58 per cent, besides trade with

* It is practically impossible to give the accurate gold equivalent of these sums. First, because silver falls so rapidly that a calculation of exchange is obsolete before it gets back from the printer; and second, because the purchasing power of silver in the East has not fallen to anything like the same extent as its exchange against gold. The average exchange of the Haikwan or Customs tael for 1893 was 3s. 11¼d., and the British Consul calculates at this figure, making the total foreign trade £27,418,388. In dealing with the figures of the Chinese Imperial Maritime Customs later on I have reckoned the tael at 3s. 4d., as a nearer approximation.

other parts of the British Empire which it is impossible to calculate separately. The direct trade with Great Britain, both
imports and exports, has fallen off greatly during the past twenty
years, largely because the Suez Canal has brought the southern
ports of Europe into closer communication with China. But the
trade between China and India is growing rapidly, although the
export of opium to China from Indian ports is falling steadily
and will ultimately all but disappear.

It is curious that by the "Land Regulations," which form
the Constitution of Shanghai, the Chinese are forbidden to
reside or hold property within the Foreign Settlements, and
yet there are 175,000 of them afloat and ashore; and I fancy
even Shanghai itself would be astounded if it could be told
exactly what proportion of the whole property is in their hands.
There has been a good deal of talk about this, and in reply to
a "Cassandra" who wrote to the papers that nothing could save
Shanghai but amalgamation with the Chinese, a local writer
produced some witty verses, telling how in a vision in the
twentieth century—

> "I passed a lawyer's office, on the shingle
>   Was ' Wang and Johnson, Barristers-at-law ';
>   Where'er the nations had begun to mingle,
>   Chinese came first, I saw.

> "A steamer passed; a native gave the orders;
>   An English quartermaster held the wheel;
>   The chain-gang all were white, the stalwart warders
>   Yellow from head to heel."

Physically, at any rate, the Chinese are undoubtedly crowding out the Europeans. The wealthy Celestial keenly appreciates the fact that his person and his property are infinitely
securer under the Union Jack and the Stars and Stripes than
under the rapacious and unrestrained rule of the representative
of the Son of Heaven. He is therefore prepared to pay whatever may be necessary to secure a good piece of property within
which to live and trade in the foreign settlement. Whenever
such a piece comes into the market it is almost sure to be

knocked down to a Chinese purchaser. "Very many retired and expectant officials now make their homes in Shanghai, also many merchants who have made money. As a result, the best paying property is Chinese occupied, and of that the best is the property on which stand the pretentious establishments which furnish amusement to the Chinese *jeunesse dorée*—a class which in pre-Taiping days counted Soochow and Hangchow earthly paradises, and which now finds that the pleasures of those capitals are as abundantly supplied in the Foochow Road. This influx of Chinese has had the effect of compelling foreigners, and especially those of small means, to seek every year dwellings farther away from the busy centres, which the Chinese now monopolise. The rents of foreign houses in the Settlements are gradually rising, for as each old foreign building is pulled down Chinese houses take its place." *

Another very great and indeed vital change has come over Shanghai of late years. Formerly business was done by real merchants—that is, traders who bought to sell again. Those were the days of quickly-realised and enormous fortunes—of the merchant-princes of the Far East, whose hospitality, formerly famous the world over, is now but a golden tradition, since "luxurious living is practised by old-timers rather in obedience to ancient custom than justified by present affluence." Now the merchant, if not already extinct, is rapidly becoming so, and his place taken by the commission agent. Competition and the incalculable and ruinous fluctuations of exchange are the two factors which have brought about this result. Both as regards the character of business done, and the *personnel* of those who do it, the change is for the worse. Little or no capital is necessary, as every detail of the transactions is fixed beforehand by telegraph—the price of the goods, the freight, and the rate of exchange. It is therefore possible to do business on a very small margin, with the result that men under-bid one another

* Mr. R. E. Bredon's very able Report on Shanghai, Chinese Imperial Maritime Customs, Decennial Reports, 1882-1891.

down to the last fraction, and the further result that an
unscrupulous member of the trading community is tempted to
get business of this kind by any and every means. It is obvious
that more intimate relations between the Chinese themselves
and the European markets would soon result in the elimination
of the foreign agent altogether.

Two other causes are also appearing to transform the
Shanghai of old time, and indeed all the business relations
between foreigners and Chinese. The first is the growth of
Chinese manufactures. The Chinese Cotton Cloth Mill Company, the Chinese Spinning Company, the Shanghai Paper Mill
Company, the Min-li Ginning Mill Company, and the Yuen-chee
Ginning Mill Company, are all Chinese concerns, with Chinese
capital and under Chinese management, with foreign technical
assistance. The first-named of these is supposed to be financed
by the Viceroy Li Hung-chang himself. It was recently completely destroyed by fire, but is being rebuilt on a much larger
scale than before. These enterprises have not yet paid much
in the way of dividend, owing probably to inexperienced direction, but there is no reason to suppose that they will not be
successful in the end. And their success would probably mean
a nearly proportionate amount of European failure. The reader
will naturally ask at once why foreigners have not started such
concerns themselves. The answer is based to a great extent
upon the supineness of a recent British Minister to China. The
Chinese claim—without any justice, so far as I can make out—
that the treaties give no right to foreigners to manufacture
within the treaty limits, and their claim has never met with
serious official resistance. They even go so far as to prohibit,
without a special permit, the importation of machinery on
foreign account, which is ridiculously in contradiction of plain
treaty rights. It is to be hoped that one among the innumerable results of the present war will be the settlement of this
question in favour of Europeans. The benefits to Chinese con-
sumers would be incalculable, and the whole world might well

gain an enormous and unexpected advantage from the opening of China which would almost necessarily ensue, since, as has been truly said,* if China were only fairly open to foreign enterprise, there is room in her vast territories and among her millions of inhabitants for all the surplus silver of the world for many years to come.

In connection with this probable cause of a change in the future of Shanghai must also be mentioned the great and increasing amount of purely Chinese capital invested, not only in native enterprises within treaty limits, such as those I have mentioned, but also in foreign companies, with foreign management, and known by foreign names. The China Merchants' Steam Navigation Company, with its fine fleet, represents a large native investment, in which the Viceroy Li is again prominent, and it is freely said that many ships trading under foreign flags are in reality Chinese property. Moreover, although this is a well-kept secret, a surprising proportion of the deposits in foreign banks is believed to stand in Chinese names. In view of all this extensive and constantly growing Chinese investment in property, mortgages, shipping, manufacturing enterprises, and banking deposits, it is inevitable that those who thus pay the piper should claim more and more the right to call the tune. The second cause of the change to be anticipated is Japanese competition with European firms for the foreign trade of China. This is a factor of the greatest future importance, but discussion of it will come more appropriately in a later chapter. Though Shanghai may change, however, and indeed must change, there is no reason to despair of its future as an outpost of British Trade. The openings for foreigners and foreign capital may both decrease, but the bulk of trade will increase. Mr. Commissioner Bredon says, "I think the future of Shanghai depends on China and the Chinese and their interests, and that foreigners would be wise to run with them," and his opinion should carry great weight. Two

* By Mr. Consul Jamieson, F. O. Reports, Annual Series, No. 1442, p. 23.

events, on the other hand, may open up for Shanghai a future brighter than its brightest past. The Chinese railway may make it into the link between the whole of China and the rest of the world; or the present war may end by throwing China open at last, in which case the unequalled situation of Shanghai would give it the lion's share of the enormous trade that would arise.

The first sight of Hongkong, the farthest outpost of the British Empire and the fourth port in the world, is disappointing. As you approach it from the north you enter a narrow and unimposing pass: then you discover a couple of sugar-refineries covering the hills with smoke; and when the city of Victoria lies before you it is only St. John's or Vladivostok on a larger scale. It is piled up on the steep sides of the island without apparent purpose or cohesion; few fine buildings detach themselves from the mass; there is no boulevard along the water-front; and the greater part of the houses and offices in the immediate foreground, though many of them are in reality large and costly structures, look a medley from a little distance. In one's disappointment one remembers Mr. Howell's caustic characterisation of the water-front of New York—that after London and Liverpool it looks as though the Americans were encamped there. The face of Hongkong is not its fortune, and anybody merely steaming by would never guess the marvel it grows on closer acquaintance. For a few weeks' investigation transfigures this precipitous island into one of the most astonishing spots on the earth's surface. By an inevitable alchemy, the philosopher's stone of a few correlated facts transforms one's disappointment into stupefaction. Shanghai is a surprise, but Hongkong is a revelation.

When you land at the city of Victoria (it is strange, by the way, that almost everybody at home and half the visitors there are ignorant that "Victoria" is the name of the city and "Hongkong" of the island), the inevitable 'ricksha carries you through a couple of streets, far from being beautiful or well-

managed, but you forget this in the rush of life about you.
Messengers jostle you, 'rickshas run over your toes, chair-poles
dig you in the ribs. The hotel clerk smiles politely as he in-
forms you that there has not been a vacant room for a month.
Later on your fellow-passengers envy you the little rabbit-hole
of a bedroom you have secured at the top of the Club. When
you come down again into the hall you find it crowded with
brokers of many nationalities, making notes, laughing, whisper-
ing, drinking, but all just as busy as they can be. The Stock
Exchange of Hongkong was the gutter, the local Rialto extending from the Club for about a hundred yards down the
Queen's Road, and it was filled with Britishers, Germans, Anglo-
Indians, Chinese from Canton, Armenians from Calcutta, Parsees
from Bombay, and Jews from Baghdad, and with that peculiar
contingent known as the "black brigade," recognisable by the
physiognomy of Palestine and the accent of Spitalfields. And
on the Club walls and tables are a dozen printed "Expresses,"
timed with the minute at which they were issued, and the mail
and shipping noon and afternoon "extras" of the daily papers,
announcing the arrivals and departures of steamers, the distribution of cargoes, the sales by auction, and all the multi-
tudinous movements of a great commercial machine running at
high pressure. For, to apply to the Far East the expressive
nomenclature of the Far West, this colony "just hums" all
the time. At least, it hummed in this way on the many occasions when I was there, as it will hum again, though just at
present, what with the utter reaction from over-speculation, the
general depression of trade, the fluctuations of silver, and
the paralysing effect of the plague, Victoria is a depressed
and rather unhappy place. Then the chair a friend has
sent to take you to dinner arrives, with its four coolies
uniformed in blue and white calico, and by another twist
of the kaleidoscope you find yourself, three minutes after
leaving the Club, mounting an asphalte roadway at an angle
not far short of forty-five degrees, hemmed in above and on

either hand by great green palms and enormous drooping ferns
with fronds yards long, among which big butterflies are playing
round long scarlet flowers. For as soon as you begin to ascend,
the streets of Hongkong might be alleys in the tropical con-
servatories at Kew.

Hongkong is built in three layers. The ground-floor, so to
speak, or sea-level, is the commercial part of the Colony. The
"Praya" along the water's edge is given up to shipping, and is
altogether unworthy of the place. It is about to be changed,
however, by a magnificent undertaking, now in progress,
the "Praya Reclamation Scheme," originated and pressed to
a successful issue by the Hon. C. P. Chater, by which the
land frontage will be pushed out 250 feet, and a depth
of twenty feet secured at all states of the tide. The next
street, parallel to it, Queen's Road, is the Broadway of Hongkong, and all the business centres upon it. In the middle
are the Club, post-office, courts, and hotels; then come all the
banks and offices and shops; past these to the east are the
different barracks, and as one gradually gets further from the
centre, come the parade-ground, cricket-ground, polo-ground, and
race-course, and the wonderfully picturesque and pretty cemetery, the "Happy Valley." In the other direction you formerly
passed all the Chinese shops for foreigners and then got into
Chinatown, a quarter of very narrow streets, extremely dirty,
inconceivably crowded, and probably about as insanitary as any
place on the globe under civilised rule. I never ceased to
prophesy two things about Hongkong, one of which, the epidemic, has come true indeed. The other waits, and as it is
rather alarmist it is perhaps better left out of print. The worst
parts of Chinatown have now been destroyed, literally at the
cannon's mouth, and in spite of every possible Chinese threat,
so that this blot on the Colony is erased. This is all on the
island of Hongkong. while across the harbour, in the British
territory of Kowloon, a new city is springing up—a splendid
frontage of wharves and warehouses; a collection of docks, one

of which will take almost any ship afloat; half a dozen summer-houses, a little palace among them—whose splendid hospitality is for the moment eclipsed; and the pleasure-gardens and kitchen-gardens of the community.

The second storey of Hongkong lies ten minutes' climb up the steep side of the island. Here nearly everybody lives, and lives, too, in a luxury and ease that are not suspected at home. Here is Government House, a fine official residence in beautiful grounds; Headquarter House; and the wonderful streets I have already mentioned, although one might as properly call Windsor a house as describe these palm-shaded walks and groves as streets.

Finally, there is the third layer, the top storey of Hongkong, known collectively as "The Peak." The Peak itself is one of the highest of the hundred hills of the island, rising precipitously behind the city to the signal station, 1,842 feet above the sea, where a gun and a flagstaff announce the arrival of mails and ocean steamers. But "The Peak" as a residential district means all the hill-tops where cool breezes from the sea blow in summer, where one can sleep under a blanket at night, and where, in a word, one can spend a summer in Hongkong with a reasonable probability of being alive at the end of it. Here everybody who can afford it has a second house, and so many are these fortunate people that the "top side" of the island is dotted all over with costly houses and bungalows; there are two hotels, and a steam tramway runs up and down every fifteen minutes. The fare up is thirty cents—a shilling—and down half as much. This is startling enough, but a better notion of the expense of life here is conveyed by the fact that to have a second house at "The Peak" for the summer you must rent it for the whole year, as it is uninhabitable in winter, at a rental of 150 to 200 dollars a month—about a sovereign a day all the year round for four or five months' residence. Besides this, there is the tramway fare, the cost of coolies to carry your chair up and down, and the expense of bringing every item of domestic supplies, from coals to cabbage, a forty-five minutes' climb uphill. But what is the summer climate on the second storey of Hongkong which forces people to flee from it at so much trouble and cost? To be frank, almost every man I asked before I had experience of it, described it to me by the monosyllabic appellation of the ultimate destination of the incorrigible unrighteous. One of the chief summer problems of Hongkong is to determine whether the mushrooms which grow on your boots during the night are edible or not. The damp is indescribable. Moisture pours down the walls; anything left alone for a couple of days—clothes, boots, hats, portmanteaus—is covered with mould. Twenty steps in the open air and you are soaked with perspiration. Then there are the cockroaches, to say nothing of the agile centipede whose bite may lay you up for a month. When the booksellers receive a case of books, the first thing they do is to varnish them all over with a damp-resisting composition containing corrosive sublimate. Otherwise the cockroaches would eat them before they had time to go mouldy. If you come home at night after dinner very tired, beware of carelessly throwing your evening clothes over a chair, as you would at home. If you do, the cockroaches will have destroyed them before you wake. They must be hung up in a wardrobe with hermetically fitting doors. It does happen, too, that men die in summer in Hongkong between sunrise and sunset without rhyme or reason. And the community is a pale-faced one, though it is only right to add that it numbers probably as many athletes and vigorous workers as any other. The place used to be known as "the grave of regiments"—a stroll through "Happy Valley" tells you why. Now the men are not allowed outside barracks in summer until five p.m., and there is a regular inspection to see that every man has his cholera-belt on. The "down side" of Hongkong is damp and hot; the "top side" is damp and cool. That is the difference for which people are prepared to pay so heavily. The first time I stayed at "The Peak" I noticed round the house a number of large stoppered bottles, such as you see in druggists' windows, prettily encased in wicker-work. On inquiring of my host he showed me that one contained biscuits, another cigars, another writing-paper, and so on, each hollow stopper being filled with unslaked lime in filtering paper, to absorb any damp that might penetrate inside. These bottles tell the whole tale. People run over to Macao, that Lusitanian Thule, four hours' steaming away, for Sunday, and when the summer is proving too much for them and their thoughts begin to run on "Happy Valley" and a grave there—like that of Martha's husband in Padua, "well-placed for cool and comfortable rest"—they just go on board a steamer and disembark at Nagasaki or Yokohama. Japan is the sanitarium of the Far East.

A striking feature of Hongkong is the elegance and solidity of its public works. Its waterworks at Tytam, on the other side of the island, are almost picturesque, and the aqueduct which supplies the city is the basis of a footway three miles long, called the Bowen Road, of asphalte and cement as smooth and solid as a billiard-table, which laughs at the tremendous downpours of the rainy season. "Happy Valley" is the pride of Hongkong, and the palm-shaded road I described above was a dangerous and ugly ravine called "Cut-throats' Alley" a few years ago. Speaking of cut-throats reminds me that Hongkong even now is not a particularly safe place. People avoid walking alone at night in one or two directions; every Sikh constable carries a rifle at night and several rounds of ball cartridge, and if you hail a sampan at night to go to dinner on board some ship in the harbour, the constable at the pier makes a note of its number, in case you should be missing the next day. For these sampan people used to have a pleasant habit of suddenly dropping the mat awning on the head of a passenger, cutting his throat in the ensuing struggle and dropping his pillaged body overboard. The Sikhs make admirable policemen, obedient, trustworthy, and brave, and are correspondingly

detested by the Chinese. If they sin at all, it is from too much
zeal, and I believe they take a keen personal pleasure in whack-
ing a Chinaman. There is a story to the effect that during an
epidemic of burglaries general orders were issued to them to
arrest all suspicious-looking people who did not halt when
challenged at night, especially if they had ladders. Next night
a Sikh on duty saw a Chinaman on the top of a ladder. Nothing
could have been clearer, so he challenged the man, who paid no
attention, and then fired and brought him down. It was the
lamplighter. Even now no Chinaman is supposed to be out
after nine p.m. without a pass.

Unlike Shanghai, which is an international republic, Hongkong is, of course, a genuine British colony, and in no part
of the world is the colonising genius of the British race, or the
results of its free-trade policy, better shown. It was ceded to
the British in January, 1841, as one result of the war which
broke out between Great Britain and China in 1839, and its
cession was finally recognised by the Treaty of Nankin in 1842.
At that time its population consisted of a few thousands of
Chinese fishermen, since it was to all intents and purposes a
barren island. So far were even competent judges from fore-
seeing its marvellous future, that in a valuable book on China
written by R. M. Martin in 1847, there is a chapter called
" Hongkong, its position, prospects, character, and utter worth-
lessness in every point of view to England." From the beginning, however, it has been the Aladdin's palace of commerce.
The island itself has an area of only twenty-nine square miles,
and the whole colony, including a couple of little islands and
the strip of territory known as British Kowloon on the mainland exactly opposite, just over thirty-two. Kowloon constitutes
our frontier with China in the Far East. It is two and
one-third miles in length, and is guarded in a peculiar way.
The duty on opium going into China is so high that the profits
on smuggling it have always tempted the Chinese, the most
expert smugglers in the world, to evade the Customs in any

way and at any risk. From the free port of Hongkong the greatest danger in this respect was to be apprehended. The Chinese Imperial Maritime Customs have a station at Kowloon, with the business office situated, for purposes of convenience, within the British colony. They have a small fleet of revenue cruisers to stop all junks and Chinese steamers, and they have built an impassable fence of bamboo, eight feet high, between British and Chinese territory. In this there are six gateways, each guarded by a post of revenue officers, while on the Chinese side there is a broad solid road ceaselessly patrolled night and day by a Customs force, consisting of over one hundred "braves" armed with loaded Winchester repeating-rifles, and under the command of six foreigners. To avoid possible frictions or collusions, these are all of non-British nationality. It is a curious fact, by the way, as will be seen from my photograph of the advanced French frontier-post at Monkay, that both England and France are separated from China by a rampart of bamboo, that strange and accommodating plant which serves more purposes than anything else that grows.

The situation of Hongkong has, of course, had most to do with its unexampled progress. It is the furthest eastern dependency of the Crown, and forms the end of the arm of the Empire which stretches round the south of Asia. The next step in advance northward will be forced upon us within a very short time by both commercial and strategical considerations, but nothing can seriously interfere with the importance of Hongkong as the next station north of Singapore, from which it is 1,400 miles. A coaling station and naval base at least a thousand miles further north has become a necessity if we are to hold our predominant position in the Far East, and for this purpose Port Hamilton will certainly not do. Hongkong is 79 miles from Canton, the greatest trading city of China, and an excellent service of daily steamers keeps the two in touch. Macao, of little and decreasing importance, is 40 miles away; the Philippines are 650; Saigon is 900;

Shanghai, 824; Bangkok, 1,454; Yokohama, 1,575; and Vladivostok, 1,670. The former barren and almost uninhabited island is thus the focus of the Far East to-day.

From a military and naval point of view Hongkong is one of the most important stations in the Empire. Its docks and machine-shops are worthy of its position, several large ships, and countless small ones, having been built and launched from them. The Admiralty dock is 500 feet long, 86 in breadth at the top and 70 at the bottom, and 29 feet deep. The land defences of the Colony consist of six divisions: Stonecutter's Island, Belcher's Bay, Kowloon West, North Point, Kowloon Dock, and Lyeemoon Fort. The armament of the chief of these consists of the justly-abused 10-inch and the admirable 9.2-inch guns. The place is probably quite impregnable from the sea on the harbour side, but to make sure there is need to fortify Green Island, since otherwise ships coming round the island would not be visible from Stonecutter's or Belcher's till they were almost in sight of the town. Any nation except our own would have fortified this point years ago. Hongkong is one of the few defences armed with the famous Watkins "position-finder," for which the British Government paid so much. By this all the guns of all the chief batteries can be aimed and fired by one man in a commanding and secure position. With the principal entrances mined—all preparations for which exist in the most complete and detailed manner—any hostile fleet attacking Hongkong harbour would in all human probability come utterly to grief. The weak point is well known to be on the other side. In the military manœuvres the attacking force has got in again and again. The redoubts are all planned, and there are plenty of machine-guns and a few howitzers, but with the large forces of infantry possessed by Russia in Siberia, and by France in Tongking, to say nothing of the powerful Japanese army, it is impossible to feel quite happy about Hongkong until its southern side is protected as well as its harbour. Especially is this the case if the common remark of naval men, that in the event of war the fleet would at once put to sea and leave Hongkong to take care of itself, is to be taken literally.

To my thinking, however, Hongkong is in more danger from the Chinese than from any other quarter. Kowloon City is a mass of roughs; Canton is the most turbulent and most foreigner-hating city in China; 20,000 Chinese could come down to Hongkong in a few hours; and a strike of Chinese servants would starve out the Colony. Before Kowloon was added to the Colony, a Hongkong head was worth thirty dollars, and "braves" used to come down to try and get them. The defences have lately been increased by a regiment of Indian troops, with a strength of 10 British officers and 1,014 natives of all ranks, who were raised in a marvellously short time, and have been brought to a high point of discipline and efficiency, and besides those there is always a regiment of British troops and a force of engineers and garrison artillery stationed there. As an example, however, of the power of the Chinese, it may be remembered that when it was found necessary to isolate and fumigate the horrible Chinese quarters during the recent outbreak of plague in the Colony, this could only be done under the guns of the fleet, and the actual work was performed by British volunteers.[*] Asia—always excepting Japan—never has been civilised and never will be, till a greater change comes than this age is likely to see, otherwise than at the mouth of the cannon and the point of the bayonet. At home this statement will doubtless be regarded by many excellent people with feelings akin to horror, but all who know the East will know it to be true.

This question of the relations of foreigners and Chinese presents much the same general aspect in Hongkong as it does in Shanghai. Here, too, the Chinese merchant is

[*] It is to be hoped that the permanent committee of the Sanitary Board, and the soldiers, will receive some official recognition of their efforts, for it was chiefly by them that the plague was eradicated.

crowding out the British middleman; here, too, it cannot be very long before the bulk of the real estate of the Colony is owned by Chinese. Every day they are advancing further into the European quarter, and Chinese merchants are among the richest men in the community. "In every dispute between the Chinese and the Government," said a well-informed resident to me, "the former have come off victorious." By and by, therefore, we .shall have virtually a Chinese society under the British flag, ruled by a British governor. Such is "Empire," and I see no particular reason to regret the fact, even if it were not impossible to do anything to alter it. The Empire depends upon trade first of all, and such a community must always form the strongest trading link between Great Britain and China. By means of trade alone the Empire stands for the welfare and civilisation of the greatest number, and these are undoubtedly to be found in the direction here prophesied. At any rate, whether we like it or not, and whether we welcome it or oppose it, this change is inevitable.[*]

Besides this "danger," however, if it be one, there is the real danger arising from the unruly and criminal Chinese. In spite of all denials, piracy is still rife in the waters round Hongkong. Chinese junks are the constant victims, and the eyes of the Colony were opened in 1890 by the piracy of the British steamer *Namoa*, which was seized by her Chinese passengers, two of her officers and a number of her crew shot, the remaining officers and European passengers imprisoned in the cabin, like another "Black Hole," for eight hours, the captain dying there, the loot transferred into six junks which came alongside at a signal, and then abandoned, after the windlass had been broken, the fires drawn, the lifeboats stove

---

[*] To escape being misunderstood, let me make it quite clear that I think this Chinese progress absolutely dependent upon British guidance and control, both political and commercial, and ask that what precedes and follows about the Chinese in our Colonies may be read in connection with my chapters about the Chinese in China.

in, and the side-lights thrown overboard. A long time afterwards a number of men were beheaded in Kowloon for the piracy, among them being at least one man who had been concerned in the piracy of the *Greyhound* years before. Only a few months ago disturbances broke out in Hongkong between the members of two rival clans, the Sze Yap and the Tun Kun, and work among many coolies was suspended for a time in consequence, and many steamers delayed The police were kept very active and the military under arms, while a guerilla warfare was carried on among the rival clans " the combatants watching for victims of the opposite party, and attacking them individually in quiet places, or shooting them from the tops of houses." Another piece of terrorism occurred when five hundred men employed on the new reservoir were frightened from their work. " A military procession," said a local paper, " with a few small dragons in the shape of field and Maxim guns, would probably exercise a wholesome influence upon the Cantonese swashbucklers who now fancy they can work their own sweet will in this British Colony." Hongkong is. in fact, an Arcadia for the criminals of the neighbouring province, who first plan their outrages there and then take refuge in it when their *coup* has been effected. If the hue and cry after them becomes too hot, they commit some small offence against the laws of the Colony, with the view to getting committed to prison for a few months, under which circumstances they are absolutely safe against the pursuit of detectives from their own country. Even if they are discovered, arrested, and formally charged, the difficulties in the way of their rendition are so great that they have a good chance of getting off after all. For as the British authorities know very well that torture and punishment await all whom they give up, they are naturally chary of handing prisoners over, notwithstanding any assurances of fair trial that may be given, and they therefore insist that a man shall be proved guilty *prima facie* before he is surrendered, with the result that the Chinese authorities regard British law as a means whereby their own criminals escape punishment, as many of them undoubtedly do.

The population of Hongkong in 1893 was 238,724, of whom the whites were 8,545, the Indians 1,001, and the Chinese 210,995. This included the strength of the garrison. In addition there was a boat-population of no fewer than 32,035 Chinese. The expenditure of the Colony was 1,920,523 dols., and its revenue 2,078,185 dols.,* the latter showing a net decrease of 158,000 dols. and the former of 422,000 dols. The assets of the Colony are put down at 2,417,054 dols., and its liabilities at 928,031 dols. Its military contribution is £40,000, paid in quarterly instalments. The ascending scale of Colonial contribution in the present state of silver may be judged from the statement that the four quarters of 1893 were paid in the following amounts of dollars—72,000, 72,000, 75,000, and 77,000, and that for 1894 the total will amount to 400,000 dols., or one-fifth of the entire revenue. Hongkong being a free port there

* It is useless to attempt to translate these figures into sterling, as explained in footnotes elsewhere. During 1893 the Mexican dollar fell from 2s. 8½d. to 2s. 8¾d., and now stands at 2s. 1½d., with entire uncertainty as to the future. The Chambers of Commerce of Hongkong and Singapore have petitioned in favour of a British dollar, and it seems clear that such a coin should be introduced. There is not the slightest reason for the persistence of the Mexican dollar, and many against it, and a British dollar is the only alternative to the legalisation of the Japanese yen, the objections to which are too obvious to mention. It is preposterous that the Power doing beyond all comparison a preponderance of trade with the Far East should be dependent upon foreign coins like the Mexican dollar and Japanese yen. A British dollar, now a rare coin, was introduced in 1866, but time was not allowed for its general acceptance, and the Hongkong mint was closed two years later and its machinery sold to Japan. (See Chalmers's "History of Currency in the British Colonies," pp. 375 sqq.—a work of great industry and ability.) The British dollar should, of course, be the metallic counterpart of the familiar "Mexican," and it is to be hoped that among the opportunities for reform offered by the results of the present Japanese war with China, this question may not fail of solution. As an example of the inconvenience now prevailing I may add that when I was preparing for the exploration of the unknown north of the Malay Peninsula, of which an account is given in a later chapter of this book, I was indebted to the courtesy of the Penang branch of the Chartered Bank of India, Australia and China for a supply of the old "pillar" dollars which alone are accepted there, and that I had to pay a premium of nine per cent. for them. [Since the above was in type, the coinage of a British dollar has been sanctioned.]

are no custom-house statistics available, but the record of shipping gives some idea of the trade of this astounding place. The total shipping entered and cleared in 1893 was 14,023,866 tons, of which the British flag covered 7,732,195 tons. This is already an extraordinary proportion, but a little investigation shows it to be far more striking than thus appears. The non-British shipping of the Port of Hongkong remains from the above figures at 6,291,671 tons, but of this Chinese ships carried 4,389,551 tons. Excluding Chinese ships, therefore, the British shipping trade of Hongkong was 7,732,195 tons, against 1,902,120 tons carried by all other foreign nations put together.

In spite of all its commercial progress, however, and its vital position in the Empire, Hongkong is in many respects curiously behind the civilisation of its time. One may say roughly, for instance, that the law of the Colony to-day is the law—both Common and Statute—that was in force in England on April 5, 1843. I saw several Europeans in Hongkong gaol for debt. There is no Married Women's Property Act in force, although this actually exists in Chinese law. There is no copyright for British authors under their own flag, and I saw the counters of the foreign book-sellers crowded with pirated reprints of contemporary authors. An Englishman living in the foreign settlement at Canton— Shameen—is under one law; an Englishman living in Hongkong under another. Hongkong is still—or to be quite exact, was when I was last there—under the Bankruptcy Acts of 1849 and 1861. A petition had been presented, signed by all the Chinese merchants of the Colony, suggesting amendments suitable to local circumstances, but the authorities would have none of them, so it was referred home, and the Secretary of State ordered the suggestions to be introduced. This was already six years ago, and nothing had been done. The amalgamation of Law and Equity has never been introduced in fact, whatever may have happened in theory. " Our law," said a leading local lawyer to me, " is antediluvian. You cannot even get a copy of the Hongkong Ordinances—that is, of the

complete law of the Colony.　If Hongkong had not been blessed
with reasonable judges, we could never have got on at all."
Hongkong has long desired a Municipality, to deal with all
local matters except such—the defences, for example—as are of
a purely Imperial nature, but this justifiable ambition has been
snubbed again and again.　A growing dissatisfaction, however,
has been shown with the system of official and unofficial
membership of the Legislative Council.　The former all vote as
they are required by the Governor, and the latter are in a
minority　The official members once showed some signs of
voting according to their own views, but the Governor promptly
put his foot down upon such insubordination.　"Gentlemen,"
he said to the official members at the next Council meeting,
" you are quite at liberty to speak and vote as you like; but if,
holding official positions, you oppose the government, it will be
the duty of the government to inquire whether it is for its
advantage that you should continue to hold those positions."
Official salaries, therefore, are consequent on official votes.
Among my notes about Hongkong I find this remark was
made to me: "An official member has never made a full and
free speech on any subject since Hongkong was a Colony."
The spirit of free criticism, however, has now sprung up,
thanks chiefly to the independence and tenacity of one unofficial member, the Hon. T. H. Whitehead　From the time
of his election, five years ago, as the representative of the
Chamber of Commerce, he has refused, in spite of every species
of pressure and influence, to fall into line with the old tradition
which prescribes that the unofficial member should make a
speech, including a mild protest in extreme cases, accept with
a deferential bow the Governor's assurance that " the honourable member's remarks shall not fail to receive every consideration," and then let the matter drop.　Mr. Whitehead, on the
contrary, has been unkind enough to make the lives of government officials burdens to them by his insistence upon expla-
nations, justifications, facts, statistics, records and appeals to

the higher authorities in England. It is not supposed, to adapt Mr. Kipling's amusing verse, to be good for the health of an unofficial member to hustle a Colonial Governor, but Mr. Whitehead has thriven greatly in the exercise. He holds a position which gives him an intimate knowledge of the affairs and finances of the Colony, and it is doing him bare justice to say that he is on the way to revolutionise the management of official matters. He is strongly supported by the commercial community, whose interests he thoroughly understands, and the Chinese gave him such farewell honours when he left the Colony the other day for a holiday in Europe as have never been seen there before.

Mr. Whitehead has devoted himself to exposing the weakness and defects of the existing system of government and the constitution of the Legislative Council, and has just brought home a petition, signed by nearly ninety per cent. of the British ratepayers, praying for a measure of local self-government equal to that possessed by the smallest community at home and by colonies abroad with not a fraction of the wealth, importance, or experience of Hongkong. This petition explains the position of the unofficial inhabitants of the Colony so clearly, and sets forth their grievances so temperately, that I cannot do better than reproduce it almost *in extenso*, especially as its prayer will have to be granted sooner or later. It runs as follows :—

It is a little over fifty years since the Colony was founded on a barren rock, the abode of a few fishermen and pirates. To-day it is a city and settlement with upwards of a quarter of a million inhabitants ; a trade estimated at about forty millions of pounds sterling per annum, and a revenue of some two millions of dollars, wholly derived from internal taxation. Hongkong is a free port, through which passes upwards of fourteen millions of tons of shipping per annum, and it ranks amongst the very first in the list of the great seaports in Her Majesty's dominions. It is the centre of enormous British interests, and is an extensive emporium of British trade in the China seas, and, while it remains a free port, it is destined to expand and develop, and to continue to be the centre of vast traffic and of constant communication between Europe, the Australian Colonies, the United States, and Canada on the one hand, and China, Japan, the Philippine Islands, British North Borneo, Java, Indo-China, Siam, the Straits, and India on the other. Hongkong has attained to its almost unequalled commercial position, through the enterprise, skill, and energy of British merchants, traders, and shipowners;

through the labours of Her Majesty's subjects who have spent their lives and employed their capital on its shores; through the expenditure of many millions of dollars in roads, streets, and bridges; in buildings, public and private; in extensive reclamations; in docks, piers, and wharves; and last, but not least, in manufactures of great and increasing value. The prosperity of the Colony can best be maintained by the unremitting exertions and self-sacrifice of your Petitioners and the valuable co-operation and support of the Chinese, and only by the continuance of Hongkong as a free port.

Notwithstanding that the whole interests of your Petitioners are thus inextricably and permanently bound up in the good administration of the Colony, in the efficiency of its Executive, and the soundness of its finance, your Petitioners are allowed to take only a limited part or small share in the government of the Colony, and are not permitted to have any really effective voice in the management of its affairs, external or internal. Being purely a Crown Colony, it is governed by a Governor appointed by Her Most Gracious Majesty the Queen, and by an Executive and a Legislative Council. The former is composed wholly of Officers of the Crown, nominated and appointed by the Crown; the latter consists of seven Official Members, selected and appointed by the Queen, and five Unofficial Members, two of whom are nominated by certain public bodies in the Colony, while the other three are selected by the Governor, and all are appointed by Her Majesty.

The Executive Council sits and deliberates in secret. The Legislative Council sits with open doors, and its procedure appears to admit of full and unfettered discussion, but there is virtually no true freedom of debate. Questions are considered, and settled, and the policy to be adopted by the Government in connection therewith is decided in the Executive Council. They are then brought before the Legislative Council, where the Government—the Official Members being in a majority—can secure the passing of any measure, in face of any opposition on the part of the Unofficial Members, who are thus limited to objecting and protesting, and have no power to carry any proposal which they may consider beneficial, nor have they power to reject or even modify any measure which may in their opinion be prejudicial to the interests of the Colony.

In the adjustment and disposal of the Colonial revenue it might be supposed that the Unofficial representatives of the taxpayers would be allowed a potential voice, and in form this has been conceded by the Government. But only in form, for in the Finance Committee, as well as in the Legislative Council, the Unofficial Members are in a minority, and can therefore be out-voted if any real difference of opinion arises.

Legislative Enactments are nearly always drafted by the Attorney General, are frequently forwarded before publication in the Colony or to the Council for the approval of the Secretary of State, and when sanctioned are introduced into the Legislative Council, read a first, second, and third time, and passed by the votes of the Official Members, acting in obedience to instructions, irrespective of their personal views or private opinions.

The Legislation so prepared and passed emanates in some cases from persons whose short experience of and want of actual touch with the Colony's needs, does not qualify them to fully appreciate the measures best suited to the requirements of the Community.

Those who have the knowledge and experience are naturally the Unofficial Members, who have been elected and appointed as possessing these very qualifications, who have passed large portions of their lives in the Colony, and who either have permanent personal interests in it, or hold prominent positions of trust which connect them most closely with its affairs, and are therefore the more likely to have been required to carefully study its real needs, and to have thoroughly acquainted themselves with the methods by which these are best to be met. On the other hand the offices occupied by the Official Members are only stepping stones in an official career; the occupants may be resident for a longer or a shorter period in the Colony, and for them to form an opinion on any question which arises, different from that decided upon by the Government in Executive Council, is to risk a conflict with the Governor, and they are therefore compelled to vote on occasions contrary to their convictions.

Your Petitioners humbly represent that to Malta, Cyprus, Mauritius, British Honduras, and other Crown Colonies, more liberal forms of Government than those enjoyed by your Petitioners have been given: unofficial seats in the Executive Council; unofficial majorities in the Legislative Council; power of election of Members of Council; and more power and influence in the management of purely local affairs: in none of these Colonies are the commercial and industrial interests of the same magnitude or importance as those of Hongkong. Your Petitioners, therefore, pray your Honourable House to grant them the same or similar privileges.

Your Petitioners fully recognise that in a Colony so peculiarly situated on the borders of a great Oriental Empire, and with a population largely composed of aliens whose traditional and family interests and racial sympathies largely remain in that neighbouring Empire, special legislation and guardianship are required. Nor are they less alive to the Imperial position of a Colony which is at once a frontier fortress and a naval depôt, the headquarters of Her Majesty's fleet, and the base for naval and military operations in these Far Eastern waters; and they are not so unpractical as to expect that unrestricted power should be given to any local Legislature, or that the Queen's Government could ever give up the paramount control of this important dependency. All your Petitioners claim is the common right of Englishmen to manage their local affairs, and control the expenditure of the Colony, where Imperial considerations are not involved.

At present your Petitioners are subject to legislation issuing from the Imperial Parliament, and all local legislation must be subsidiary to it. Her Majesty the Queen in Council has full and complete power and authority to make laws for the island, and local laws must be approved and assented to by the Governor in the name of the Queen, and are subject to disallowance by Her Majesty on the recommendation of Her Principal Secretary of State for the Colonies.

Your Petitioners recognise the necessity and propriety of the existence of these checks and safeguards against the abuse of any power and authority exercised by any local Legislature, and cheerfully acquiesce in their continuance and effective exercise, but respectfully submit that, subject to those checks and safeguards, they ought to be allowed the free election of representatives of British nationality in the Legislative Council of the Colony; a majority in the Council of such elected representatives; perfect freedom of debate for the Official Members, with power to vote according to their conscientious convictions without being called to account or endangered in their positions by their votes; complete control in the Council over local expenditure; the management of local affairs; and a consultative voice in questions of an Imperial character.

This power to control purely local affairs is but the common right of every Englishman, and to deny it to Hongkong—the

4

absolute authority of the Crown over all purely Imperial matters being safeguarded—is without a shadow of justification. Besides being signed, as I have said, by ninety per cent. of the British ratepayers, this petition has the strongest support of the entire Chinese community, who pay nine-tenths of the whole taxation. The inhabitants of Hongkong claim that nothing could have shown more clearly the necessity for municipal government than the muddle made by the Government in dealing with the plague. This cost Hongkong a million dollars, thousands of lives, many thousands of its Chinese inhabitants, and inflicted a loss hardly calculable upon its vast shipping interests. Much of all this, it is declared, could have been saved by proper management. As an example of a state of things against which the Hongkong press and the unofficial members of Council have constantly protested, it may be pointed out that at this most critical period of the Colony's history it was administered by a Government most of whose officials were "acting" men, and many of them, therefore, necessarily less competent than the holders of their offices should be. "Why is it," asked the *Daily Press*, "that so large a number of officials can claim leave all at once? . . . It should not be possible for any administration to become so depleted of its responsible members as this Colony is at the present moment." Without the actual list of the "acting" officers the state of affairs would not be believed. It is as follows: Acting Colonial Secretary, Acting Chief Justice, Acting Puisne Judge, Acting Attorney General, Acting Director of Public Works (an untried junior), Acting Assistant Registrar General (who was really Acting Registrar General), Acting Clerk of Councils, Acting Postmaster General, Acting Police Magistrate, Acting Clerk to Magistrates, Acting Sanitary Superintendent, Acting Superintendent of Civil Hospitals, Acting Assessor of Rates, Acting Registrar, and Acting Deputy Registrar. This list by itself is enough to show that something is seriously wrong. By appealing single-handed to the Home Government, over the heads of the Governor and his officials, Mr. Whitehead has also obtained the appointment of a Retrenchment Commission, of which it has been truly remarked that if its recommendations bear any resemblance to the Report just issued by a similar Commission in the neighbouring Colony of the Straits Settlements, which has recommended economies to the extent of nearly a quarter of a million dollars *per annum*, Hongkong will have reason to be thankful.

Above all other considerations and criticisms, however, it is the greatness of this outpost on the edge of the Empire that must always finally recur to any Englishman who has studied it. I doubt if there can be a more remarkable view in the world than that of the city of Victoria and the ten square miles of Hongkong harbour from "The Peak." At night it is as if you had mounted above the stars and were looking down upon them, for the riding-lights of the ships seem suspended in an infinite gulf of darkness, while every now and then the white beam of an electric search-light flashes like the track of a meteor across a midnight sky. By day, the city is spread out nearly 2,000 feet directly below you, and only the ships' decks and their foreshortened masts are visible, while the whole surface of the harbour is traversed continually in all directions by fast steam-launches, making a network of tracks like lacework upon it, as water-spiders skim over a pool in summer-time. For Hongkong harbour, as I have said, is the focus of the traffic of the East, though what this means one cannot realise until one has looked down many times into its secure blue depths and noted all that is there—the great mail liners, the P. & O., the Messageries Maritimes, the North German Lloyd, the Austrian Lloyd, the Occidental and Oriental, the Pacific Mail, and the Canadian Pacific; the smaller mail packets, to Tongking, to Formosa, to Borneo, to Manila, and to Siam; the ocean "tramps" ready to get up steam at a moment's notice and carry anything anywhere; the white-winged sailing-vessels resting after

their long flights; the innumerable high-sterned junks plying
to every port on the Chinese coast; and all the mailed host of
men-of-war flying every flag under heaven, from the white ensign
of the flagship and the black eagle of its Russian rival, to the
yellow crown of the tiny Portuguese gunboat or the dragon
pennant of China.   On one day, the Governor told me, no
fewer than two hundred and forty guns were fired in salutes in
the harbour.   All these vessels cross and recross ceaselessly in
Hongkong harbour, living shuttles in the loom of time, bearing
the golden strand of human sympathy and co-operation between
world and world, or like the Zeitgeist in *Faust*, "weaving the
garment divinity wears."   I am not prepared to say that divinity
would always find itself comfortable in the garment that is woven
in Hongkong, but one thing I can affirm, and that is that a visit
to our furthest Colony makes one proud to belong to the nation
that has created it from nothing, fills the word "Empire"
with a new-born meaning, and crystallises around it a set of
fresh convictions and resolves.

CHAPTER II.

A SCHOOL OF EMPIRE: THE STRAITS SETTLEMENTS.

SINGAPORE, says an old chronicler, "presents to the eye of the voyager a scene that has repeatedly excited the most rapturous admiration." The rapture probably began with the descendant of Alexander the Great, who—the story goes—came over from Sumatra and founded it, the first Malay settlement on the Peninsula, exactly a century after the battle of Hastings, naming it Singhapura, " The City of the Lion," from a lion-like beast he saw on landing. Camoens felt the rapture, too, when he sang—

> "But on her Land's end framed see Cingapur,
>   Where the wide sea-road shrinks to narrow way;
> Thence curves the coast to face the Cynosure,
>   And lastly trends Auroraward its lay."

And diluted to the thinner consistency of a less impressionable age, the same rapture is experienced by every traveller who enters the harbour. But his eye soon falls from the setting of exquisite green hills to the marvellous multi-coloured wharf of Babel awaiting the touch of the steamer. There Malay jostles Chinaman, Kling rubs shoulders with Javanese, Arab elbows Seedy-boy, and Dyak stares at Bugis, all their dirty bodies swathed either in nothing to speak of, or else in scarlet and yellow and blue and gold. Among them a dainty English lady, come to meet her husband or brother or lover, her eyes full of laughter or tears, and her face flushed with anticipation, looks so white and fair and frail that one marvels in pride at the thought that she and such as she are the mothers of men who impose the restraints and the incitements of Empire upon the millions of these dark races of the earth.

If it is unnecessary to describe Shanghai and Hongkong, because of the hosts of people who visit them and the super-abundance of books which discuss them, still less is it needful to give a detailed account of Singapore. The Colony, however, has several points of interest peculiar to itself, besides those which it shares with other parts of the Far East, and though a glance at the latter will suffice, the former call for considera-tion at greater length. Singapore is interesting for its remark-ably beautiful situation; for its history, so full of vicissitudes and bloodshed until it finally came under the administration of Bengal in July, 1880—as an example of vicissitudes, Malacca was captured by us from the Dutch in 1786, restored in 1801, retaken in 1807, restored in 1818, resumed for good in 1825; for its geographical situation as the extreme southern limit of continental Asia, and the "corner" between the Far East and the rest of the world; for the fact that it was the first free-trade port of modern times; and very interesting, of course, as one of the keystones of Imperial defence. To a casual observer, however, Singapore does not present such striking features as many other places. The business town is two or three miles away from most of the private residences; these are not in groups but in units, each solitary in its own charming grounds; you cannot make a call under half an-hour's drive, and until you have learned a little Malay it is a most difficult community in which to find your way about; and the Club is practically closed at seven o'clock, and if you make arrangements to dine there, your single lighted table only emphasises the surrounding darkness.

This evergreen island, almost on the equator, where neither Christmas nor Midsummer Day brings much change to the thermometer, and in whose tropical jungles the cobra and

hamadryad live and a stray tiger is occasionally found, is the seat
of a large number of very ticklish problems of government, and
the visitor would be surprised indeed if he could see for a
moment, through the eyes of the Governor of the Straits Settlements, the variety and responsibility of the questions requiring
decision and action every day. It is a singularly complicated
problem, to begin with, to govern the city itself, with its six
thousand Europeans and Americans (including the garrison), its
four thousand Eurasians, its four thousand Javanese, its sixteen
thousand Indians, chiefly Klings (natives of India, from the
Coromandel coast), its thirty thousand Malays, its hundred and
twenty thousand Chinese and all its mixed mass of Bengalis and
Bugis, Jawi Pekans and Boyanese and Burmese, Persians and
Arabs and Dyaks and Manilamen. These native peoples are quiet
enough when left alone, but a single unpopular ordinance is
sufficient to bring them rioting into the streets. A few years
ago Singapore was in the hands of a mob for two days—in fact,
until the government gave way—because it was decided to make
the causeways clear for passengers. The city used to be the
headquarters of several of the principal Chinese Secret Societies,
the most inscrutable and ruthless and law-upsetting organisations in the world. These were suppressed by formal enactment
on the initiative of Sir Cecil Smith, four years ago, and a
" Chinese Advisory Board " created to deal with their legitimate
work, but it may well be doubted whether a system to which the
Chinese have an irrepressible tendency has not been made more
secret rather than extirpated. Mr. Wray, the "Protector of
Chinese," in his latest report, says that " sporadic attempts are
still made, and will always be made where Chinese congregate
in large numbers, to start illegal organisations," but he believes,
or perhaps one should say, hopes, that " secrecy is impossible
amid a heterogeneous society like ours, and incessant vigilance
and prompt action on the part of the Chinese Protectorate are
all that is necessary in such cases." The chief societies were
the Ghee Hin, the Ghee Hok, and the Hok Hin. The former

was the original and the most powerful one, and when it was suppressed, after great difficulty and many disputes among its members concerning the distribution of its property, its membership in Singapore was thirty thousand and in Penang forty thousand. The other two have been "registered" and permitted, as they are ostensibly only Chinese mutual benefit societies. There is still not the slightest doubt, however, that they stand between their members and the foreign law. Professional bailers attend the courts to bail out any member of their society, and they help their members in all sorts of ways to flee from justice. A chapter, and a most romantic one too, might be written about these societies. They have, for example, the most elaborate system of signs for mutual recognition. One of them bases its signs upon the numeral three. At table, a member wishing to make himself known to any fellow-member present places three glasses together in a certain way, or passes a cup of tea held peculiarly with three fingers. A man fleeing from justice and praying for refuge, puts his shoes outside another's house, side by side, with the heels turned towards the door. If the owner turns one shoe over on the other, the fugitive knows he can take refuge there. In spite of the suppression, I fancy that *Hoan Cheng Hok Beng*—"Upset Cheng," the present Manchu dynasty of China, "restore Beng," the former dynasty—still has a magic and compelling significance in Singapore, for these are the pass-words of the famous Triad Society, which honeycombs China and has more than once put the throne in terror. The Triad consists of the characters *Thien Tay Hoey*—"Heaven, Earth, Man."

To appreciate Singapore as a city of Orientals, one must spend a day or two in the native quarters, and this is just what the ordinary visitor fails to do. From this point of view it is certainly one of the most astounding communities in the world. To begin with, it is enormous. For days you may wander about without ever turning on your track, through miles upon miles of semi-native houses and shops, through crowded

streets, in variegated bazaars, with all the merchandise of all
the East spread out endlessly before you. Each race has its
own quarter—there is "Kampong Malacca," "Kampong Kling,"
"Kampong Siam," "Kampong China." In one spot you are
dazzled with the silks of India ; in another the *sarongs* of Java
are spread out like a kaleidoscope ; in another you are suffocated with an indescribable mixture of Eastern scents ; in another
an appalling stench meets you, strange rainbow-like birds utter
raucous cries, and the long thin hairy arm of a gorilla is
stretched out between bamboo bars in deceptive friendliness ;
in another there is such a packed mass of boats that
you hardly know when your foot has left dry land. And all
this mixed humanity exists in order and security and sanitation, living and thriving and trading, simply because of the
presence of English law and under the protection of the British
flag. Remove that piece of bunting from Government House,
and all that it signifies, and the whole community would go to
pieces like a child's sand-castle when the tide rises. Its three
supports are free trade, fair taxation, and even-handed justice
among white, black, brown and yellow, and these exist in the
Far East under the British flag alone. At least, I have been
almost everywhere else without finding them. Of course, in all
this the Chinese enormously preponderate. The foolish opinion
is sometimes heard at home that this Chinese community
represents China—that it is a specimen of what China may
become, a standing bond of union between ourselves and China.
The very opposite is the case. This community has grown up
and exists precisely because it is *not* China—because the conditions of its existence are precisely the antithesis of Chinese
conditions. The Straits Chinaman would not exchange his
British nationality for anything else in the world ; he plays
cricket, football, and lawn tennis ; he has his annual athletic
sports ; the recreation ground, and indeed every open space, is
covered in the afternoons with Chinese engaged in these games ;
he goes to the Free Library and he reads the newspaper ; he

attends a Debating Society and he carries off prizes at the
Raffles School ; he eats foreign food and imitates foreign vices.
When he has prospered he drives through the streets in a
carriage and pair with a European coachman on the box.   He
knows that he is the equal of the Englishman before the law,
and considers that he is slightly superior to him in other
respects.   He looks upon the Civil Service as *his* servants, upon
the Governor as *his* ruler, upon the forts as *his* protection, upon
the whole place as *his* home.   A Chinaman is one of the most
influential members of the Legislative Council.

Mr. George C. Wray, the Protector of Chinese, whom I have
already quoted above, writes as follows in his last report : " We
have developed an ever-growing, permanent, law-abiding, Straits-
born population, who are proud of being British subjects, give
their children a liberal English education, and are rapidly con-
solidating themselves into a distinctive, loyal subject-race, of
whose abilities and behaviour our Government may well be
proud."   The number of these Straits-born Chinese, according
to the census of 1891, was 12,805 in Singapore, and 84,757 for
the whole Colony, and they are rapidly increasing.   The
business of the European firms—and this is true of almost the
whole Far East—could not be carried on for a week without
their Chinese " shroffs," " compradors," and clerks.   Between
the census of 1881 and that of 1891 the Chinese inhabitants of
Singapore had increased from 86,766 to 121,908.   During the
year 1898 there were no fewer than 144,558 Chinese immigrants
into Singapore alone, to say nothing of the 68,751 who went to
Penang, to which the same remarks apply.   It is therefore not
surprising that even the lethargic Chinese Imperial Government has at last been struck with this new and strange China
growing up under a foreign flag, and that it has despatched
commissioners to inquire into the reasons why Chinese who
make money in the Straits never come back to their own land,
and has published an invitation to its self-exiled citizens to return,
and an order to its own officials to refrain from interfering with

them when they do so. The hilarious scorn, however, with which this invitation has been received, and the almost brutal frankness of the reasons given in reply to the inquiries, show at the same time the value the well-governed Chinaman sets upon his privileges, and his opinion of the prospects of reform—even when backed by Imperial command—in his native land. Even to the Chinese woman who is a prostitute in China, Singapore is by comparison a paradise. Mr. Wray says: "There being no supervision or means of redress in China, women of the lower classes better themselves by coming to a land where debt-slavery is not tolerated and where the mere act of reporting to the nearest official means immediate freedom." *

* It would not be fitting to discuss here the whole question of the relations of the prostitute class to the Colonial authorities, but I must put my opinion on record somewhere in this book. I am profoundly convinced, after much study of statistics and careful investigation into the question in the Far East, that the action of Parliament and the Colonial Office in over-riding the repeated requests and protests of the highest and most responsible local authorities is so seriously wrong that the word "blunder" is wholly inadequate to describe it. From the point of view of morality it is as wrong as from the point of view of administration it is improper. The conditions of life and character are so utterly different in Europe and Asia that any comparison between them for the purpose of justifying recent legislation is not only impossible but absolutely ridiculous. What may be wise and imperative laws for the women of Europe, may quite well be wrong in every respect for the women of Asia. Hongkong and Singapore were in this respect two of the healthiest communities in the world; they are rapidly becoming, if indeed they are not already, centres for the propagation and distribution of pestilence. From this the native society and the British garrisons suffer in identical proportions. As for the fate of the unfortunate women themselves, the pen of Dante would be required to describe what it will soon become again. To the familiar horrors of the slave-trade, add an equal amount of other and indescribable horror, and you will have some notion of what life will be for the thousands of Chinese women under the British flag but without its protection. Anybody who desires to inform himself upon the normal condition of Eastern prostitutes should pursue inquiries into the lot of the young women who are sold into this slavery, even by the female members of the Siamese royal family, and who pass a great part of their lives in the district of Bangkok known as Sampeng, behind barred windows and padlocked doors, from which they never emerge until, dead or alive, they leave the place for good. The action of Parliament and the Colonial Office has simply condemned thousands of Chinese women to a fate of almost unimaginable woe, from a great part of which they were previously shielded. As the Protector of Chinese in Singapore says, to suppress the evil altogether is utterly impossible, though it may be greatly mitigated. All that this legislation does is to afford a certain relief to the consciences of partially informed people at home, at the cost of enormous and unnecessary suffering to

The Straits Settlements, which were incorporated as a Crown Colony in 1867, having previously been under the jurisdiction of the East India Company, consist of the large island of Singapore; the smaller island of Penang; Malacca and Province Wellesley on the mainland; another strip of territory and the island of Pangkor—together known as the Dindings; the Cocos Islands, and Christmas Island. The three latter call for no special mention; Province Wellesley is a sugar-growing district, which may become of importance if a railway runs into the inland side of it; and Malacca is reposing, after its varied history and its former prosperity as the outlet of the products of the Peninsula, in a condition of peaceful stagnation. Its colourless condition is well typified by its sole product—tapioca, produced in large quantities by Chinese labour and capital. Commercially, as the Governor has recently said, it is "a mere suburb of Singapore," and it will remain so until the Chinese develop its strip of very fertile land, which its own Malay inhabitants are far too lazy to do. Camoens wrote of—

> "Malacca's market grand and opulent,
> Whither each Province of the long seaboard
> Shall send of merchantry rich varied hoard."

Three centuries ago Malacca was "the great emporium of the Eastern Archipelago." * But its walls were "blown up at great expense in 1807," and its history virtually ceased long ago. There are compensations, however, for the quaint and quiet little place, for its Resident Councillor has just described it as "a favourable example of a prosperous agricultural district, where crime is almost unknown and the people are happy and contented." Penang, on the contrary, has been a discontented community lately. Singapore has

many thousands of natives in the Colonies. And it is of no use for the people who hold a contrary opinion to denounce those who express this one, having formed it after conscientious inquiries favoured by unusual opportunities.

* Lucas: "Historical Geography of the British Colonies," L 107—a work of which it would be impossible to speak too highly.

inevitably taken away much of the advantageous trade Penang formerly enjoyed with the neighbouring . Protected States; it claims that it has contributed more than its fair share toward Colonial expenditure, and received less for its own purposes; and it has been refused the large amount it desired for the erection of wharves. Much bitterness between the two chief partners in the Colony has thus been aroused, and a wordy war in paper and pamphlet, and even in Parliament, has followed. The Government also declined to grant the Royal Commission of inquiry which Penang desired. According to the Acting Governor's annual report, however, this discussion is now at an end. Mr. Maxwell writes: "A number of real or supposed grievances were also ventilated, but when the chief ground of complaint had been proved by a reference to statistics to be without foundation, the agitation, to which some of the Penang Chinese had somewhat blindly given their support, rapidly died away." It is probable that the growing influence of the Chinese, which is even truer of Penang than of Shanghai or Hongkong, and the great depression of trade, were as much as anything else the causes of the discontent of Penang. Last year the expenditure of the municipality exceeded the revenue by 17,000 dols., and the cash balance was reduced from 24,107 to 6,860 dols., while its municipal indebtedness is 850,000 dols. This, however, is a very small matter compared with the fact that the revenue of Penang, as a whole, has increased yearly since the "low-water mark" of 1891 by 3,000,000 dols., and this although no new sources of revenue have been established. And the figures of Penang's trade, 87,608,854 dols., are the highest for the past five years. The outlook, therefore, does not warrant any particular depression of spirits. In regard to the question of municipal expenditure (for all parts of the Straits Settlements have their municipalities, unlike Hongkong, which is still in official leading-strings), I may add that in every case, and not in that of Penang alone, the expenditure last year exceeded the revenue. With regard to Singapore, a few statistics are of much interest. The total trade for 1898, excluding the movements of treasure, was 260,982,169 dols., an increase over 1892 of more than 26,000,000 dols. In spite of this, however, owing to the depreciation of silver, these same figures for the two years, translated into sterling at the average rates for each year, give £37,135,141 for 1892, and £36,769,590 for 1898—a silver increase of 26,000,000 dols. thus appearing as a gold decrease of £365,551! It would be difficult to find a more striking object-lesson of the position of a silver-using colony in regard to a gold-using mother country. That the trade of Singapore is healthy enough, apart from the question of silver, is evident from the shipping returns, which were 6,944,846 tons entered and cleared in 1898, an increase of nearly half a million tons over 1892.

In the finances of Singapore, however, one question far out-weighs in importance, both Imperial and Colonial, all others— that of the military contribution. Upon this matter Singapore has been on the verge of revolt—hardly too strong an expression to describe the bitterness aroused in the Colony by the action of the home authorities. This is the more to be regretted since to an outsider studying the dispute it seems eminently one which could have been amicably settled by a compromise. When the Straits Settlements desired to be removed from the jurisdiction of India in 1867, and formed into a Crown Colony, the British Government assented on the understanding that the Colony should bear the cost of its own defence. At this time, however, there was a distinction made between the troops and their accommoda-tion at Singapore, Malacca, and Penang, for the defence of those places; and other troops and their cost and accommodation at Singapore, for Imperial purposes—the latter being maintained by the home Government. Up to 1890, the Colony had paid a yearly contribution of £50,145 towards its defence, but in that year the Secretary of State for the Colonies suddenly de-manded that the contribution be raised at once to £100,000 per annum, with an addition, first, of £28,976, being one-half of the alleged loss of the Imperial Treasury by exchange on previous payments; and second, of an indefinite sum for further barracks. Now here, beyond any possible doubt, the Colonial Office made an initial blunder. Admitting that an increased contribution was necessary, and admitting that the sum asked for was entirely just, to send a peremptory demand that it be voted immediately by the Legislative Council, without having extended the courtesy of an inquiry beforehand as to the views of the Colony upon a matter so seriously affecting its income, was an act to arouse resentment in the most loyal community in the world. Its instant result might have been foreseen by the least imaginative person. The Governor of the Straits, Sir Cecil Smith, passed the vote as ordered. "For my own part," he wrote to Lord Knutsford, "I found myself wholly unable to conscientiously support the justice of all the claims which Her Majesty's Government had made, and the same views which I held were shared in by every member of my Council. My instructions, however, were perfectly clear, and I had to require each member of the Executive Council to vote against his conviction and in support of the claims of Her Majesty's Government." And in reporting the vote, he wrote: "It is very important that I should not omit to point out that the course which has been followed on this occasion has placed the Executive in very strained relations with the Legislative authority, and has tended to imperil good government. The constituted authorities in this Colony have been required by Her Majesty's Government to meet a money claim without having had an opportunity of having their views on the justice and correctness of the claim considered. Such a case is, so far as I am aware, wholly without precedent." In studying the history of British colonial administration, the student occasionally comes across acts on the part of the mother country which might have been inspired by some demon of mischief, so deliberately unfortunate do they seem. The method of this demand is one of them.

Protests, appeals, minutes, and resolutions of public meetings, were of no avail, and Lord Knutsford simply replied that "Her Majesty's Government would have been glad if they could have allowed themselves to be influenced by arguments put forward so temperately and so fully;" and somewhat sarcastically added he had learnt "with satisfaction" that the Colony had included a similar vote in the estimates for the ensuing year. For the four years ending December 31, 1893, therefore, the Straits paid a regular contribution of £100,000 a year, during which time the Colonial revenue was further decreased by depression of trade and dislocated by the fall of silver. Public works in the Colony had to be abandoned, and almost imperative improvements postponed, and at last a loan had actually to be raised. "The financial arrangements," said Sir Cecil Smith to his Legislative Council on October 15, 1891, "have been completely upset; and although every endeavour has been made, and is being made, to reduce our expenditure, it has been found necessary, in order to meet our liabilities, to dispose of all our realisable assets—namely, the investments in gold amounting to 1,013,762 dols., and in Indian stock amounting to 350,000 dols." Even this state of things did not move the stony heart of the home authorities, and the people of Singapore made one more desperate set of appeals at the beginning of 1894, when the first series of payments came to an end. In response the Colonial Office removed £10,000 by way of solatium, and added £20,000 for additional barrack accommodation—thus meeting the appeals of the Colony by raising the total contribution for the present year from £100,000 to £110,000!

A little calculation shows the situation of the Straits Settlements to be as follows :—The revenue of the Colony for last year was 8,706,308 dols., an increase on 1892. Its expenditure was 8,915,482 dols., a decrease from 1892. Thus there was a deficit of 209,174 dols. The military contribution is therefore increased at a time when there is positively a financial deficit. To see, however, how bad the case really is, we must look at the effect of the depreciation of silver. The average Singapore

exchange at sight of the Mexican dollar for 1892 was 2s. 10⅝d. At
the moment of writing it is 2s. 1⅞d. To remit £100,000 to London
in sterling during 1892 would therefore have cost the Colony (say)
700,000 dols.; to remit the same sum home to-day would cost
932,000 dols. That is, the military contribution of the Colony
has risen between 1892 and 1894 by 232,000 dols., apart from
any act of either the British Government or the Colonial
authorities. Finally, the amount to be paid during the present
year, at the present rate of exchange, is 1,025,200 dols.—rather
more than twenty-seven and a half per cent. of the total revenue
of the Colony! It is hardly surprising that such a state of things
"tends to imperil good government."

Yet, as I have said, the question at issue seems one which
should be settled without much difficulty on the time-honoured
principle of give and take. Everybody admits, to begin with,
that each part of the Empire ought to bear its proper share of
the defence of the whole. Unfortunately, many parts escape doing
so. Singapore, on the contrary, has always been eager to subscribe
its proportion. Lord Knutsford will remember, I am sure, how
in the famous confidential Colonial Conference of 1887 he held
up Singapore as a shining example to the lagging Australian
colonies. The Secretary of State bases his claim upon the
"colossal trade" of Singapore. The Colony retorts that at
least three-quarters of this trade merely passes through the
harbour on its way to other parts of the Far East, and that
therefore it is Imperial trade and not local. This is an indisputable fact. Lord Knutsford wrote: "The large stores of
coal which your trade requires, of themselves invite attack."
Singapore replies, first, that this coal belongs to ship-owners in
London, and that therefore it is they who should be asked to
pay for its defence; second, that it is used chiefly for the transit
trade aforesaid; and third, that by common consent and the
definite statement of a Royal Commission, Singapore is an Im-
·perial coaling station second in importance only to the Cape
itself. And I may here remind the Colonial Office that when

the Russian "scare" broke out in 1885, the home authorities instantly telegraphed to the Governor of Singapore asking how much coal was there. He replied, 200,000 tons; whereupon they fell into a panic lest the Russians should get it and our ships be deprived of it, and telegraphed in all directions for ships to go and guard it. And this was the origin of Imperial interest in the speedy and efficient arming of Singapore. The Colonial Office has made one very misleading statement in this controversy, namely, that the batteries of Singapore were armed with heavier guns at the special request of one of its own officials. But this official was, at the time of his recommendation, lent by the Colony to the Imperial Government, and was therefore an Imperial officer, acting in the interests of the Empire as a whole. Singapore is, of course, a link of the greatest value in the armed chain of Empire. Without it, or some similar place not far away, Great Britain could not pretend to hold her position in the Far East. On the other hand, the Colony has been hitherto a very flourishing one. In it, therefore, Imperial and local interests are pretty well divided. This is exactly what the Colony says. It has built forts (which were kept waiting a long time for their guns) at a cost of £81,000; it has paid £28,976 to recoup the Imperial Treasury for loss on exchange; for four years it has contributed £100,000 a year, though its allowance of troops has generally been below the strength promised; and now, though its revenue shows a deficit and its public works and imperative improvements are at a standstill, it offers to pay gladly one-half the cost of its defence, say £70,000 a year, notwithstanding the augmentation of this sum by the ceaseless fall of silver. If this is not a fair and indeed a thoroughly loyal offer, then facts and figures have no value, and the people of Singapore are right when they declare that the home Government exacts this contribution simply because the Colony is able to pay it, and for no other reason whatever. Before the British Government finally refuses the appeal of the Colony, let the authorities ask themselves what would be their feelings if the inhabitants of the Straits Settlements absolutely refused to pay it, and requested that the forts which they themselves have built should be dismantled and the garrison withdrawn. This has already been suggested. When the despair in Singapore was at its height, I asked a highly-placed official at home if there were anything more the Colony could possibly do or say to avert their fate. "No," he replied, "the matter is settled—unless, perhaps, they were to do one thing." "What is that?" I asked eagerly. "Shoot the Governor," he said. The joke was heightened by the fact that there never was a more deservedly popular governor than Sir Cecil Smith. There are less desperate steps than this, however, in the power of any Colony, which would still be very disturbing to the Colonial Office; and while we are straining the loyalty of Hongkong in one direction by refusing it the measure of self-government which its neighbours possess, it is to be hoped that we shall not strain that of Singapore too much in another direction. Our pride in those *propugnacula imperii* should be too great to permit us to treat them unfairly.

CHAPTER III.

ANOMALIES OF EMPIRE: THE PROTECTED MALAY STATES.

IN point of size the Straits Settlements are dots on the map of
the Malay Peninsula. One dot is Singapore; a little way up
the coast Malacca is another; still following the coast the Dindings form a third; Penang and Province Wellesley are two more.
Around and beyond these is a vast expanse of country of which
Europe may be said to know virtually nothing. Yet the lower
part of it is the scene of a successful experiment in government
second in interest to none in the world, while of the upper part,
Mr. Alfred Russel Wallace's statement made in 1869 that "to the
ordinary Englishman this is perhaps the least known part of the
globe" is still literally true.* Omitting the Straits Settlements
the Malay Peninsula may be said to be divided into two parts by
what has been aptly called "the Siamese *bunga mas* line," that
is, to the north of the line lie the great Malay States whose independence is only impaired by their annual offering to the
Siamese Government of the *bunga mas*—"Golden Flower"—in
acknowledgment of nominal suzerainty. It is the latter which are
still as unfamiliar as the remotest parts of Africa to the foreign
explorer, and the journey I made through several of them, some
parts of which covered ground visited by no white man before,

* An admirable little handbook, edited by Capt. Foster, R.E., and issued in 1891
by the Intelligence Division of the War Office, under the title "Précis of Information concerning the Straits Settlements and the Native States of the Malay Peninsula," should be better known than it is. Its information about the native States
is very meagre, but Capt. Foster conscientiously collected all that was then
accessible. Very few Europeans have travelled there.

will be found described in later chapters. It is the so-called
Protected Malay States lying between these semi-independent,
unknown regions and the flourishing British Colony discussed in
the preceding chapter, that I propose to consider here.

If the traveller from Singapore should embark on a steamer
and land at one of several ports along the coast without any
previous knowledge of the existence of the Protected States, he
would be greatly puzzled to explain his environment. He would
arrive at a perfectly appointed foreign wharf; his landing would
be supervised by a detachment of smart Sikh and Malay police;
he would buy a ticket exactly as at a small country station at
home, and be conveyed to the capital town by a line of admirably
managed railway. There he would find himself in a place of
tropical picturesqueness and European administration. Man-
grove and bamboo-clump, coconut palm and sago-tree, would
meet his eye on every side; Malay in *sarong* and *baju*, Kling in loin-
cloth and turban, Chinaman in the unvarying dress of his race,
and Englishman in helmet and white duck, would rub shoulders
with him in the street; the long-horned, slow-stepping buffalo
harnessed to a creaking waggon, and the neat pony-cart of his
native land, would pass him in alternation; he would drive away
along streets metalled and swept in foreign fashion and lined
with buildings of Eastern material and Western shape. This,
he would say, is not a British Colony, it is not a native kingdom: what is it? The answer would be, It is one of those
political anomalies, a Protected State of the Malay Peninsula.

Of these there are five—Perak, Selángor, Sungei Ujong and
Jelebu, Pahang, and the Negri Sembilan. Each was formerly
a Malay State or congeries of States, and is now a British
possession in all except the name. To each a British Resident
is appointed, who is nominally the adviser to a Malay ruler, but
practically administrator of the whole State, subordinate only to
the Governor of the Straits Settlements and the Secretary of
State for the Colonies. Each Protected State is theoretically
ruled by a Council of State consisting of the Sultan, his

"adviser," the British Resident, several of the principal chiefs of the former, and the higher administrative officers of the latter. This meets perhaps half a dozen times a year to give final sanction to new laws and changes of local policy. Its meetings, however, are merely formal, since, although the Sultan might be consulted as a matter of courtesy upon a new law affecting natives, it is out of his power to place any effective opposition in the way of an ordinance drawn up by the Resident and approved by the two superior authorities I have mentioned. The Sultans receive a liberal allowance from the finances of the States for their personal expenses, and their principal officers either receive a proportionate allowance or a salary if they perform under the British Resident any of the duties of government. These five States have become protectorates in the familiar and inevitable method of Imperial expansion—in several cases at their own request. Perak received a Resident in 1874 in consequence of a prolonged series of hostilities between rival groups of Chinese tin-miners, in the course of which British interests and investments were jeopardised. The first Resident was Mr. J. W. W. Birch, who was treacherously murdered in the following year. The Perak War, which followed, will be remembered by many people. Three native officials who had planned the murder were hanged, and others, including Sultan Abdullah, were banished to the Seychelles. The protection of Selángor and Sungei Ujong dates also from 1874, and was equally due to internecine warfare. The large State of Pahang was for many years a thorn in the side of these two, owing to the disorderly condition of its inhabitants and the hostility of the Raja towards British subjects. This culminated in the unprovoked murder of a Chinaman, a British subject, in the streets of Pekan, the capital, in 1888. Whereupon the Colonial Government, at the limit of its patience, placed the State under British protection. The fifth, in order of time, the Negri Sembilan—two Malay words meaning simply "nine countries"—quarrelled among themselves to the destruction of their prosperity and begged to be taken under British protection in 1889, which was done.

The change in the condition of each State as it was removed from native maladministration and placed under British control has been one of the most astounding spectacles in the history of the British Empire. Pahang, as I shall explain later, lags behind the rest, but the others have surpassed the condition of even the Protected States of India, and present most of the features of a British Colony in a population composed entirely of Malays and Chinese. They possess hospitals, both paying and for paupers, leper hospitals, lunatic asylums, and dispensaries; there is a State store, a State factory, and even State brick-fields; there are sanitary boards and savings banks, fire brigades and printing offices; waterworks, roads, and railways; post offices, telephones, and telegraphs; schools and police; and vaccination, which is compulsory, though there is no necessity for compulsion, is performed with "buffalo lymph," obtained from the Pasteur Institute in Saigon. Order is preserved by forces of Sikhs linked with an equal strength of Malays, and all the duties of administration are carried out under the Resident by a mere handful of Europeans, forming an uncovenanted civil service, directing a native staff. The revenues have risen by almost incredible leaps; two of the States have large credit balances. One hundred and forty miles of railway have been built by them, and their extraordinary prosperity shows no sign of diminution. As Sir Andrew Clarke has said, "The result of our policy of adventure is one of which England may well be proud. A country of which in 1873 there was no map whatever, has been thrown open to the enterprise of the world. Ages of perpetual fighting and bloodshed have ended in complete tranquillity and contentment." All this has been accomplished by the administrative genius of literally a score of Englishmen.

To exhibit the condition of the Protected States at a glance and thus save much unnecessary description, I have compiled

the following table, which shows the area, population, revenue
(with its increase), expenditure, volume of trade (with its increase),
and the present credit or debit balance in the assets and liabilities of each State. With two exceptions marked below the
figures are all taken from the Residents' reports for the
year 1893.

	Area square miles.	Popula- tion (1891)	Revenue Dollars.	In- crease over 1892	Expendi- ture. Dollars.	Total Trade. Dollars.	In- crease over 1892	Assets and Liabili- ties. Dollars.
Perak	19,000	214,254	3,094,094	344,529	2,895,899	24,897,923	3,963,124	+ 444,534
Selángor	3,500	81,592	2,795,951	652,902	2,895,599	19,545,459	4,092,375	+1,090,925
Sungei Ujong and Jelebu ..	1,690	29,602	592,975	94,972	576,562	4,204,107	592,617	– 195,899
Pahang	19,000	57,402	98,652	32,644	278,592	(1893) 672,509	—	– 948,700
Negri Sembilan.	3,500	41,617	190,999	12,899	122,097	No returns.	—	– 257,254

From this table it will be seen that Perak * is at the head of
the Protected States. Its area is much greater than any except
Pahang, its population is nearly three times that of any other,
and its revenue and volume of trade are much larger. Its
credit balance has been reduced chiefly by heavy and at present
unproductive expenditure in extending its railway system, of
which sixty-eight miles are now open for traffic. Perak has
been called the "child of Penang," but much more truly should
it be called the child of the two enlightened men who have in
turn directed its administration, first, Sir Hugh Low, and
from 1884 to 1866, and from 1889 to the present time, Mr.
F. A. Swettenham. The former of these set Perak on the
right road, and to the foresight and administrative ability of
the latter the present happy condition of the State is largely
due. Mr. Swettenham has been connected with Perak since it

* The word perak (of which the last letter is not pronounced) in Malay means
"silver." There is, however, no silver found in the State, and the word is supposed
to refer to the silver-like masses of tin which are its principal product.

came under British influence. He was three times sent on special missions there in 1874. He took an active combatant part in the Perak War, and with Lieutenant Abbott and a handful of men defended the Residency, after the assassination of Mr. Birch in 1875, until it was relieved by British troops sent hastily from Singapore, for which service he was three times mentioned in despatches. At the conclusion of the war he was placed in charge of the Residency for a time in succession to Mr. Birch. He is one of the two or three best Malay scholars living, and his annual Reports are models of administrative ability. As an example of the progress of Perak the following passage from the report to the Resident by the magistrate of the district of Kinta is instructive:—"The advancement of this district is almost incredible. Ten years ago it was little more than a vast stretch of jungle, unapproachable except by a shallow and rapid river, and possessing not a single mile of first-class cart-road nor a village of any importance." During the year, 4,492 acres of mining land were taken up, and 822 acres of agricultural land; 15,847 acres of mining land and 2,958 acres of agricultural land were about to be assigned to applicants; 29,143 acres of land had been applied for, and fresh applications poured in every day. Mr. Swettenham has proposed a scheme for the irrigation of 50,000 acres of rice-growing land, and experts lent by the Indian Government reported favourably upon it. The First Battalion of the Perak Sikhs, which has a strength of 685 of all arms, has attained a high pitch of discipline and efficiency under Lieut.-Colonel Walker, and conducted itself with great credit on several occasions when it has had to take the field, especially in suppressing the recent revolt in Pahang.

In Selángor, substitute for the name of Mr. Swettenham that of Mr. W. E. Maxwell, at present Colonial Secretary in Singapore, and the history of the State might be told in the same words. It has a yearly trade of over twenty millions of dollars, and possesses in its treasury or on loan to other States a balance of over a million. During the past year no fewer than 47,778 Chinese immigrants arrived within its borders. Its railway pays over 12½ per cent. interest, and would have paid more, as Mr. W. H. Treacher, the present Resident, explains, but for a deficiency of rolling stock, owing to the traffic having increased beyond expectation. Selángor has always been the rival of Perak in the race for the best show of prosperity, and it is difficult to say to which the palm belongs.

The allied States of Sungei Ujong and Jelebu are administered by an Officer-in-Charge, who reports to the Resident of Selángor. The total number of tin-mines in these two States is 150, covering 4,176 acres, and employing 4,000 Chinese miners, and Sungei Ujong contains the most flourishing example of coffee plantation in the Peninsula. This is the Linsum Estate, and its crop in 1898, upon 210 acres, some not in full bearing, was no less than 94,796 lbs. of clean coffee. The Negri Sombilan occupy the district between the last-named and Malacca, and have already attained a sufficient degree of prosperity to enable them to pay the interest upon their loan. In these States, as the Resident writes, " a population of 40,000 Malays is controlled by three Europeans and a few police," the remainder of the police being required for the Chinese coolies at work in the mines and on the estates.

The story of Pahang, the great State which extends from the borders of all the above to the eastern coast of the Peninsula, is unfortunately a very different one. When it was taken under British authority its population was reduced to almost the lowest level by Oriental rule. Mr. Rodger, the first Resident, described its condition prior to his arrival in 1888, in the following words :—"A system of taxation under which every necessary as well as every luxury of life was heavily taxed ; law courts in which the procedure was the merest mockery of justice, the decisions depending solely on the relative wealth or influence of the litigant, and where the punishments were utterly barbarous ; a system of debt-slavery under which not only the debtor but his wife and their most remote descendants were condemned to hopeless bondage ; an unlimited *corvée,* or forced labour for indefinite periods, and entirely without remuneration ; the right of the Raja to compel all female children to pass through his harem — a right which has desolated almost every household in the neighbourhood of Pekan,—such are some of the more striking examples, although the list is by no means exhaustive, of administrative misrule in a State within less than twenty-four hours of Singapore. and immediately adjoining the two Protected States of Perak and Selángor. The condition of the Pahang *ryot* may be briefly expressed by stating that he had practically no rights, whether of person or property, not merely in his relations with the Raja, but even in those with his immediate District Chief."

The distances in the State are enormous, and no means of communication existed, while the most promising part was that situated a considerable distance from the sea-board, around the headwaters of a river rendered almost unnavigable by rapids. The Sultan, moreover, a man of violent and depraved character, conspired secretly against the authority of the Resident while openly professing to support him. Two revolts subsequently broke out, each of which had to be suppressed at great expense and by prolonged fighting, with the result of plunging the State heavily in debt to its neighbours and the Colonial Government. To add to its embarrassment, during the year before the arrival of the Resident, the Sultan had given away vast tracts of his territory in concessions to Europeans, who used them for speculative purposes, as thousands of investors in England have good reason to know. Enormous districts were thus shut out from native or Chinese development, while the European concessionnaires were endeavouring to dispose of them for preposterous sums. One of the first acts of the Resident was to give notice that all concessions thus granted, which had not been actively taken up by a certain date, would be cancelled, and accordingly twenty of these were annulled a short time ago.

Owing to the monsoon and the lack of harbour accommodation, the entrance to the rivers of Pahang is closed from the sea for nearly half a year, from about November, and the State is only accessible by a long and difficult overland route, when some small steamer cannot be found to take the considerable risk of attempting to cross the bar. During 1898 the pitiful sum of 21,205 dollars was spent on public works, and the whole trade of Pahang only amounted to 672,869 dollars. Of this the output of gold was 9,616 ounces, and of tin 265 tons. The only road in Pahang is an 8 ft. bridle-path 52 miles in length, which affords an instructive comparison with the 200 miles of good metalled roads and the 68 miles of railway of Perak. This State is, in fact, the "sick man" of the British possessions in the Malay Peninsula. It is heavily in debt, with no prospect of being able to discharge its liabilities, and all the money that it can raise is expended on administration, leaving little or nothing for the Public Works which alone would ensure its development. Its native inhabitants have suffered so much from their past, that even in so simple a matter as the procuring of a better species of rice seed and planting it, Mr. Hugh Clifford, the present Resident, says, "they are at once so ignorant and unenterprising that it would be futile to look to them to take the initiative in such a matter." Although the State has thousands of square miles of extremely fertile land, it imports all the rice used by the non-agricultural class. During the speculative period of 1889, houses were erected at Pekan, beyond any possible need. At the present moment many of them are deserted and are actually falling into ruin. The Sultan resides at Pekan, therefore this is the capital, although the true centre of the State ought to be moved, as Mr. Clifford shows, in the very able Report from which I have already quoted, to Kuala Lipis. In the interior are tribes of semi-wild natives, called Sakais and Semangs, who are treated with the greatest barbarity by the Malays, and for whom British administration has done nothing. There is undoubtedly great mineral wealth in

Pahang, and the notorious Raub gold mines are at last actually paying interest upon their capital. Little can be done with this so long as the present system of administration continues. The native of Pahang is, of course, in a vastly happier state than he was seven or eight years ago, and the changes effected by British rule must be looked for almost entirely, as Mr. Clifford says, " not in a vastly improved system of communication, nor yet in a very marked advance in the material prosperity of the State, but rather in the great improvement noticeable in the condition of the bulk of the native population." The fertile and stanniferous lands of Pahang are no better than those open in Perak and Selángor, and it is therefore unreasonable to expect settlers for the former until all the latter are taken up. Year after year like the past two or three may go by without any improvement in Pahang, and therefore, to quote Mr. Clifford once more, " no one having the interests of Pahang at heart can pretend to regard the continued adoption of the present policy with any degree of satisfaction." The salvation of this great tract of the Peninsula must come, if at all, from a much wider scheme of reform.

The present Sultan of Perak, His Highness Raja Idris ibni almerhum Raja Iskander Shah, C.M.G., succeeded on April 5, 1889. He is the twenty-eighth of his dynasty in succession from Merhum Tanah Abang, who was buried by the Perak River four hundred years ago. " Before that time," says Mr. Swettenham, " Perak was known as Kastan Zorian, and the Malays of Perak had not then embraced the religion of Islam." His Highness is a man of attractive character and agreeable presence; and a conversation I had with him at Kuala Kangsa, where he resides, showed him to be a keen and appreciative observer of foreign ways. He visited England in 1882, and told me that what most struck him was the fact that in London there were " ten thousand times ten thousand carriages." The two things that had interested him most were the making of great guns at Woolwich, and the instrument-room at the General

Post Office. He was also much impressed by the urbanity of British royal personages in general, and of the Prince of Wales in particular. "In five minutes," he said of the latter, "I felt as if I had always known him. A Malay prince not worth five cents would make a thousand times more fuss." The Sultan has written a very lengthy account of his life, beginning with the genealogy of his own family, with the object of instructing other Malay Rajas; though, he adds, it will make them very angry, because it says, for example, that the lavatories of Western peoples are better than the palaces of the Malays. "The Malays," he continued, "are like the frog under the coconut-shell—they think there is nothing but what they can see. But Malaya is waking up—look at Perak and Selángor." His Highness remembered the guidance of Sir Robert Meade, of the Colonial Office, and desired that his respects might be presented to him. As an example of the friendliness existing between the protected and their protectors, I may quote Mr. Swettenham again, who wrote in his Report for 1890: "As regards my relations with His Highness, I do not think they could be more cordial than they are," and "His Highness's interest in the administration is as great and intelligent as ever, and his unvarying sympathy and good feeling are of the greatest assistance to me in my work." The extent to which bygones are bygones in the British protection of these States is sufficiently shown by the fact that two sons of the ex-Sultan Abdullah, who was banished for complicity in the murder of Mr. Birch, occupy posts in the Government service on the same terms as Europeans, and fill them faithfully and well. The Sultan himself has recently put on record his opinion that the Residential system has "vastly improved the material condition and prosperity of the Perak Malays of all classes." One fact may be adduced in support of this loyal admission. The Government of Perak now pays more than 180,000 dols. a year in allowances and pensions to Malays, whereas when the State was taken under British protection its total revenue did not reach 80,000 dols. yearly.

These figures should be interesting to the Aborigines' Protection Society. The truth is that the British Government is the best aborigines' protection society that has ever existed.

The State of Johor is neither a Colony nor a Protected State in the same sense as the preceding, but it must be mentioned here to complete the survey of this part of the Peninsula. Johor forms the point of the Peninsula, and contains about 9,000 square miles and 200,000 inhabitants, of whom the Chinese outnumber the Malays by four or five to one. The capital, Johor Bahru, is fifteen miles from the town of Singapore, and less than a mile from the island. Its ruler is His Highness Abu Bakar,* G.C.M.G., whose father was *Temenggong*, or Chief of Police, to the Sultan Ali, and was placed on the throne by the Indian Government, when the latter was deposed in 1855. He succeeded in 1885, and receives a considerable annual subsidy from the British Government, which controls the foreign relations of the State. He will probably be the last of his line, as Johor is understood, by the terms of his will, to pass to the British Crown on his decease. The Sultan is a familiar figure in certain circles in London, and he is well known to the inhabitants of Singapore as an exceedingly genial and hospitable potentate, who is always ready to entertain a distinguished visitor, or lend the use of his territory for a horse-raffle or other mild form of dissipation not sanctioned by the laws of the Colony. But his State offers a painful comparison with the other Malay States under British influence. It is undeveloped, without roads, without any modern system of administration ; it contains only two towns, the greater part of it is virgin jungle, and it differs from the ordinary Malay State only by the absence of actual misrule. The Sultan, however, has rendered great services to the Straits Government as go-between in many negotiations with other Malay rulers, although the latter do not regard him as an equal, on account of his far from royal birth.

Such, in its briefest form, is the remarkable history of those

* Hence " Mr. Baker," in Brighton.

political anomalies, the Protected Malay States, down to the present time. For the future, however, their history will have to proceed along other lines. The experiment has been an extremely successful one, but not much more success—possibly only retrogression—can be looked for in the same direction. The States have now outgrown the Residential system. While they had yet everything Western to learn, and their affairs were on a comparatively small scale, the personal rule of the Residents was the best education and control they could have, though even this would not have shown such good results if the Residents themselves had not happened to be men of unusual ability and courage. But now that the original Malay population is exceeded in numbers by the Chinese settlers, that the finances deal with millions of dollars, that to the protected areas have been added huge tracts of country which cannot possibly pay their way for a long time to come, and that inter-State co-operation is therefore absolutely necessary, I am convinced that the administration can no longer profitably be left in the hands of half a dozen men, necessarily often antagonistic to one another, none of whom possesses any higher nominal standing than that of servant to a native ruler. While the problems were small, the Residents were left almost unhampered in their decisions, and their rule therefore showed all the advantages of the " free hand." Now, however, they have at once both too much and too little authority. In details their control is virtually absolute, and it is they who must invent and propose every important policy. This will be, of course, of a piece with their action in small matters. At this point, however, they sink back into the position of merely subordinate officials. First, the Governor of the Straits Settlements investigates the matter with much less experience and knowledge than the Resident who has proposed it; and if he disapprove, there is an end at once. If he approve, the question goes before the Secretary of State for the Colonies, with still less ability to pronounce upon its merits—sometimes with not even enough local knowledge to enable him to pronounce correctly

the name of the place whose destinies are in his hands. The
usual conclusion is that the Resident is either overruled, or his
policy sanctioned with such conditions as deprive it of nearly all
value. As against the Governor and the Secretary of State, the
Resident is helpless, and all he can do is to wait two or three
years for the opportunity of pointing out in his Report how much
better it would have been if his original suggestions had been
sanctioned. The Protected States, therefore, must be governed
by a man whose position enables him to deal direct with the
Secretary of State at home, and with much more authority than
at present.

Another reason for a change is that the less flourishing
States can only be set upon their feet with borrowed capital,
and as the Colony has none to lend them, while two of
their neighbours have substantial cash balances, it is easy
to see where this must come from. But Perak and Selángor
will be extremely unwilling to lend money to Pahang, unless
they are able to bring their knowledge and experience to bear
upon the spending of it, and under the present system they
would have no more control than if they lent the money to
Argentina. They might see their own savings being employed
just across their borders in a manner which they knew to be
futile, yet they could not stir a finger. In his Report for
1893, the Resident of Perak says: "As Perak has no direct
interest in Pahang, and could profitably spend in Perak all the
revenue likely to be raised here, financial help can only be given
by making some sacrifice. There is no security for the advances
made, beyond what can be hoped for from the future development of Pahang; and it is therefore only reasonable that, if the
idea of advising the native rulers in the administration of the
Malay States is to be maintained, those States which now find
the means of financing Pahang should have a preponderating
voice in the expenditure of their own money, and the schemes
to which it is applied." But if the Residents of Perak and
Selángor direct the spending of practically all the money spent

6

in Pahang, then it is they, and not the Resident of Pahang, who control the latter State; and why keep up the fiction of separate control? For this reason also, therefore, the time appears to me to have come for the substitution of one head for five.

But there is a further consideration in support of this view, which far outweighs in importance both those I have mentioned. It is this: the prosperity of the Protected States rests upon such an insecure basis that having risen as brilliantly and conspicuously as the rocket, it may come down as rapidly and irrevocably as the stick. It is based solely upon the products of the tin-mines. The Perak Report shows this clearly, though indirectly. The total value of exports for 1898 was 14,499,475 dols., and of this no less than 11,895,465 dols. was tin and tin-ore—82 per cent. The total revenue collected was 8,034,004 dols., of which Customs—"that is, duty on tin"—amounted to 1,842,741 dols.; and of course many of the other receipts are dependent upon the tin industry. The Selángor Report puts the truth more bluntly: "The revenue of the State hangs directly on the output of tin." Now all prosperity dependent upon mining is precarious, but that dependent upon alluvial tin-mines—and lode-mining hardly exists—must be the most precarious of all. It may be replied, however, that mining is a very good basis upon which to start; that California, for instance, owes its present agricultural wealth to the original attractions of its gold-fields. Undoubtedly, but the Malay States are not attracting a class of people who will develop into agriculturists. At present, when a tin-mine is exhausted, its neighbourhood becomes a desert. A paragraph in the Report for Sungei Ujong illustrates this: "The valuable tin-mines at Titi were in part worked out, and the mining town which sprang up there so rapidly has begun to dwindle." If the prosperity of these States is to continue, it is therefore clear that something else must be found and cultivated to take the place of mining when this becomes less profitable or ceases altogether. This something must, of course, be agriculture, and fortunately there are no more fertile lands in the world than are here open to every comer on the best possible terms. I have given one example of coffee-growing, and it would be easy to multiply testimony. The manager of the Waterloo Estate in Perak writes: "The cultivation of coffee promises well, and where land is judiciously selected and opened, it cannot, in my opinion, fail to be a success." The Officer-in-Charge of Sungei Ujong reports: "Liberian coffee will grow on almost any kind of soil here. I have seen it growing on the 'spoil bank' of an old tin-mine, and at the present prices no form of agriculture could be more remunerative." And what is true of coffee is equally true of tea, pepper, gambier, tobacco, and rice. The States governments have done everything in their power to dispel the general ignorance of British settlers and planters about Malaya, and they offer the very warmest welcome to any who will come. Certainly no part of the Empire presents a better field for the agricultural investment of capital and personal efforts, yet what was said by the Resident of Perak in 1889 is still only too true: "Ten years ago, when almost nothing was known of the capabilities of the Malayan soil and climate, it seemed likely that the field just opened would attract many experienced European planters and a considerable amount of European capital. Now that the possibilities of agriculture have been to a large extent proved, communications greatly extended, and many facilities offered which did not then exist, the State seems to have lost its attractions for the planter."

To assure the future of the Protected States, therefore, it seems to me imperative that they should be formed into some kind of separate confederation—the Crown Colony of the Malay Peninsula, for example. This would remove them from the jurisdiction of Singapore, which now hampers and robs them; place them on a strong footing before the Secretary of State for the Colonies; enable their problems to be solved in a uniform manner, instead of by the conflict of interests; group their resources so that the stronger can afford the needed help to the weaker in the wisest and fairest shape; develop and advertise their agricultural possibilities; protect their forests; codify their laws, and place the administration of them under a British judge; and finally, present a firm and permanent foundation upon which to build when the inevitable moment comes for the absorption of the rest of the Malay Peninsula.

FRANCE IN THE FAR EAST.

CHAPTER IV.

IN FRENCH INDO-CHINA: LEAVES FROM MY NOTEBOOKS.

IT is one of the curious and significant facts of the Far East that to get to a French possession there you must go in either an English or a German boat, with the single exception of the heavily subsidised Messageries Maritimes. I went to Tongking the first time in the little *Marie*, hailing from Aponrade, wherever that may be. As soon as we had crossed the restless Gulf of Tongking and were in sight of a low-lying green and evidently fertile country, wholly different from the rocky and forbidding coast of China, Captain Hundewadt hoisted the German flag, and the pilot came off. There are two bars, one hard, which must not be touched, and the other soft mud, upon which a ship can rush at full speed and either get over or stick, as the case may be. We stuck.

Within gunshot of us as we lay in the mud was a large white European house, built on the point of an elevated promontory. It is the summer house Paul Bert built for himself, just before death put an end to all his plans and ambitions for Tongking. It has never been occupied, and the Government was thinking of turning it into a sanitarium for the forces near the coast. Once over the bars we steamed a mile or two up the river, past half a dozen odd-looking river gunboats, and dropped anchor off Haiphong. The port of Tongking is now a pretty little town, with excellent broad streets, planted with trees on each side, with spacious warehouses and solid wharves, with one Boulevard of extensive shops, many pleasant bungalows, and an astonishing

hotel. At six o'clock its *café* holds a hundred people, taking
their pre-prandial drink. To see them it is difficult to realise
that you are at the other end of the earth from Paris, and there
could not be a better illustration of the saying that a Frenchman
takes France with him wherever he goes. The business part of
the town consists of several crowded streets of Chinese houses,
and the native town, which is miserable and very dirty, lies on
the other side of a narrow creek. There are three excellent newspapers, one daily, one bi-weekly, and one weekly, and almost
every characteristic of a French town, including the duel,
which flourishes greatly in Tongking. Not a little money and
much intelligent labour have been expended to transform the
original malarious swamps into this bright and pleasing little
place, reminding one of Algiers, with its broad green and white
streets and constant sunshine. But I fear that both the labour
and the money must be looked upon as little better than wasted.

There is nothing to detain one in Haiphong. An afternoon is
enough to see it all. So next morning at eight I went on board a
big, powerful, twin-screw steamer, *Le Tigre*, for the trip to Hanoi,
the capital and largest town, upwards of a hundred miles up
the Red River. The navigation is extremely difficult in places,
owing to the mudbanks and sharp turns, but the twin-screw and
the Chinese pilot between them managed every twist but one.
There was no European captain, only a purser, and the Chinaman was apparently in sole command. A stack of Snider rifles
stood in the saloon, and a plate of half-inch iron was suspended
on each side of the pilot and the two men at the wheel, completely shielding them from bullets fired from the shore. We
had a capital breakfast, and a charming French priest, in
Chinese dress and pigtail, who was returning to his inland
station in China *viâ* Tongking, told us string after string of
adventures and incidents of his work among the Celestials. For
hours the trip is monotonous. The banks are flat, the country
is always green and fertile, the water-buffaloes wallow in the
mud, and enormous flocks of teal rise in front every few minutes.

A diversion came at one o'clock in the shape of a little post of soldiers halfway between the seaboard and the capital. The steamer came slowly alongside the high bank, a plank was thrown out, and the garrison invited us on shore. They were an officer, two non-commissioned officers, half-a-dozen privates, and about fifty native troops. The post was a strongly stockaded little place a hundred yards from the river, well able to keep off any ordinary attack. But the garrison was a sorry-looking band. The officers were in pyjamas, and the men's old thick blue and red French uniforms were only recognisable by their shape, nearly all the colour having long ago departed. Their coats were patched, their trousers torn and ragged, their boots split. As for their faces, anæmia of the most pronounced character was written plainly across them. I have never seen such a ragged and worn lot of soldiers. The arrival of the daily steamer is the only distraction of the little force, and they were profusely grateful for a bundle of illustrated papers. We also gave them a little more entertainment by running aground just opposite their post when we left.

The steamer reached Hanoi at midnight. The only hotel was closed; vigorous hammering at the door produced no effect whatever, and I was beginning to contemplate the prospect of spending the night in the street, when a jolly captain of artillery came past, evidently fresh from a good dinner, showed me a back way into the hotel, and even accompanied me, because, as he explained, I probably did not yet know how to treat the natives. Certainly if he did, I did not, although his method was simplicity itself. We discovered six " boys " sleeping sounder than I ever saw human beings sleep in my life, on a table in the dining-room. With one shove he pitched the whole lot in a heap on the floor, and as they even then showed unmistakable symptoms of an intention to finish their nap as they lay piled up on one another, he fell to work on the heap with his cane so vigorously that he soon had them scampering all over the room like a nest of disturbed rats. " Tas de cochons," he said, and resumed his homeward way.

Like almost every city of the Far East, so far as my experience goes, Hanoi is less interesting than you expect. The foreign town, of five or six hundred inhabitants, is little more than one street, named, of course, after Paul Bert, and even that is disfigured by a narrow, irregular tramway, running down the middle and carrying military stores all day long. There is a small lake in the centre of the city, with a curious islet and pagoda, that gives one pretty point of view, and the ride round the walls of the Citadel, a square mile or so of enclosed land, is interesting for once. And the " Pont de Papier," where the ill-fated Rivière met his fate so wretchedly on the afternoon of May 19, 1888, with the tiny pagoda just beyond it, where the brave Balny disappeared, are historically impressive if one has the whole story of those days in mind. But Hanoi makes a poor showing as the capital of Tongking. The Hotel Alexandre is the very worst I ever set foot in. The monuments are second to those of an ordinary Chinese town. The advent of the foreigner has killed native art and handicraft, without contributing anything to replace it. You may walk the length of the " Rue des Brodeurs " without finding a piece of embroidery worth carrying home. There is a " Rue des Incrusteurs," named after the workmen who inlay mother-of-pearl into ebony, but I spent half a day there before picking up a decent piece, and that was made before the French were thought of. The native metal-work, that sure test of the art-tendencies of an uncivilised people, has vanished with their independence. Even the Governor-General apologised for his surroundings. " I shall be able to receive you better," he said courteously, " when you come to Saigon." But there is this compensation for Hanoi as compared with Haiphong. The faster Tongking prospers, the faster will Haiphong decay ; while Hanoi always has been the capital, and nature has so placed it that it always will be, and the two will prosper, if at all, together.

Of the native inhabitants, of whom Hanoi has 70,000, there is much that might be said. After China, with its hundreds of thousands of great brown coolies, and its slim ones who will walk all day up-hill under burdens that would break down a European athlete on the level, the Annamites strike the visitor as a nation of pigmies. Their average height must be under five feet; they are narrow-chested and thin-legged, their mouths are always stained a slobbering filthy red with the areca-nut and lime they chew unceasingly, and they are stupid beyond the power of words to tell. Whether it is in any degree due to the fault of their conquerors or not, I cannot say, but they appear to be a people destitute of the sense of self-respect. At anyrate, the French treat them as if they had none. The first time I went into *déjeuner* at the hotel at Haiphong one of the "boys" had left a dirty plate on the little table to which the host showed me. "Qu'est ce que tu fais, toi?" demanded the latter, pointing to the plate, and smack, a box on the ears followed that you could have heard fifty yards off. And this in the middle of a crowded dining-room. You would no more think of striking a Chinese servant like that than of pulling a policeman's nose in Piccadilly. Before a Frenchman, an Annamite too often appears to have no rights.

Both men and women in Tongking wear their hair long and twisted up into a kind of chignon on the top of the head. It is of course always lanky and jet-black. Their dress is of the most simple. The men wear a loose jacket and short trousers, and the women a long, straight shift reaching from neck to heels. The Annamite man is a very poor creature, and it is only among the upper classes that one sees occasionally a well-formed or handsome face, with some elevation or dignity of expression. The women are much better looking, and would often be pretty except for the stained mouth and teeth, which renders them horrible to a European eye. But in figure they are the most favoured of any I have seen in the Far East, as my illustration may go to show, and in the course of a walk in Hanoi you may meet a dozen who are straight enough and strong enough and shapely enough to serve as a sculptor's models. Their native

dance is a burlesque of the Japanese, to the accompaniment of
a fiddle six feet long. The few women you see with clean
mouths and white teeth are almost sure to be the mistresses
of Europeans.

The most curious of the surface impressions of Tongking is
the language you must learn to talk with the natives. Your ear
becomes familiar with "pidgin English" before you have spent
a day in the East, and, *pace* Mr. Leland, a horrid jargon it is,
convenient, no doubt, but growing positively repulsive after a
while. But "pidgin French," or "petit nègre," as it is called,
comes as a complete surprise. And it is all the funnier because
of the excellent native pronunciation of French. "Petit nègre"
is characterised, as compared with French proper, by four
features—omission of the auxiliary verbs, ignoring of gender,
employment of the infinitive for all moods and tenses, and
absence of words taken bodily from the native, like "maskee,"
"man-man," and "chop-chop," in Pidgin. The one expression
which recurs again and again with an infinity of meanings is
"y-a-moyen," or "y-a-pas moyen." And after this comes
"fili," for "fini," nearly as often. The "You savvy" of Pidgin
is "Toi connaitre?" The "My wantchee," is "Moi vouloir."
The native servant is everywhere called by the English word
"boy," pronounced "boi-ee," in two syllables. And the
language is further enriched by a number of words recalling
the nursery, like "pousse-pousse," for jinrikisha, "coupe-coupe,"
for a big knife, and so on. "Beaucoup" does duty for "très"
and "bien," so one is constantly hearing sentences like these:
"Moi beaucoup vouloir avoir sampan," "Soupe beaucoup mauvais—moi donner vous beaucoup bambou," and "Toi beaucoup
imbécile." "Petit nègre" is of course much younger than
Pidgin; for one person who speaks it a hundred thousand speak
the latter; and it is not capable of the flights of oratory to
which the accomplished speaker of Pidgin can soar. Nor will it
ever become what Pidgin has long been—the *lingua franca* of
communication between vast numbers of people otherwise

acquainted with only a score different dialects and tongues. I may add here that "Tongking" is the same word as "Tokyo," meaning "Eastern Capital," and that the former is the only correct spelling to express the Chinese sounds. "Tonquin" and "Tonkin" are indefensible, either in French or English.

The northern part of the peninsula of Indo-China is Tong-king, the French territory adjoining China; the central part is Annam, which was formerly a long narrow strip of coast, but by the recent Convention with Siam stretches back to the Mekong; and the southern end of the peninsula is Cochin-China, with Cambodia lying behind it. Of all the possessions of France in the Far East, Cochin-China is the most imposing, as it is also the oldest. Saigon, the capital, was first captured by a combined French and Spanish expedition in 1859, and held by a small garrison until 1861, when Cochin-China was finally taken by France. For inhabitants it had in 1891, 1,758 French, 207 other Europeans, 6,600 Annamese, and 7,600 Chinese. It is connected by a steam tramway with the Chinese town of Cholon, three miles away, which has 40,000 inhabitants. The severe fighting which took place in and around Saigon practically destroyed the original native town, and the French were therefore able to rebuild it on their own lines. The result is that the Saigon of to-day is virtually a French town. It is laid out on the chess-board pattern familiar to all who have visited the western towns of the United States, and French taste has made it very attractive in appearance. The streets are lined with rows of trees, the roads are just like those of any European city, the public buildings are numerous and stately, the shops have all the external appearance of the *magasins* of Paris, the *cafés* are at every corner and are patronised with true French conviviality, and there is a very good reproduction of the Jardin d'Acclimation. The Palais du Gouvernement cost twelve million francs, and except perhaps the European-built "Audience Halls" of Bangkok, is the finest edifice in the Far East. The Cathedral is

almost equal to it, and every house is a little earthly
paradise in its trim garden. But Saigon has many draw-
backs to set against these advantages. The climate is
simply appalling. Hundreds of people avoid the journey
home from Shanghai or Hongkong by the comfortable Messageries Maritimes line, simply because they have once had
experience of a night passed in the river off Saigon. I have
seen a passenger fall on the deck, struck with heat-apoplexy
under a thick double awning, and I have twice paced the deck
for a whole night, fan in hand, sleep being out of the question
because of the heat and the mosquitoes. And except for the
Chinese, there is little commerce worth the name. It is a city
of *fonctionnaires*, and nine out of ten Frenchmen are occupied
in purveying either French luxuries or French personal services
to the official and military classes. Take away the shop-keepers,
the barbers, the tailors, the wine merchants, the tobacconists,
and the restaurant keepers, and there would be virtually no
Frenchman left who was not a soldier, a sailor, or a Civil
servant. Even many of the former have recently left the place.
While I was at Bangkok the foreign community learned with
pleasure that a French barber had arrived, and everybody went
to him at once, thankful to escape from the doubtful comb and
fingers of the native. He had left Saigon in despair, thinking
that even in the Siamese capital he might do better. Like other
French colonies, Saigon is the victim of protection and of the
inability of the *colon* to shake off the depressing conviction of
exile.

I paid a flying visit to another French colonial town, and it
left an ineffaceable impression on my mind. I was on board a
private ship sailing down the coast of Annam, when we ran
short of medicine for one of our party who was down with fever.
So we anchored off Tourane, and two of us went ashore in the
ship's boat. It was in the middle of the afternoon on a week-
day, but the main street of the town was almost deserted. Not
a score natives were about, hardly a European was to be

seen, except a group of officers sitting in front of a *café*. It was half an hour before we could transact business at the post-office. The whole town was a spectacle of stagnation, though it is one of the Annamese ports described as "ouverts au commerce international." Tourane, in fact, was a vivid commentary upon the words of Pierre Loti about precisely this part of the Far East—" C'est le voile qui se tisse lentement sur les choses trop éloignées, c'est l'anéantissement par le soleil, par la monotonie, par l'ennui."

One very pleasant reminiscence of Cochin-China I have. The city of Saigon is situated 60 miles from the mouth of the river, where there is the well-known light of Cape St. James. There is a charming little hotel there, where the Saigonnais come to seek refreshment from the dreadful heat of the town. One of the most important stations of the Eastern Telegraph Company is at the Cape, for there the cable between Hong-kong and Singapore touches land,* and connects with the French cable to Tongking and the land lines to Cambodia and Siam. It is a curious little colony at Cape St. James, a dozen Englishmen for the service of the English cable, three or four Frenchmen for the French cable, half-a-dozen pilots, and the few invalid Saigonnais who come to the hotel. The electricians get their supplies in a launch from Saigon every Sunday morning, and for the rest of the week their only communication with the great world is by the zig-zag line which trickles interminably out of the tiny siphon of Sir William Thompson's recorder. And this tells them little, for even news messages come in code. The great French mail steamers pass them twice a week, and the few

* At last a direct cable connecting Hongkong, Labuan, and Singapore has been arranged for and is now being laid. In the interests of the Empire this means of communication, independent of foreign soil, was absolutely essential. The next step, which ought not to be delayed a single day, should be to separate entirely from the British office in Hongkong the foreign employés of the Danish Great Northern Company. Their presence might conceivably constitute an Imperial danger of great magnitude. It should not be forgotten that the King of Denmark once took an attitude in this connection hostile to British interests.

other steamers which ply to Saigon for rice pick up a pilot.
The Company keep them well supplied with newspapers, and
they have an excellent billiard-table, but their life is not a
happy one. On Sundays, when the fresh supplies are in, they
feast. On Monday they feast again, for all meat must be
cooked at once. On Tuesday, cold meat. On Wednesday,
hash. On Thursday, back to tinned meats, and by Friday
there is probably neither bread nor ice at the Cape. Then,
too, fever makes its regular round among them. Their pale
faces, scarred with prickly heat and other physical nuisances of
a damp tropical climate, are a painful reminder that our
convenient telegrams, like everything else we enjoy, mean
sacrifices on somebody's part. The staff of the Eastern Company are everywhere among the most intelligent and hospitable
compatriots that the British traveller in the Far East can meet,
and the station at Cape St. James became like a home for me
for a few days. A good deal of romance is connected with this
remote pulse of the great world. Not many years ago, for
instance, the clerks used to work with loaded rifles beside them,
and on one occasion the sleeping staff were aroused in the night
by the report of a rifle, and on rushing out found that the night
operator had been visited by a tiger while working at his
instrument. The neighbourhood is still supposed, with more
or less scepticism by those who live there, to be infested with
tigers, and the government offers a standing reward of one
hundred francs for the destruction of one. During the few
days I spent at Cape St. James I made the acquaintance of an
Annamite hunter, named Mitt. He was a grave and sedate
man, extremely poor, and stone deaf, but his knowledge of
the jungle and its inhabitants might have rivalled that of
Mowgli himself. In the course of a long talk about *shikar* I
consulted him on the possibility of getting a tiger, though I had
already found that even in tiger lands tigers are not so common
as one's imagination at home pictures them. And moreover,
whenever there is a tiger there are a hundred men of his

locality bent on trapping him, or poisoning him, or snaring him with bird-lime, or, if needs must, on shooting him. My first hopes had been set on Vladivostok. There are the woolliest tigers in the world, and before reaching that remote spot I had been filled with stories of how they were in the habit of coming into the back yard for the scraps, and how men never walked abroad at night in parties of less than a dozen, all armed to the teeth. But once in Russian Tartary, I found the tiger was a tradition, and the leading merchant told me he had standing orders from three different high officials to buy any tiger-skin that came into the market, at almost any price. So I transferred my hopes to Korea. Was not the tiger a sort of national emblem of the Hermit Kingdom? And is there not a special caste of tiger-hunters, the very men who once gave such a thrashing to a foreign landing-party? In a ride across the country, therefore, I might well hope for a chance. From sea to sea, however, I never caught sight of even the hunter; only with much difficulty did I succeed in finding and buying one poor skin, and the most satisfactory response I could get to my earnest inquiries was the information, "There are two seasons in Korea: one in which the man hunts the tiger, the other in which the tiger hunts the man. It is now the latter; therefore you must come at another time." So in Northern China, so, too, in Tongking, though there I once actually saw a tiger's footprint at the entrance to a coal-mine. Mitt was disposed to be encouraging, and at last he declared, "Moi aller voir." So he disappeared for a couple of days, and returned one morning with instructions for me to be ready in the afternoon, and we started at five o'clock, Mitt walking and running ahead and I following him on a pony.

For a time we followed a road through the woods and then struck off into the bush. An hour later Mitt motioned me to dismount. A coolie waiting for us jumped into the saddle and galloped off. We were on a small rising ground, dotted with bushes, in the middle of a rough tangle of forest and brush-

wood. I looked everywhere for the *mirador*, and not finding it,
I yelled an inquiry into Mitt's ear. He pointed to a tree fifty
yards away and I saw how marvellously he had concealed it.
He had chosen two slim trees growing four feet apart, behind
these he had planted two bamboos at the other corners of the
square, and then he had led two or three thickly-leaved creepers
from the ground and wound them in and around and over a
little platform and roof, till he had made a perfect nest of live
foliage. The floor was about twenty feet from the ground, and
it looked perilously fragile to hold two men. But it was a
masterpiece of hunting craft. In response to a peculiar cry
from Mitt, two natives appeared with a little black pig slung on
a pole, yelling lustily. The *mirador* overlooked a slight depression in which an oblong pond had been constructed for the
buffaloes to wallow in, as these creatures cannot work unless
they are allowed to soak themselves in water two or three times
a day. By the side of this the pig was securely fastened. The
two natives took themselves off with their pole, Mitt gave me a
" leg up " into the *mirador*, which shook and swayed as we
climbed gingerly in, and we arranged ourselves for our long
watch. We loaded our rifles at half-past six, and till half-past
ten we sat side by side like two stone Buddhas. Then five wild
pigs came trotting down to the water to drink, which was an
intensely welcome break in the monotony. At half-past eleven
Mitt made signs to me to go to sleep for a while and he would
watch. At half-past twelve he woke me and immediately fell
back in his turn, fast asleep. It had been moonlight, but the
moon was now hidden behind clouds. On the horizon broad
flashes of summer lightning were playing. There was a chorus
of frogs in the distance, night-birds were calling to one another,
the great lizards were making extraordinary and grotesque
noises, and it was so dark that I could no longer discern the
black patch of the pig's body on the ground twenty yards away.

This is not a book of sporting adventures, though there are
many such memories upon which I should like to dwell, so

I will only say that at two o'clock, suddenly, in perfect silence and without the slightest warning, a big black object flashed by the far side of the little pool. It was like the swoop past of an owl in the starlight, like the shadow of a passing bird, utterly noiseless and instantaneous. I fired, and a minute afterwards a loud cough showed that the bullet had found its place. At daylight we descended and sought everywhere on the hard ground for footprints. The search brought us for a minute to the edge of a stretch of tall grass. That moment came very near being the last for one of us. While we were peering about, the tiger suddenly sat up in the grass not ten feet away, and, with a tremendous roar, sprang clean out into the open. He was so near that it was out of the question to shoot. If I had flung my rifle forward it would have fallen on him. I could see his white teeth distinctly and the red gap of his throat. I remember even at that moment wondering how he could possibly open his mouth so wide. Mitt and I were perhaps eight yards apart and the tiger leaped out midway between us. Instinctively the Annamite made a wild rush away on his side and I on mine. The tiger had evidently walked just far enough into the grass to be hidden and had then lain down. His presence there took us so completely by surprise that we were helpless. If he had been slightly less wounded than he was, it is perfectly certain that in another instant he would have sprung upon one or the other of us, as we had not the remotest chance of escaping by running away. But the first spring was evidently all it could manage, for it turned immediately and sneaked back into cover. It was evident that the beast was no longer in fighting trim, so after a few minutes we followed it into the grass and I despatched it with a couple of shots. Every sportsman knows that at such a moment one is ridiculously happy. It turned out to be a tigress, a little under eight feet long, and very beautifully marked. Six coolies carried her on crossed poles; the natives came out and "chin-chinned" her to Cape St. James, for the tiger is "joss" to them; her skin went to Rowland Ward's; her

claws were mounted as a necklace by a Chinese goldsmith ; her
body was eaten by the Annamites, and I had a reward of a
hundred francs from the French Government for killing an
animal nuisible. With that reward and a little addition Mitt
was able to settle down for life as a landed proprietor. Since
then I have found out a place where a dozen tigers may
certainly be shot in a week or two, but this is for another
time.

The French war with China—or the "reprisals," as it was
called by France—has left many a memory in the Far East.
Some of these are instructive for the future, some of them should
be put on record for the historian, while some are too dreadful
to tell at all. Among the first-named are the advantages
attaching to the state of "reprisals." During the war the
bullocks for victualling the French forces used to stand in the
streets of Hongkong. The Hongkong coolies at first refused to
work for the French, and the French mail steamers were loaded
by "destitutes" from the Sailors' Home. Hongkong was on
the eve of a general strike of the Chinese. The coolies refused
under threats from China, but when they saw that the French
could get on without them, and that the coolies who replaced
them were getting a dollar a day, they returned to work. The
French fleet established coaling-stations in the Pescadores, and
at the anchorage of Matsu, a few miles north of the mouth of
the river Min, and at these points they were regularly supplied
with coal from a non-British firm in Hongkong. The same
firm were dealing at the same time with the Chinese government. One curious incident of the war was narrated to me by
the chief actor in it. There was an American-built craft of five
hundred tons, named the *Ping-on*, sailing under the British flag.
She was sold by her owners to the Chinese government to be
delivered in Foochow, and sailed for that port with nine hundred
Chinese soldiers on board. They mutinied and refused to be
taken to Foochow, and forced the captain to take them to
Taiwan, in Formosa, which he did, receiving there the first

payment of seventeen thousand dollars. There the Chinese put another captain on board, and in some unexplained way, succeeded in getting her to sea still under the British flag. For some time she ran between Amoy and Formosa, until one day, with a full load of Chinese soldiers, she ran into the midst of the French fleet in Rover's Channel, in the Pescadores. This was a very curious " accident " for an experienced navigator to make. As soon as the Chinese saw their position a number of them jumped overboard, and the *Ping-on* was captured and taken to Saigon. That there was something very wrong about her right to fly the red ensign is proved by the fact that the British Government took no steps whatever on her behalf, as they did, for instance, in the case of the *Waverley*, which was captured by the French and given up again. The blockade of Formosa gave rise to many strange and painful incidents. Before Keelung was taken, one of my informants had seen thirty-two heads of French soldiers in the market-place, all having either deserted or been captured at the unsuccessful attack on Tamsui, where French troops in heavy marching order were landed with three miles of paddy-fields between them and the enemy, whereas a mile above the fort they might have found an excellent landing-place. Being over their knees in mud they were of course simply mown down by the Chinese riflemen. For every one of these heads a reward of a hundred taels had been paid. The foreigners in Formosa protested so strenuously against this barbarity of the Chinese that the reward was altered to a hundred taels for a live Frenchman, and I have talked to the man who had thirty under his charge at one time. They were then treated very well, most of them being ultimately given a free passage to Amoy, and a few entering the Chinese service, where some remain to this day. These thirty had all deserted from the French ships, and all but two or three were men from Elsass-Lothringen and spoke little but German. " You may guess," added my informant, who was a foreigner occupying a high official position, " how miserable they must

have been on board, for them to desert to a place like Formosa!"
As an example of the way the Chinese were swindled by certain
foreign purveyors, I may mention that they were supplied from
Europe with five hundred thousand rounds for Winchester rifles,
and that the whole of this ammunition was found to be worthless,
when a foreign officer examined it, and was destroyed. Another
dreadful incident of which I find all the details in my notebooks,
arose from the necessity the French found or believed themselves
to be in to shoot a number of women in Keelung. An alarming
number of French soldiers were being reported as missing, and
it was alleged that these women had decoyed them into houses
and there made away with them in horrible ways. Twenty
women were identified and found guilty, and they were all shot.
In judging of any acts of punishment or retaliation by Europeans
against Chinese, it must never be forgotten that acts of appalling
and almost incredible barbarity are the common accompaniment
of all Chinese warfare. If it were not that the details are indescribable I could give a blood-curdling list of horrors that have
been described to me. And as I have more than once had a
narrow escape myself at the hands of Chinese ruffians, I speak
not altogether without personal experience.

There is one other event of the Franco-Chinese "reprisals"
upon which public opinion, particularly in France, is ill-informed,
and which, in the interests of history, should be recognised in its
true light. I mean the engagement between the French and
Chinese fleets at the Pagoda Anchorage in the Min river, off
Foochow, on August 23, 1884. This is generally regarded as a
battle, and as Admiral Courbet's greatest achievement: in fact,
it was a massacre. M. Pierre Loti calls it "la grande gloire de
Fou-tchéou," and all French writers follow in the same strain.
For weeks the Chinese fleet had lain at anchor, covered by the
shotted guns of the French fleet, and considering the utter and
instant cowardice shown by the Chinese when the critical
moment at last came, it can only be supposed that they were
under the impression that the French would not really attack

after all. The Chinese ships numbered eleven, all of wood, mounting forty-five guns, only a few of which were of large calibre, and carrying 1,190 men. The French ships were nine armoured vessels and two torpedo boats, with seventy-seven guns and 1,830 men. The signal for the engagement was given immediately on the arrival of the *Triomphante*, by the hoisting of the red flag on the *Volta* at fifty-six minutes past one o'clock. At three minutes past two all was over. Two Chinese vessels sank in a few seconds. Two others ran ashore in attempting to escape. Two more were so moored that their big guns could not be fired, and they were immediately adrift in a sinking condition. Three more were disabled at the first discharge. One, the *Yangwu*, fired her stern chaser once, killing several men on the bridge of the *Volta* and almost killing Admiral Courbet himself. Before she could reload, a torpedo-boat from the *Volta* reached her and she was blown to pieces *within twenty-seven seconds* of the beginning of the fight. One Chinese vessel alone may be said to have been fought. This was the little *Chenwei*. "Exposed to the broadsides of the *Villars* and the *d'Estaing*, and riddled by a terrific discharge from the heavy guns of the *Triomphante* as she passed, she fought to the last. In flames fore and aft, drifting helplessly down the stream and sinking, she plied her guns again and again, till one of the French torpedo boats, dashing in through the smoke, completed the work of destruction."[*] "The captain reserved one loaded gun till the last moment, and then as the battered and shot-rent ship gave the last mournful roll, he pulled the lock-string and sent hissing on its errand of hate the last farewell of the unfortunate *Ching Wai*."[†] "Though in *seven minutes* from the firing of the first shot every Chinese vessel was practically disabled, the French continued to pour in shot, shell and Hotchkiss fire,

---

[*] Imperial Chinese Maritime Customs, Report of Mr. Deputy Commissioner Carrall, which may be regarded as an official account of the engagement.

[†] "The French at Foochow," by James F. Roche and L. L. Cowen, U.S. Navy, which confirms the above in all essential details.

regardless of the wounded and helpless men in the crippled ships.
. . . The casualties on the French side were 5 killed and 15
wounded, and on the Chinese side 419 killed and 128 wounded,
and 51 missing, besides 102 killed and 22 wounded on board
war junks." Such is the true story of the Foochow fight. Of
course war is war, and the French Marshal was right when he
said, "Quand je fais la guerre je laisse ma philanthropie dans
les armoires de ma femme." And it is the business of a fleet to
disable the fleet of the enemy in the shortest possible time.
But with the exception of the *Chenwei* on one side and the
ten men on the torpedo-boat of the *Volta* on the other, the less
said about "gloire" on this occasion the better. French
soldiers did cover themselves with glory when their commander
made his fatal blunder before Tamsui, and many a time in
Tongking, but Foochow belongs to another category.

I have in my notebooks the following striking story of the
death of Rivière, which I took down in these words from the
lips of the narrator, who sufficiently describes himself. It will
be remembered that Commandant Rivière, an extremely gallant
but very nervous man, ambitious of literary honours, who had
said, "Je m'en vais par le Tonkin à l'Académie," had been
compelled to spend nearly a year in possession of the citadel of
Hanoi, while the Chinese Black Flags came in thousands into
the town and gathered in impudent strength in the neighbourhood. At last the reinforcements he had prayed for came, and
slight hostilities began at once. Then the Black Flag leader,
the famous Liu Jung-fu, issued his challenge to the French
commander. "You send out teachers of religion," it said, " to
undermine and ruin the people. You say you wish for international commerce, but you merely wish to swallow up the
country. There are no bounds to your cruelty, and there is no
name for your wickedness. You trust in your strength and you
debauch our women and our youth. . . . He who issues this
proclamation has received behest to avenge these wrongs. . . .
But Hanoi is an ancient and honourable town. It is filled with

honest and loyal citizens. Therefore could he not endure that
the city should be reduced to ruins, and young and old put to
the sword. Therefore do I, Liu Jung-fu, issue proclamation.
Know, ye French robbers, that I come to meet you. Rely on
your strength and rapine, and lead forth your herd of sheep and
ours to meet my army of heroes, and see who will be master.
Wai-tak-fu, an open space, I have fixed on as the field where I
shall establish my fame." * This was stuck up one night upon
the gates of the citadel and all over the stockades, and was
followed by an attack next day. So much by way of introduction: now for the story which was told to me. My informant
said: " Rivière was at Hanoi doing nothing, in spite of the fact
that the Chinese were known to be gathering round the place.
People talked a good deal about it, and one day the challenge
came from Liu Jung-fu. So Rivière said, 'That's nothing but
humbug—I'll show you.' And next morning he went out with
four hundred men, himself in a carriage and pair, for he had
been suffering from fever. It was to be just a morning's walk—
nothing else. Berthe de Villers was with him, and when they
reached the Pont de Papier he came up and said, ' Vous feriez
bien, Commandant, de faire fouiller ces bois.' ' Vous avez
peur ? ' asked Rivière. ' Je n'ai jamais peur,' replied Villers,
and turned to walk off, when a volley was fired from the wood.
Villers was hit in the stomach, and a quarter-master, standing
close by, in the chest. Rivière sprang out, placed Villers and
the man in the carriage and ordered it back to Hanoi at
once. The horses were turned, bolted, and carried the two men
at full gallop back to Hanoi, where they arrived locked in each
other's arms in the death-grasp. In the meantime the volleys
had continued and men had fallen by dozens and lay in heaps
along the road. Rivière rushed ahead to get a gun on the bridge
turned round so that it could be brought back, when he was
struck mortally in the side and fell. A lieutenant named

* For the whole proclamation see J. G. Scott, " France and Tongking," 1885,
p. 82, and C. B. Norman, " Tonkin," 1884, p. 210.

Jacquis ran up, and Rivière, seeing that he had made a horrible and fatal mistake, and that he was mortally wounded, ordered Jacquis to kill him. 'Jacquis, brûle-moi la gueule!' 'Je ne veux pas, Commandant.' 'Je vous le commande!' 'Je ne peux pas, Commandant.' Then Rivière drew his revolver and blew his brains out, and Jacquis, seeing it, did the same. Rivière's head was carried away after the *sauve qui peut*, and was only recovered a long time afterwards after much negociation. It had been put in spirits of wine in a kerosine oil tin, and was perfectly recognisable, whiskers and all. I slept on that tin for several nights. Then I was a member of the committee who drew up the *procès verbal* uniting the head to the body. He had shot himself in the mouth and the bullet had come out behind the left ear." With regard to this story I can only say that I repeat it exactly as it was told to me in Tongking by a thoroughly respectable informant. Of course Rivière's sortie, the rout of the French, the return of the defeated troops into Hanoi, the distribution of wine, the consequent drunkenness of the over-strained men, the officers themselves doing sentry-go on that "black night" of May 19, 1883, the seizure of Rivière's head and the subsequent surrender of it, are matters of history. With this strange story I close my notebooks so far as souvenirs of the war are concerned.

One of the most remarkable romances of modern Eastern history is connected with these French colonies. In the spring of 1889 there appeared at Hongkong a tall, well-built Frenchman, with a bushy brown beard and very long legs, who called himself Marie David de Mayréna, and distributed visiting-cards with the words " S.M. le Roi des Sédangs " printed upon them. He had had an adventurous career in the Far East, in the course of which he had more than once displayed great personal courage in guerilla warfare. At last his wanderings brought him to the region of the Sedangs, a tribe inhabiting part of the *Hinterland* of Annam, a region not so well known then as it has since become. By these people he had been elected king, and of the

genuineness of his election there can be no doubt whatever.
He was at first recognised by the French missionaries and
by the French authorities, and I have myself seen correspondence and treaties which establish his claim beyond
question. Of these treaties there were a score signed between
Mayréna and the chiefs of the different tribes; with the
Hallongs and Bràos, signed by Khen on June 3, 1888; with
the confederation Banhar-Reungao, signed by Krui, President ;
with the Jiarais, signed by Ham on August 19, 1888, promising tribute of " un éléphant domestique dressé "; with the
village of Dak-Drey and half-a-dozen others, signed by Blāk,
chief, translated and witnessed by P. Trigoyen and J. B.
Guerlach, " missionnaires apostoliques "; and finally, a treaty
of alliance between " les R. P. Missionnaires et les Sédangs,"
concluded " entre Marie, roi des Sédangs, et le R. P. Vialleton,
supérieur de la Mission des Sauvages Banhar-Reungao." This
treaty provided that " à partir d'aujourd'hui, toutes les tribus ou
villages qui ont reconnu ou qui reconnaitront a l'avenir l'auto-
rité du Roi des Sédangs seront les amis et alliés des villages
des Pères Missionnaires. En cas d'attaque des Missions, ils
préteront aide et secours." I should add that I give these
details not only for their romantic interest, but also because
when Mayréna was thrown over by the French authorities
and the missionaries, he was poohpoohed as a common liar,
and now that he is dead and the whole strange adventure at
an end, I take a pleasure in showing that he was not wholly an
impostor, in spite of his vanity and his follies. It should be
added in explanation of certain phrases that his French was
by no means always above reproach. To continue, the relations which had subsisted between Mayréna and the priests
are clearly shown by the following passage in the treaty,
which, like most of this strange history, is now published for
the first time so far as my knowledge goes: " Considérant que
si nous detenons la couronne du Royaume Sédang, nous la
devons aux RR. Pères Missionnaires de la Société des Missions

Etrangères de Paris ; que c'est grâce à leurs concours que nous
avons pu expliquer notre volonté et parcourir le Royaume
avant d'être élu ; que ce sont eux qui ont servi d'intermédiaires
entre nous et les chefs pour traduire nos pensées "—complete
liberty to preach is granted, all religions are promised toleration,
but that of the Roman Catholic Church is declared the official
one ; the right of refuge is given, too, in chapels, and finally
lands for a new town to be *chef-lieu* of the province of Kon
Trang, and to bear that name, are conceded to the R. Père
Trigoyen. This treaty is dated Kon Jéri, August 25, 1888.
The " Constitution " is dated July 1, 1888, and its Article III.
reads, " M. de Mayréna, déjà élu Roi des Sédangs, portera le
titre Roi Chef Suprême," and Article V., " Le drapeau national
sera bleu uni avec une croix blanche à l'étoile rouge au centre."
It was signed by thirty-seven chiefs, of whose names I copied
only the first and the last—Kon Tao Jop and Pelei Tebau.
When Mayréna first turned up in Hongkong, he was vouched
for by the French Consul and introduced by him to everybody,
including the Governor, in consequence of which his social position was sealed by an invitation to dinner at Government House.
At this time he was an astounding figure, when in his royal
attire. He wore a short scarlet jacket with enormous *galons* on
the cuffs, a broad blue ribbon, a magenta sash in which was
stuck a long curved sword worn across the front of the body,
white trousers with a broad gold stripe, and a white helmet with
a gold crown and three stars. He distributed broadcast the
" Order of Marie I.," beginning with the captain of the little
Danish steamer *Freyr*, in return for the hoisting of his royal
standard in Haiphong harbour, and continuing with the
Governor of Hongkong, who was caused no slight embarrassment in getting rid of the impossible ribbon and cross. He
used notepaper with a huge gold crown and coat-of-arms upon
it, gave large orders for jewellery, and conducted himself
generally like a crowned head. I have seen a private letter he
wrote at this time, from which the following passage is perhaps

worth putting on record : " Il est un ait bien certain, c'est que entre l'Annam et le Siam il existe un vaste pays qui a nom Laos. . . . Or, les Sédangs et les Hamongs sont (illegible), je parle des chefs marqués au bras et dans le dos par le roi du Laos. La France a-t-elle quelque droit sur le Laos ? Non ! . . . Le Laos . . . n'a aucune rélation avec les nations Européennes." Mayréna succeeded in getting a few Hongkong merchants to enter into an arrangement with him, by which he conceded to them the right of developing the country of the Sedangs, in return for certain duties upon trade and exports. But the collapse came, of course, when the French authorities changed their policy and took a line of direct opposition to him. Even the missionaries who had enabled him to secure the treaties of which they themselves were the official witnesses, denounced him as an impostor. He then offered himself and his country to the British, who would naturally have nothing to do with him, so he next tried the Germans, and was actually indiscreet enough as to send a telegram to Berlin in open German, offering his allegiance, forgetting that this must pass through a French office in Saigon. Of course it was read and reported from there and orders were issued for his arrest. He believed that he was condemned to be shot for high treason, so he went to Europe by the German mail steamer, a few of his acquaintances in Hongkong passing the hat round to pay his passage. After he had left, the police succeeded in recovering most of the jewellery he had presented and failed to pay for. A man of this stamp, however, is never very long without money, and after spending some time in prison in Ostend for debt he next turned up in Paris and lived there in luxury for awhile, the French press not being quite sure what to make of him. Finally, he returned to the Far East, settled down with one male companion and two or three female ones on an uninhabited island off the coast of the Malay Peninsula, where a cobra brought his strange career to a sudden end by biting him in the foot. All that remains of " Marie I., King of the Sedangs," is the set of postage stamps he issued, which are among the most prized curiosities of the philatelists. Such is the true story of a " man who would be king," and it is perhaps worth telling as an illustration of the fact that even in these late days there may be as much romance in reality as in fiction, at least in the wonderland of the Far East.

CHAPTER V.

ON THE FRANCO-CHINESE FRONTIER.

I WAS particularly fortunate in having the opportunity of making a flying trip to the frontier between China and the French possessions. This is far off the beaten track; no vessels go there except to carry military supplies, and no private boat-owners could be induced to go for fear of the pirates. I had been to see the coal mines of the "Compagnie française des Charbonnages du Tonkin," and the Managing Director, M. Bavier-Chauffour, was good enough to place his steam yacht, the *Fanny*, at my disposal. The trip was one of great interest, and at the time of my visit no Englishman had been there, except Mr. James Hart, who represented China on the Commission to delimit the frontier.

From Hatou, where the coal mines are, we steamed due north along the coast, entering almost at once the unique scenery of Along Bay. For hours here we threaded our way among rocks as thick as trees in an orchard—enormous towering hills a thousand feet high, great boulders hanging over sea-worn caves, tall trembling steeples, tiny wooded rock-islets, shimmering grottos, and an infinite number of grotesque water-carved forms —the monk, the inkstand, the cap of liberty. All the afternoon there was one of these within gun-shot on each side. This is the pirates' haunt, and it is indeed a glorious thing to be a pirate king when you can run from your pursuer into Along Bay and disappear instantly at any point. On our way down we came across a fleet of sampans, carrying a thousand wood-

cutters to their work, convoyed by a gunboat. The commander
hailed us, and we went on board. "I engage you to be
cautious," he said; "there is a well-armed band of pirates
reported on the coast. I would come a little way with you, but
I have just received telegraphic orders to stand by these boats.
However, keep a good look-out."

By the evening of the second day we were close to our
destination—the mouth of the river separating Tongking and
China. It was very foggy intermittently, and the pilot was
about at the end of his knowledge. He believed us, however,
to be just off the mouth of the river. So we held a council of
war on the bridge, and decided to anchor. The word was hardly
out of our host's mouth when—scrunch, scrunch, under the keel
told us it was too late. Full speed astern, anchors laid out,
everybody on board run backwards and forwards across the
vessel—none of these things moved us. We were high and dry,
on a falling tide. Then the fog lifted for a moment, and we saw
where we were—far beyond the mouth of the river, within a
quarter of a mile of the mainland of China, and in probably the
very worst spot for the very worst pirates in the whole world.
And in these seas there is only one tide in the twenty-four hours.
For twenty hours we should be on the sandbank, in two or three
hours we should walk round the launch; never in their lives
would the pirates have had a chance at such a prize as the
Fanny; and they could come in any number from the mainland.
We tried to laugh at our bad luck, but the situation was
decidedly unpleasant. One of our party knew the country very
well, and the natives, as he speaks Annamese, but we all knew
enough to know one thing—namely, that it would never do to
be taken alive. To blow one's brains out if necessary is one
thing; to be skinned alive is another. So we made preparations for our defense. No craft travels in these waters without
being armed; and we were particularly well off. We had each
his gun, rifle, and revolver; three Sikh guards from the mines
had their rifles, and there were six Winchesters in the rack in

the saloon. The Chinese captain and crew could all be depended
upon; so we posted a sentry forward, one aft, and one on the
bridge, to be relieved every two hours, with orders first to
hail and then to fire at anybody or any boat that might approach.
Then, after dinner, we laid our revolvers on the table and
commenced an all-night game—the second time in my life that
I have assisted at the unholy union of poker and pistols. Once
only were we disturbed. About two o'clock the Sikh in the
bows shouted " Sampan! " In an instant we were on deck,
and there, sure enough, was a big black boat approaching from
the sea. We waited till it was within a couple of hundred
yards—long enough to see that it was full of men, and was
being rowed in unusual silence; then our Annamite-speaking
member shouted, " If you don't show a light instantly we shall
shoot." There was no answer, and still the boat came on.
He shouted again, and the rifles were at our shoulders, when
the boat showed a lantern. Then slowly it disappeared back
into the darkness.

So ended our desperate affair with the pirates. Their existence is no joke, however. Numbers of native junks fall into
their hands, and a few months before I was there several
Europeans had been murdered by them, and two or three others-
with sums of money in their possession, had completely dis
appeared. A fortnight previous two redoubtable pirate chiefs
were captured, two hundred men with 120 breechloaders, after
an expedition costing seven thousand dollars and a hundred
killed and wounded. At a place called Caobang they are still
formidable in the field, kept by their leaders under strict
discipline and training, and, when hard pressed, make their
escape across the frontier into China, where the mandarins help
them. And, of course, every junk that leaves the Canton river
is heavily armed with brass cannon, and every European
steamer that plies on it has an open stack of loaded rifles in
the saloon for the passengers' use.

It is a long row up the river to the little frontier town of

Monkay. This is—or rather was—a very peculiar place. It
was built half on each side of the little stream that forms the
actual frontier. Two halves had different names, the Tongking one only being called Monkay, and the Chinese town
Trong-King. (The reason for using the past tense will be
plain presently.) The town had no poor quarter; its streets
were mathematically laid out; its houses were all of brick and
stone, with richly carved and ornamented lintels and eaves;
its inhabitants were all rich. In some way or other, this was
the outcome of the alliance of piracy and smuggling. When
the French came they did not interfere with the town on their
side of the stream, but on the top of a sugar-loaf hill, three-
quarters of a mile back, they began to build a little fort, and
under its guns they laid out a " citadel," inside which to locate
the barracks, officers' quarters, magazines, &c. Among the
first to be sent there was a civilian officer named Haitce. One
day they were attacked by a band of Chinese soldiers. They
resisted as long as possible and then fled; some were shot, some
escaped, Haitce only was captured. He was taken back to a
house in the principal street of the model little town of Monkay,
tied down upon a table, and skinned alive.

Now, at this time, the famous Colonel Dugenne was in command of the Foreign Legion in Tongking. Everybody knows
what the Foreign Legion is—almost the only force in the world
where a sound man is enlisted instantly without a question
being asked. No matter what your nationality, what your
colour, what your past, you are welcome in the Foreign Legion.
A man may even desert from the regular French army and
re-enlist, unquestioned, in this heterogeneous force. In return
for this preliminary indulgence, however, you must put up with
many inconveniences—the worst climates, the hardest work, the
front line of the attack, the forlorn hope, and the most iron
discipline. Once out of civilised parts, and there is practically
only one punishment in the Foreign Legion—the punishment
that can only be awarded once. To keep such a body of men

in order, this is perhaps necessary, and the officers to enforce
it must be hard men—men with bodies of steel and hearts of
stone. And the hardest of them all was Colonel Dugenne.
Some day I must tell the stories I heard of his methods of
pacification in Tongking. When the authorities learned of the
outrage I have described, they understood that it was no use to
wipe it out with rose-water. So they sent Colonel Dugenne and
his "children." He came and looked at the place. "Burn it,"
said he. But it wouldn't burn, being all brick and stone. "Blow
it up," said Colonel Dugenne. And they did—they blew the
whole town literally to bits. Compared with Monkay, Pompeii
is in good preservation. You need an alpenstock to get through
the streets. And the house where Haitco was tortured is now
a hole in the ground twenty feet deep.

You are not long in discovering that Monkay is not like other
places. As we were rowing up, a big red pheasant was sitting
in a tree not twenty yards away. I picked up my rifle to try
and shoot its head off, as I have done with partridges in the
Maine woods. "Don't fire here," I was told; "the people at
the fort would think there was trouble, and probably turn out a
lot of men." The Resident, M. Rustant, walked down to meet
us and take us to the Residency. This proved to be an old
temple, or *pagode*, as the French call all native buildings, divided
into rooms by board partitions, and very meagrely provided with
modern furniture. Outside a six-foot moat was dug, and lined
with spikes of bamboo so thickly that a hen could hardly walk
about in it. On each side of the moat was a stockade built of
heavy bamboo, eight feet high, and sharpened to a spike at the
top. At each corner a look-out was built of sods and bamboo,
in which a sentry stood always with a loaded rifle. The front of
the Residency faced the river, where a little gun-boat lay at
anchor. The back of it looked towards the frontier, and therefore the back entrance, with the kitchen and offices, was further
protected with thick walls of sods *en échelon*, to guard against
the bullets fired across at it from long range. The Resident's

guard consists of a hundred and twenty native militia, under two
European officers.   But at night as we sat at dinner in the
cold, bare, cob-webbed, bat-tenanted central hall of the former
temple, the door was pushed noisily open, and a night-guard of
thirteen men and a sergeant of the Foreign Legion tramped
past our chairs to an ante-room, and grounded their arms with
a crash on the stone floor.   At midnight we were awakened by
the same tramp and crash as the guard was changed.   And
there is no " show pidgin " about this : all these men and their
ball-cartridges may be needed at any minute.

Next morning we went to pay our respects to the commanding
officer, and look round.   First we climbed up to the *fortin* on
the top of the sugar-loaf hill, where there were half-a-dozen
light guns and a small force of French artillerymen, and into
which no native is ever permitted to set foot.   The frontier river
winds along like a silver thread three-quarters of a mile off   the
citadel is just below, and the half-dozen houses of the foreign
population ; and through a glass you can see the Chinese guns
and soldiers in their own fort, on a similar hill, a couple of
miles off, or less.   All these guns, of course, are trained straight
at one another.   And over the hills you can see the telegraph
wire connecting the furthest extremities of the Chinese Empire,
stretching down into the town, a solid and prosperous-looking
little place, like Monkay on this side before Colonel Dugenne
blew it up.   The French have no telegraph, but a line of helio-
graph to within a few miles of Haiphong, only allowed to be
used for official messages.   Indeed, there is nobody else to use
it, although the Resident was kind enough to allow me to
receive a private message from home by its aid.

Then we walked, always with an escort, through the ruins
of the town down to the river.   As we entered the street the
quick eye of the Commandant caught sight of new marks on a
blank brick wall.   Climbing into the inside we discovered that
somebody from across the frontier had come, probably during
the preceding night, and actually loop-holed the wall for rifles,

so that they could steal across the next moonlight night and pick off the sentries at the fort ! From the arrangements made then and there, I fancy those gentry would get a reception to surprise them. The river which constitutes the actual frontier is only about forty yards wide, and can be forded at low tide. On the French side the bank is high, while the Chinese town is built almost down to the water's edge. As soon as we were seen on the opposite bank the Chinese soldiery came down to the river in crowds, in their bright yellow and red jackets, to stare at us, and when I set up my camera they evidently became rather nervous, thinking it a new engine of war. Indeed, the Commandant said, "Don't stay there any longer than is necessary; it's just possible they might take a pot-shot at us." Across this river, of course, not a soul ventures. If a Frenchman should try, his head would be off his shoulders, or worse, in five minutes. With a good deal of difficulty, I bribed a Chinaman to take a telegram across, addressed to Sir Robert Hart, in Peking, but they refused to despatch it, and sent it back. In fact, the relations between the French and Chinese are about as strained as they can possibly be. The Commandant pointed out to me a small cleared and levelled spot on the top of a hillock, and told me its gruesome story. Two months before my visit a block-house had stood there, garrisoned by a sergeant and six French soldiers and eight native regulars. One night the people at the fort suddenly heard rapid firing, and shortly afterwards the block-house burst into flames. The night was pitch dark, and it was no good for them to move out to the rescue, as they did not know that there were not a thousand Chinese, and, as the block-house was burning, their comrades had either escaped or been killed. At daylight they marched down and found the eight natives and five Europeans dead, the sergeant headless and horribly and indescribably mutilated, and one European missing—evidently carried off into China, as he was never heard of again. No wonder that a Chinaman from across the river who falls into French hands here gets a very

short shrift—generally about as long as it takes to pull a
trigger. In fact, I believe any Chinaman at Monkay at night
is shot on sight. The Chinese who come across on these
murdering expeditions are not pirates at all, or "black flags,"
or dacoits, or anything of that kind; they are Chinese regulars,
who leave their jackets behind and resume them on their
return. And, of course, if the practice were not encouraged or
at least winked at by the Chinese officials, it could not go on.

The native troops are not very smart soldiers, but they take
kindly to the loose French discipline, and on several occasions
they have fought very well indeed. Their dress consists of
dark blue cotton knickerbockers and jacket, a little pointed
bamboo hat, and a sash. They wear no shoes; and the only
difference between the militia or civil guards and the regulars is
that the sash and hat of the former are blue and of the latter
red. At Monkay the total strength at the time of my visit was
about seven hundred and fifty men—three hundred and fifty
Europeans and four hundred natives—not nearly enough, the
Commandant complained bitterly. Once as I stood with him
in the fort he showed me a valley miles off, and said, "There are
five hundred pirates over there. The day after to-morrow I am
going out to say 'Bonjour' to them." And two days after I
got back to Hongkong, I read in the newspaper that he had
made his expedition, the Chinese had attacked his camp during
the night, and that he had been the first man shot. "Don't
forget to send me some of your photographs," he had said to me
at the same time, when I was taking those which now illustrate this chapter; "they will be very dramatic." A Customs
officer named Carrière was captured and carried off by pirates
last year. Three Frenchmen, MM. Roty, Bouyer, and Droz-
Frits were captured at different times in 1892, and kept prisoners
for many months before their surrender was effected. And in
August of the present year the Chinese made a raid at Monkay,
killed a M. Chaillet in his own house, and carried off his wife
and child. So the Franco-Chinese frontier is still a place
that "repays careful avoidance."

CHAPTER VI.

A STUDY OF FRENCH COLONIAL ADMINISTRATION.

SOCIETY in French Indo-China is sharply divided into three classes, and each of the three is at daggers drawn with the other two. They are the official, the military, and the civilian —the Governor-General, the Colonel, and the Colonist. To the official eye the military class is constantly endeavouring to usurp functions to which it has no right, and the civilians are an unreasonable body of incapable people, impossible to satisfy. The military class are furious against the Government, represented by the officials, for their reduced numbers, and cling all the more tenaciously to privileges which only belonged to them as an army of occupation ; and they desire to be allowed a free hand to "pacify" the country by the only means known to them —the sword. The civilian colonist, finally, detests the military, in the conviction that if he could only once get rid of nearly all of them the country would "pacify" itself fast enough by commerce and agriculture, which it will never do so long as it is a happy hunting-ground for crosses and promotions. And how can he feel either respect or sympathy for the Governors who come and go like the leaves on the trees, and who must needs hold the helm in Hanoi with their eyes fixed on the Quai d'Orsay ? Society in the French colonies of the Far East is a perpetual triangular duel.

Let me give a few of the experiences upon which this analysis is based. The first person with whom I had any conversation after setting foot of Tongking was a well-informed, intelligent bourgeois who had passed six years there. I began by saying I was sorry to hear of the heavy casualties of a column then operating in the interior, a hundred men having been lost in one action. "He'll arrive, all the same," replied my acquaintance, speaking of the officer in command. "He wants his third star, and what does he care if it costs him five hundred men? He'll get it, too, *allez!*" There is the civilian's view of the military. Now for the functionary's view, and I should not tell this story if M. Richaud's terrible death—let me throw a word of recollection and respect over his "vast and wandering grave"—had not untied my tongue. When I was at Hanoi I asked him, on the strength of my French official letter, for an escort of a few men to accompany me to a place one day's march into the interior. "Certainly," he replied, "with pleasure. They shall be ready the day after to-morrow." The same evening I was dining with him, and when I entered the drawing-room he took me on one side and said, "By the way, about that escort, I am exceedingly annoyed, but it is impossible." And answering my look of surprise, for my official letter had been given for the very purpose of making such facilities certain, he continued: "The General replies that he has not five men of whom he can dispose at this moment. Frankly, you know, you should properly have asked him in the first place, and not me." The Governor-General's annoyance and embarrassment at having to acknowledge to a stranger this humiliating snub were so visible that of course I dropped the subject, and his secretary's whispered request afterwards not to reopen it was unnecessary. But I could not help asking him next day as we were driving whether in French colonies, as in English, the chief civil authority was not *ex officio* commander-in-chief. He saw the point instantly and replied, "Yes, that is my title too," and after a pause—"*seulement, je délègue mes pouvoirs.*" After thus being refused an escort, I was refused permission to go alone at my own risk, so my proposed journey was doubly impossible. At the time the General had not five men "disponibles" there were, of course, twenty times that number kicking their heels in barracks. The Governor had promised the escort, therefore the General refused it. That was the only and the universal explanation offered me. And it was the true one.

To pass on again to the civilian colonist. Half way up the river between Haiphong and Hanoi I noticed heaps of fresh mud lying along the bank. "Then you have been dredging, after all?" I asked. "Hush," was the reply; "we have been doing a little of it at night, because the Administration would not allow us to do it openly, and we stuck here every day." Why not? Heaven only knows. It is simply incredible, and therefore I will not waste time in attempting to enumerate what " l'Administration" denies. It is, as Mephistopheles described himself to Faust, *der Geist der stets verneint.* Whatever you want, though it cost the Government not a penny, though it be a boon to the community, though it be the opening-up of the country so enthusiastically toasted, the authorities are absolutely certain to refuse your request. Said a French civilian, "Les consuls français ne sont bons que pour vous donner tort quand vous avez raison." This is no joke—if you think so, stop the first man, not a "functionary," you meet in the street in Haiphong and ask him. It is almost as easy to get into Parliament in London as to get a concession of land for any purpose whatever in Tongking, although the whole vast country is on public offer, although the land almost throws its crops and its minerals in your face, and although the inhabitants are "pirates" by thousands simply and solely for the employment and sustenance which welcomed capital and encouraged enterprise alone can furnish. This point has been urged frankly and strongly by a French critic who is intimately acquainted with Tongking:—
" Soyez certain que si la pacification du Tonkin est si longue. cela tient surtout à ce que nous n'avons pas su empêcher la misère qui pousse les indigènes au brigandage. Si l'on avait laissé le champ libre à l'esprit d'entreprise, si l'on avait appelé

l'élément indigène, à tous les degrés de l'échelle sociale, à par-
ticiper au développement de notre nouvelle colonie, la pacification serait bien avancée, sinon achevée.   Au lieu de nos 15,000
hommes pourchassant des pirates, nous verrions, à l'heure qu'il
est, ces mêmes pirates employés paisiblement à des travaux
publics, car, il ne faut pas nous le dissimuler, nos ouvriers de
demain sont les pirates d'aujourd'hui, les cultivateurs d'hier,
chassés de chez eux par nos procédés belliqueux de ces dernières
années."

It is the fact, though it seems almost incredible, that after all
these years of French administration, the scores of military
expeditions, the spending of countless millions of francs, the
loss of tens of thousands of lives, Tongking is only "pacified"
so far as the delta is concerned.   The rest of the country is not
safe from one day to another, and almost every transport of
valuables has to have a military convoy.   Within the last year
a number of Europeans have been carried off and only a few
weeks ago a train was actually stopped and pillaged while but a
short distance from the capital.   Mr. Consul Tremlett, whose
Report from Saigon is dated February 25, 1894, writes of Tongking as follows :—" The delta may be considered as being fairly
under control, but, apart from that, the province is continually
raided by so-called pirates.   There are now at least three
Frenchmen in captivity of whose fate the public knows nothing;
they are no doubt being held for ransom."   One of these, an
official, was captured at Sin-gam, not 40 miles from Hanoi,
upon a line which is running several trains a day, and not a
hundred yards from a military post.   And at the close of 1893
the *Courrier d'Haiphong* said : " Since two years, not a month,
not a week has passed without reports of shots exchanged,
gangs of ' pirates ' broken up, engagements more or less bloody.
The number of ' pirates ' has certainly not diminished, and their
audacity has increased."   For my own part, I should not be
surprised to hear at any time of a new outburst of " piracy "
on a large scale, supported by the Chinese across the frontier.

If the government of Tongking were administering a hostile province which it desired to crush out of existence, it could not do much better than follow the tactics pursued almost without interruption since the colony was created. I have told how it refuses privileges, and when it does give them, what are they, too often? Shortly before my arrival, a concession had been given for the "Magasins Généraux" at Haiphong, a monopoly of Custom-house examination in the warehouses and on the wharves of one firm, to whom and whose terms everybody was obliged to come. In vain the whole community protested and protested. The monopoly was granted, and Chambers of Commerce of both Haiphong and Hanoi immediately and unanimously resigned, and the Chinese merchants sent in a declaration that unless this additional restriction were removed they would leave in a body. And a single example will show the practical evil of this monopoly. The storage of coal per ton per month cost at that time (for comparison I employ French currency) at Hongkong (Kowloon Godowns) 20 centimes; at Shanghai (Jardine, Matheson & Co.) 28 centimes; at Haiphong (Magasins Généraux) 4 francs! One resolution of the Chambers of Commerce was truly pathetic. The Government consulted us, they said, and then took no notice whatever of all our representations. It is therefore useless to maintain an institution whose powers are purely illusory. Please let us go.

Again, take the matter of railways. Everybody you meet in the Far East will assure you that the jobbery in connection with the extension of railways in Tongking passes description. I cannot, of course, speak from personal or certain knowledge upon this point, but the reader may be invited to consider for a moment the scale of railway concessions now pending there. M. de Lanessan has sanctioned the following: To MM. Vézin and Raveau, a line of 700 kilometres from Hanoi to Hué and Tourane; to MM. Soupé and Raveau, a line of 800 kilometres from Saigon to Tourane and Hué; to the same, a line of steam

tramway from Hanoi to Phu-lang-thuong; to M. Portal, who
represents the Kebao mines and a syndicate of Paris capitalists,
first, a line of 450 kilometres from Kebao, on the coast, to
Laokay, on the Chinese frontier; second, a line from Kebao to
Langson; third, a line from Haiphong to Sontay (one would
have supposed this to be almost a physical impossibility);
fourth, a line from Hanoi to Thai Nguyen; fifth, a line from
Kebao to Monkay, on the frontier. A condition of this last set of
concessions is that all the materials for the railways shall be
supplied from France, and that the locomotives shall consume
only fuel mined in Tongking. Thus a premium is put upon
failure to begin with. The railway from Saigon to Khone,
again, is to cost about 16,500,000 francs for 410 kilometres, the
Colony having agreed to pay 500,000 francs per annum for it, if
the home Government will pay the remaining seven-eighths of
the cost. And another concession is promised for a line from
Tien-Yen, on the coast, via Seven Pagodas and Hanoi, to
Laokay (obviously including one of the concessions mentioned
above), to cost 40,000,000 dollars. Now I say nothing, for I
know nothing, about jobbery in these concessions, but I am at
liberty to ask what prospect there is of any capital being
honestly put into such enterprises, and what prospect there is
of their paying their way, in view of a few facts known to everybody. Take the case of the "Compagnie Française des Charbonnages du Tonkin." After the most tenacious and romantic
efforts, a concession was obtained in 1887 by M. Bavier-
Chauffour to develop the coal mines of Hongay. The course of
the negociations reads like a chapter from an Oriental "Arabian
Nights." To make an indisputable legal tender a ship was
chartered to carry 100,000 silver dollars to Tongking, where the
whole foreign population turned out armed to escort the bullock-
carts carrying the twenty-five wooden cases through the streets.
Refused there, the dollars were taken on board again and carried
to the court of Annam, the ship narrowly escaping destruction
in a typhoon. Then they were brought back to Haiphong,

where the authorities finally accepted them. Now this concession appears to be—I speak, of course, without the least claim to expert knowledge—of the greatest value. At a place called Campha, I have seen a "boulder-stream" of remarkably pure antimony, 8,000 yards long with an average thickness of 20 feet, and I have stood on a solid block of pure oxide of antimony weighing 16 tons. In the same concession I saw a vein of oxide of cobalt measuring 100 yards by 500 by one yard. And from a little further north I have seen remarkable specimens of copper ore. Infinitely more important, however, than all these, are the coal-fields. For years the existence of these was well known, and many times the commanders of French gunboats, who had been struck by the multitude of outcrops, sent home reports calling attention to them and to the enormous advantages which would accrue to France if they could be successfully worked. The Société has spent millions of francs upon these, it has built lines of railway, it has created a town and a harbour, it has employed thousands of miners, it has erected machinery, sunk shafts and driven galleries under the direction of the most experienced engineers it could secure. I have been over the whole of the workings twice and into every one of the galleries, and even taken photographs of the miners at work. So I can speak with some confidence. As regards the quantity of coal, it is practically inexhaustible. There are millions of tons in sight and nobody can guess how much lies below. I have been in a score galleries, each of them in a solid seam from 10 to 20 feet thick. At Hatou there are seven seams side by side, aggregating 54 feet of coal. And yet these were merely the preliminary works of prospecting. The "Marguerite Mine" at Hongay is simply a great mountain of coal.

A few years ago the French Ministries of Marine and the Colonies sent out a distinguished mining engineer, M. E. Sarran, on a special mission to report upon the mines of Tongking. After tests in the laboratory, at sea, and upon briquettes, he wrote of the Hongay coals as follows: "Our opinion is that

Tongking possesses an immense wealth of excellent combustible that the navy may employ with marked advantage over all other coals of the China seas and Australia, rivalling Anzin and Cardiff by its extreme purity, by the absence of iron pyrites, and by a development of heat at the very least equal to that furnished by these coals." These coals are selling at a first-rate price in Hongkong to-day, they have been supplied by contract to a number of British lines and to the French navy, they have been reported favourably upon by British men-of-war, and there is no longer any possible doubt as to their value. The Société has recently set up machinery for making briquettes, or patent fuel, out of the coal-dust, and a preliminary order was given for 10,000 tons by the French Government for the navy. The first two lots offered were refused as not up to the required standard, but were accepted at a lower price, and on April 19th of this year new trials were made in the presence of M. Jaouin, Engineer of the Navy and Director of the Workshops. The following were the results obtained : Weight of water vaporised by a kilo of briquettes, 7·57 (the contract demanded 6·50, and the first trial had given 5·698) ; ash and clinkers, 8·11 per cent. (the contract allowed 27 per cent., and the first trial had given 56·80 per cent.). The Superior Commission of Examination unanimously recommended the acceptance of the consignment. I am not in possession of the latest returns, but the output from the Hongay mines from January 1 to April 22, 1894, was 85,716 tons. The actual shipments during this time were 86,721 tons, and 9,000 tons were left in stock. Of the deliveries to customers, 40 per cent. was first-class screened coal, and the rest smaller grades. Now my reason for going thus into the details of a single enterprise is simple. Here is a commercial undertaking of the very best character, the results of which are proved beyond doubt, in the French colony of Tongking, where are also the railways I am discussing. Yet from beginning to end the local authorities have done nothing but obstruct the Société in every way. The whole of the capital, with trifling exceptions, has been found by two British subjects in Hongkong, Messrs. Chater and Mody, to whom and whose money the development of this Tongking wealth is wholly due. Again and again have they tried to induce French capitalists to take a share of the burden. I believe this is now about to be accomplished, but I am speaking of the past. Moreover, the most childish restrictions have been enforced, of which one may be given as a specimen. No man not a French subject may be employed by the Société in any capacity. That is, if the directors desired to obtain a report upon the value of their property or upon the best means of developing it, from a distinguished British or American expert, they could not charge his fee to the accounts of the Société, but would have to pay him out of their own pockets as a purely private matter. Such are some of the conditions and history of investment in Tongking, while the country is starving for want of capital, and "pirates" hold possession of the greater part of it for want of opportunity to work for wages. I ask, therefore, what are the prospects of these tremendous railway concessions I have enumerated, or what reason is there to think that they are *bond fide* commercial investments? The reply is obvious.

These huge concessions have been granted right and left, apparently by the fiat of M. de Lancssau, while the really essential line from Hanoi to Langson, for which trade is actually waiting, was begun in 1889, and although the route is an easy one and the total distance from Phu-lang-thuong to Langson is but 72 miles, it has only reached the station of Song-hoa, a distance of 31½ miles. In addition to this, there is the stretch between Hanoi and Phu-lang-thuong, and that between Langson and Bi-ni or Lang-nac on the frontier, to be built before the trade of the district of Lungchow, estimated at 8,000,000 dollars annually, can be tapped. Yet M. Étienne officially promised to the Chamber of Deputies that the line should be completed by the end of 1891. If the French, both official and private, were really in earnest about their railways,

it is evident that they would have devoted every franc and
every effort in their power to complete their one promising
line before launching out upon a score of other questionable
lines.   Finally, in support of my whole argument, I may
quote the following passage from Mr. Consul Tremlett's latest
Report: " The Saigon-Mytho railway is always in evidence ; it
cost, although constructed along a great highway, over 200,000
francs per kilometre (crossing two rivers), or about 15,000,000
francs altogether; it has now been in existence some seven
years, but has rendered no real service to trade."

Lest it be thought that there is exaggeration or prejudice
in these suggestions of impropriety in the administration of
French Indo-China, I will reproduce a passage from the verbatim
official report of the discussion of the national Budget of 1891
in the Chamber of Deputies.   M. Étienne, Under-secretary of
State for the Colonies, was making a long and important speech
in explanation and defence of the portion of the Budget relating
to the Colonies.   He was interrupted at one moment by M.
Clémenceau, and the following conversation occurred :—

M. CLÉMENCEAU. While you are still upon the question of Tongking will you
be good enough to say a word to us about the exemptions from the customs duties ?
That is one of the important points of the Report of M. le Myre de Vilers. You
have forgotten to speak of it.

M. ÉTIENNE. M. Clémenceau points out to me that the Governor-General has
taken it upon himself to exempt from import duties certain classes of goods
intended for young industries in Tongking and Annam. He declares that the
Governor-General had not the right to deprive the Budget of the Protectorate of
these receipts. I reply that the Governor-General acted by virtue of the powers
which he holds from the State; he has done what is done—I am obliged to say it
—in the other colonies. The Councils-General, when a customs tariff has been
voted and has received the sanction of the Council of State, have the right to
reduce duties without incurring remarks from any one.

M. LETISET. In favour of private persons ?

M. ÉTIENNE. Precisely.

M. CLÉMENCEAU. Then there is no law any more.

M. ÉTIENNE. It is the Constitution.

A MEMBER OF THE LEFT. It is the absence of a Constitution !

M. ÉTIENNE. It is thus.

M. LE COMTE DE MONTFORT. Then everything is explained ! *

---

* Journal Officiel, November 28, 1890, p. 2295.

The reporter says that "mouvements divers" took place in the Chamber at M. Étienne's admission. It would have been surprising had this not been so, for it is of course obvious that when the Council-General—that is to say, the Governor-General —may exact customs duties from one person and exempt another from them, the door is opened wide to every kind of political· scandal.

I might fill pages with other examples of French administration and colonial methods. For example, a few months ago the price of the dollar was fixed at 3 francs by order of the Governor-General, at a time when the commercial price of it was from 2·70 to 2·75 francs. Some speculators purchased 200,000 dollars at the latter price and sent them to Hanoi. They were accepted by the Treasury there, and remitted at the official price of 3 francs. Thus the speculators made some 55,000 francs, while the Government lost the same sum. Again, a Paris paper tells of a contract which was given to a local firm to demolish a part of the old citadel of Hanoi. This is described as a very simple operation, the cost of which would have been met by the value of the materials accruing to the contractor. But the contractor received 40,000 dollars for his work, and a concession of nearly 100 hectares of land in the town of Hanoi to boot, the value of land there being often as much as 5 dollars the metre. Thus, adds the paper in question, the contractors received a present of about 400,000 dollars. Again, the Chinese capitation tax is the subject of much natural criticism. In one year this was farmed out for Cambodia to a Chinaman for 72,000 dollars, though his predecessor had only paid 32,000 dollars, and as the number of Chinese had not increased to any great extent it is obvious that he would make up the difference—indeed, that he was expected to make it up— by additional "squeezes" from his unfortunate compatriots.

There are in France a few publicists and politicians who have made a special study of French colonisation, and the opinions of these men are expressed with the greatest sense and moderation. But to the ordinary French writer the colonies are a sealed book. His equipment for discussing them consists of a vague sentimental idea that colonies mean strength and commerce and glory, and since he is generally actuated, as Lord Rosebery has just said, by a profound jealousy of Great Britain, and knows of her fame as a colonising nation, he insists that France must be a colonising nation too. He does not stop to reflect that everything depends upon where the colonies are and how they are administered. In despair at the difficulty of obtaining French official facts and figures in any instructive shape I recently wrote to a friend at the head of one of the most important departments of the French Foreign Office, begging him to send me any volumes he could find on the subject. After some searching he was good enough to forward to me an official work bearing this description : "Ministère des Colonies. Protectorat de l'Annam et du Tonkin. Administration des Douanes et Régies. Rapport Sommaire sur les Statistiques des Douanes et le Mouvement Commercial de l'Annam et du Tonkin en 1898." Here at last, I thought, is what I want, and indeed the volume contains many instructive figures to which I shall refer later. But it is evidently intended for popular circulation, and this is a specimen of its advice to the French emigrant :—

"We may affirm that in the very near future this country [Tongking] will offer a vast field to the emigration of our compatriots who till now have sought land and work in South America, but always under the conditions of economy mentioned above and of determined work. In the hill country and at slight altitudes the European can work in the fields all day long for five months of the year. For four other months he can work three hours in the morning and as much in the evening ; while during the three months of great heat he must take precautions at all hours of the day, on account of the sun. Under these conditions the colonist can take his personal share (*contribuer personnellement*) in the labours of clearing the land, planting, and teaching the natives he employs the use of French tools, which are greatly superior to the rudimentary tools used in the country."

It is difficult to comment upon this in fitting terms. To anybody who knows the East no comment will be necessary, and to those who do not hardly any words would bring home the truth, so wildly preposterous is the suggestion that a European agricultural labourer should go out to work in the tropics with his spade and hoe. If the author of this book had suggested to the native of Tongking that he should come to Paris and seek employment as a clerk, he would not have gone much further astray. Yet this is the kind of thing that is offered officially to French readers on the subject of French colonies.

In the preceding chapter I spoke in general terms of the proportion of "fonctionnaires," civil servants, to the French population of Indo-China. The details of this are so astonishing that they would hardly be credited from the mouth of a foreigner. I will therefore give a French official statement of them. M. Étienne, while Under-secretary of State for the Colonies and speaking in defence of the Administration, made the following remarks about the state of things in Cochin-China :—

"What is the population of that country? It is 1,800,000 souls. There is a French population of 1,600 inhabitants, of whom 1,200 are 'fonctionnaires.' How is it administered? It has a Colonial Council: elected by whom? By the 1,200 'fonctionnaires,' who have also a deputy. And you expect that confusion and disorder will not reign in that country! How, indeed, can you expect an administration to work smoothly, when thanks to this system of organisation, all this world of 'fonctionnaires' throws itself into the electoral arena, and divides itself into two, three, or four camps, one supporting the actual President of the Colonial Council, another the Mayor of Saigon, another the deputy, another the candidates for deputy? . . . In 1887 I tried to reduce the number of the 'fonctionnaires.' I did reduce the cost of them to the extent of 3,500,000 francs out of 9,000,000. I took that step in October, and in the following December the Ministry of which I was a member disappeared. Six months later, the 'fonctionnaires' whom I had dismissed had all reappeared in Cochin-China." [*] When this is admitted by the defenders of a system there is nothing

[*] Chambre des Députés, Séance du 27 Novembre, 1890.

left for its critics to say. In the very same year that the salaries
of the "fonctionnaires" of Cochin-China amounted to £960,000,
the sum spent upon public works in the Colony—the one expenditure upon which the entire productive future of such a place
must depend—was £16,000 ! But even this pitiful figure is far
from telling the whole astounding truth. When the "mouvement prolongé" which followed his words had died away, M.
Étienne continued : "And while public works in the present
year are only represented by £16,000, what do you think is the
sum allotted to the *personnel* of the public works department ?
It is £16,000—£16,000 worth of *personnel* out of £16,000 worth
of public works ! " That is, not a centime of work was
done. Moreover, during the years when millions of francs
were spent on public works in Cochin-China, what was
there actually done to show for it ? " Only a few roads
round Saigon "—" routes luxueuses," according to M. de
Lanessan elsewhere, " pour les fonctionnaires qui vont se
promener le soir autour de Saigon." It is fortunate in the
interests of truth that we have these facts from the lips of
responsible Ministers and ex-Ministers ; as I said, nobody would
have believed them from the mouth of a foreign critic. We owe
the revelations to a curious and amusing circumstance. There
is a cynical proverb to the effect that when mothers-in-law fall
out, we get at the family facts. And all this information arose
from a falling-out between M. Étienne and M. le Myre de Vilers.
As "rapporteur," the latter had bitterly attacked the financial
régime of the former. M. Étienne retorted that however bad
things might be at that moment, they were much worse when
M. le Myre de Vilers was Governor of Cochin-China. M. le
Myre de Vilers protested against the expenditure for eleven
carriages for the service of the Governor. M. Étienne replied
that his critic had himself had eleven carriages and had
spent more money upon them. M. le Myre de Vilers criticised
the sum of 12,000 francs which M. Piquet was spending as
Governor in secret services. M. Étienne retorted that M. le

Myre de Vilers himself had spent 15,000 francs. Finally, when the duel had at the same time delighted and shocked the Chamber for an hour the combatants exchanged a couple of terrific blows, and sank exhausted. M. Étienne produced a set of dreadful figures showing that expenditure had risen by leaps and bounds in all directions during M. le Myre de Vilers' tenure of office in Cochin-China. This blow his adversary made no attempt to parry, but riposted with the proof that whereas M. Étienne was posing as the reformer of administrative methods, he was himself directly and personally responsible for the extreme centralisation which had produced the very evils he was deploring. In support of this he read two despatches from M. Étienne to himself, ordering that every change in *personnel* in the Colony should in future be submitted by him to M. Étienne in Paris, before it was made. "Thus," he concluded, "M. the Under-secretary of State for the Colonies reserves to himself every nomination, and M. the Governor-General has not the right to appoint a school-master!" Such an effect did this instructive duel produce upon the Chamber that the Budget was adopted by the small majority of 85 in a total vote of 483, and this only after the Ministry had made a series of impassioned appeals to the memory of the thousands of Frenchmen who had laid down their lives for their country in Indo-China.

One recent French writer and traveller, I may add, has spoken out bluntly about Tongking. This is Prince Henri d'Orleans, who has certainly had abundant opportunities of seeing French colonial methods for himself. "Almost every-where," he says, "there exists a latent antagonism, if indeed it is not overt, between the colonist and the Government." And this is his pronouncement about French colonial administration: "It is too numerous; it is partially composed of incapables and of men with bad antecedents; it is too ignorant and meddle-some; it endeavours to raise difficulties and to check all means of action; for the most part born of favouritism, it endeavours to indulge in the same practice and displeases those who

obtain what they apply for as well as those who are passed
over." *

So much for the colonist and the Government impersonal.
What is his attitude towards the personal Governor-General?
He sees him come, he watches him while he is learning the
A B C of Tongking affairs, he reads a few official decrees, he
hears a few official after-dinner speeches, eulogizing France,
Tongking and the colonist himself, and then some day a telegram comes and the colonist sees him go. The heads of the
colonial Government succeed each other in Saigon and Hanoi
like the figures of a shadow pantomime. M. Richaud boasted
to me with a laugh that he was tolerated longer than any of his
predecessors. His term of office had been thirteen months! †
Before the Governor-General comes, he is unknown; while in
the East even his public speeches are addressed to Paris; he
returns and is forgotten. It is the merest farce of supervision,
and what wonder that the colonist sinks deeper year by year in
disgust and despair? He has described himself in a bitter
epigram: "le colon est un prétexte à banquets." Instability is
the dominant characteristic of French administration in the
Far East. Does anybody seriously believe that the solid
foundations of future prosperity can ever be laid in this shifting
quicksand? For an Englishman who cares for France it is
positively distressing to hear Frenchmen talk in Tongking.
Fifty times during my two visits was it said to me, "Ah, if only
you English had Tongking!" Matters have somewhat improved
for them lately, and a new hostility to England has sprung up,
but I seriously believe that if a secret ballot had been taken
then, a majority of the French in Tongking would have voted,

* "Around Tonkin," 1894, pp. 88 and 423.
† This is the list of Governors-General since the creation of the "Union Indo-
chinoise" by the decree of October 17, 1887:—M. Constans, Nov., '87–April, '88;
M. Richaud, April, '88–May, '89; M. Piquet, May, '89–April, '91; M. Bideau, April,
'91–June, '91; M. de Lanessan, April, '91, en congé; M. Chavassieux, March, '94,
acting; M. de Lanessan. Between December, 1884, and November, 1887, there
were ten Residents-General of Tongking—an average service of about three months.

in spite of their undying love of country, to hand over Indo-China to England. Then at least they would have been able to buy and sell, manufacture and import, create and develop, with no man to hamper them and no "Administration" to forbid. As it is, the French colonist's attitude to his government is summed up in the exclamation that I heard fall from the lips of one of them when he saw an official approaching him on duty—". Nom de Dieu !—voilà encore l'Administration qui arrive ! "

But the shadows on the picture are not yet complete. First, as to the Chinese. Nobody can advocate more strongly than I the absolute necessity of keeping them out of a civilised settled Western country. But it is as plain as the nose on one's face that no colony in the Far East can dispense with them. Their labour, their easy and willing adaptability to any job by which money can be earned, from nursing the baby to driving the steam engine ; their commercial insight and comparative trustworthiness,—these make them an ideal substratum for a new community, as Shanghai and Hongkong and Singapore and the Protected Malay States prove to demonstration. Yet Indo-China taxes them till they are giving up their established businesses, and puts a price on the head of each as he comes and again as he goes. The *impôt personnel* upon every Asiatic is from 7 dols. to 80 dols. ; the *impôt des patentes* ranges from 2 dols. to 400 dols. ; and the price of the passport without which no Asiatic can leave French territory is 2.50 dols.

Second, the port charges. Take the little steamer I returned in, the *Freyr*, 676 tons, from Randers, in Jutland. At the port of Newcastle she had paid £4 ; at Nagasaki 70 dols. ; at Yokohama 50 dols. ; at Hongkong 4 dols. ; while to get in and out of the port of Haiphong costs her every trip 302.40 dols. And this, too, is only for the ship's charges, pure and simple. The charterer must pay a dollar and a half wharfage for every ton of cargo landed—say 750 dols. for an average cargo. Thus at a port where common sense teaches that trade should be tempted

and nursed in every possible way, the authorities begin by
making trade all but impossible. There can hardly be a more
needy port in the world than Haiphong, yet it is doubtful if
there is a more expensive one. The consequences are inevitable and obvious.

Third, the enormous Customs duties of the "Tarif général."
These need no specifying. Saigon prospered exceedingly under
a free-trade *régime*, and she has been forced to give protection a
good trial. What is the position of Saigon now ? A critical, if
not a hopeless one. Yet she long ago discovered that only
one thing could save her. A unanimous report of the Chamber
of Commerce concluded with these words in big type: "We
demand the absolute abolition of the Customs régime in Cochin-
China from January 1, 1889." Yet is there the faintest shadow
of a coming change? On the contrary. In one of the last
public speeches he made, at a banquet in Hanoi, M. Richaud
exclaimed, "Renounce the chimerical hope of the return of
absolute commercial liberty!" The subsidised newspaper
added that this was followed by a "triple salve d'applaudisse-
ments." The only possible comment is, that the colonists of
Hanoi who applauded that sentiment should be refused Christian
burial, for they are suicides.

Again and again have the Colonies protested against these
duties by every means at their command, and their protests have
been supported by several of the most influential writers and
administrators in France, such as M. Leroy-Beaulieu and M. le
Myre de Vilers, but almost wholly in vain. Some slight amelior-
ations have been granted under the pressure of absolute necessity.
A series of modifications in the "Tarif Général" have been
applied to Indo-China, reducing the duties on a number of
articles and abolishing them on others. And after it had
become perfectly clear that transit trade to southern China
through Tongking would not arise so long as customs duties
were levied upon goods in transit, the authorities conceded a
détaxe of 80 per cent. upon such goods. And when this was

proved to be prohibitive they took off the tax altogether. Thus what should have been dictated at the outset by an elementary knowledge of practical economics was only conceded after a long struggle and when it was enforced by necessity. I need hardly say, I presume, that the tariff is constructed primarily to keep out the manufactures of all nations except France, but in spite of this, as I shall show later, the trade between France and her colonies in Indo-China is a mere bagatelle, not to be compared for an instant with the subventions necessary to keep the colonies going. The foreigner is regarded as an enemy, and the most petty restrictions and partialities are adopted to handicap him. Here is an example which I take from the *London and China Express*: "On a firm whose total earnings in 1892 were 182 dollars, and in 1893 749 dollars, the resident of Annam imposed the *patente* to the modest sum of 316 dollars yearly." At the port of Haiphong French ships pay fifty centimes per ton, foreign ships one franc. At the "ports ouverts au commerce" French ships pay one cent. per ton, foreign ships ten cents. Will it be believed by those who only know France in Europe, and love her gallantry, her freedom from intellectual prejudice, and her constant striving after an ideal of equality, that France in the Far East positively bars her paying hospital at her chief port against foreign sufferers by a differential tariff? Yet this is the case. In the General Hospital at Saigon foreign seamen must pay 9½ francs a day and foreign officers 13 francs —charges just double what French patients of corresponding ranks have to pay. "I addressed the Governor upon the subject," says the British Consul, from whose last Report I take the fact, "pointing out that in the hospitals of Hongkong and Singapore no distinction was made as regards nationality, but no reply has as yet been received." Is it too much to say that a nation which deliberately does this has still to learn one of the first principles of civilisation?

The result of any careful study of French colonial administration in the Far East, as I have now perhaps shown alike from my own investigations and the testimony of the best French critics both in France and on the spot, is therefore that Indo-China is grievously misgoverned. Instead of finding a helping hand, the French colonist encounters a closed fist. The "functionary," dressed in his little brief authority, has utterly forgotten that he is the servant of the colonist, that he has no other reason for existence except to aid and protect and encourage his self-exiled countryman. As it is, while the colonist is the blood of the new country, the "functionary" is the leech. Day by day the cry of the French colonial civilian goes up to heaven, "Pas tant d'Administration!" Everywhere else in the world, capital is welcomed, no matter whose pocket it comes out of. In French colonies alone gold must be stamped with "liberty, equality, and fraternity" before it is received, and a man must be a Frenchman before he is allowed to labour with the rest. The Revolution seems a joke when one learns in Tongking that one of the conditions attached to a concession is that nobody but Frenchmen shall be employed on it, and that a sick Englishman or German must pay twice as much for his bed in the hospital as a sick Frenchman. I do not believe there is another country in the world which would make such a pitiful stipulation. Does France not know what is done in her name? or is she not ashamed, remembering '89, to adopt such an attitude to-day before the world?

In conclusion I will say simply this. I believe, as every one who has looked into the matter believes, that Tongking might have a prosperous future under the control of a colonising nation. But I know, as everybody who has looked into the matter knows, that she will never reach it along the present road. A certain permanency of appointment for the Governor-General; a relaxing of restrictions upon the colonists all round; a hundred times more respect paid by officials to colonial wishes and requests; far greater consideration for native rights and sentiments; the encouragement of the Chinese; a glad welcome to capital and enterprise from any source; an immediate and equable reduction of the tariff; the decentralisation of authority;—these are some of the primal conditions of progress. If they do not come, then France may prepare for the humiliation which the very name of "Indo-China" will ultimately carry with it. In the words of the editor of the *Courrier d'Haiphong*, "To continue as at present means the loss of Indo-China—it means the ruin of French influence in the Far East."

CHAPTER VII.

THE COST OF A FRENCH COLONY.

IN preceding chapters I have endeavoured by a brief description of the external aspects of the French colonies in the Far East to place before the reader a picture of the results in life and administration which have been attained in about thirty-six years. And by my own criticisms, supported by the testimony of distinguished French writers and speakers, I have tried to show how completely France has misunderstood the problem she set herself to solve, and how persistently and wilfully her administrators have taken the wrong road. These criticisms, however, have been for the most part in general terms, whereas to produce an adequate effect they should be proved to demonstration by actual facts. What one man affirms, another may deny. Without figures a criticism may be dismissed as largely a matter of opinion. I decided, therefore, to collect from French official sources the figures relating to a typical French colony; first, concerning its cost, and second, concerning its returns: that is, to draw up a national balance-sheet for this one national enterprise, in the form of a debit and credit account.

If I had foreseen what this decision involved, I should not have attempted the task at this time. I had, however, no suspicion of the extraordinary complexities of French official finance and the difficulties, amounting almost to impossibility, which beset any one, not a professed statistician, who attempts

to disentangle the plain fact from the mountains of figures.
The French as a nation are addicted to the exact sciences, and
this national proclivity comes to its finest flower in the French
Budget. It is issued every year in a number of volumes; it is
subdivided in the most elaborate manner; it contains the
minutest details upon every possible point; it is arranged on a
theoretical system so arbitrary that a lifetime would hardly be
too long to enable one to grasp its principles. If you desire to
learn the details of the movements in the potato-market, or the
duty upon areca-nut collected in Cambodia, the French Budget
with its local additions will satisfy your curiosity at once. If,
however, you desire to calculate the cost of a French colony
through a series of years, you must unite the path-finding
instincts of a Red Indian with the patience of the patriarch and
a willingness to believe that no contradiction is involved when
1,000 francs in one book appears as 1,200 in another. Moreover, the French are never satisfied with their own official
statistics : they are constantly varying the form and polishing
the principle. And after prolonged investigation one is forced
to the conclusion that the body of statisticians desires to
remain a close corporation, and to construct out of its own
figures an impenetrable barrier to exclude the impertinent
independent inquirer. No sooner, for example, have you
discovered in what way a certain fact of finance is presented
during a series of years than you are brought up short at a
foot-note explaining that by a "mouvement d'ordre" this fact
has been transferred to another portion of the Budget and
incorporated in a wholly different series of tables. One of the
most accomplished French statisticians, M. de Foville, whose
handbook is or should be upon the desk of every writer about
France, frankly admits all this. "Nothing is more dangerous,"
he says, "than amateur statistics, where errors swarm, and
which prove everything that one desires to prove. The only way
effectually to combat this false statistic is to put true statistics
within the reach of all—to make the truth in relation to econo-

mical and social questions very accessible in the first place, and
very intelligible in the second.　But this point has not yet been
reached, especially in France.　A hundred times we have heard
men, who were certainly not the first comers, express their
regret that it is so difficult to obtain exact information upon
even the most common facts of the national life." *　And even
while I was gathering the figures which follow, M. Leroy-
Beaulieu, certainly the most capable of living Frenchmen in
such matters, has lifted up his voice in a complaint which
echoed my own growing despair.　He says: "Quite at the end
of the last session, at the sitting of July 24, 1894, M. Poincaré
laid upon the table the 'rectified project' of the Budget for 1895.
This 'rectified project,' very far from being final, is the subject
of new manipulations and rectifications.　Our unhappy Budgets
are retouched and altered to such an extent that it is impossible
to recognise them or to find one's way about in them." †　As an
example of this lack of finality, I may add that a French Budget,
whether national or colonial, is not closed until years after the
date of its appearance.　Thus the Tongking Budget of 1891,
for example, may appear in one shape in 1890, in another in
1891, in still another in 1892, and possibly even in a fourth in
1893.

After the above it will easily be understood that I put in
no claim for the completeness of my own figures.　They are
the result of many weary days of research both in London and
in the official libraries in Paris; and I doubt if there is a
contemporary French book of reference which I have not
examined.　More than once I have been on the point of
giving up the task, but I have reflected that this would be to
leave the lesson untaught, since it is very improbable that
any Frenchman will desire in the present state of colonising
enthusiasm to become the mouthpiece of facts so unpleasant
to the majority of his fellow-countrymen.　I claim only, how-

* Alf. de Foville, "La France Économique," 1887, p. 1
† Journa des Débats, November 8, 1894.

ever, that the following figures have been conscientiously sought, and I present them as an attempt to answer a question of the greatest interest, until some more skilful investigator shall correct them. Complete and final accuracy, I may add, will never be attained by anybody, since in not a few instances the official figures are hopelessly self-contradictory.*

I have chosen Tongking as the typical French colony because of the amount of discussion that has already raged around it, and because the whole of its history is included within a modern and comparatively brief period. It will be remembered that Tongking was under the suzerainty of Annam when the French became possessed of the latter country in 1862, the Annamese having driven out the Chinese long before, although China still claimed suzerainty, as she has done over every country adjoining her vast empire. The explorations of Senez, Harmand, Dupuis, and, above all, of Francis Garnier, the most gallant and devoted explorer France has ever had, filled up the interval until 1873, the year of what has been called the first Tongking expedition. Garnier seized the delta of Tongking in the winter of 1873, declared the Red River open to commerce, and was killed in an ambush on December 21st. The following years were remarkable chiefly for the explorations of M. de Kergaradec—a naval lieutenant and French Consul at Hanoi—and those of a rapidly increasing number of French officers and travellers. Up to 1882 nothing further had been accomplished, except theoretical work. In March, 1882, Rivière was despatched to Tongking with two ships and four hundred men to bring the anomalous situation to an end. He fought several actions against the Black Flags, but his force was too small to enable him to do anything of importance, and he

* "Comme nous l'avons fait remarquer dans notre précédente edition de cet ouvrage, nos documents statistiques coloniaux officiels se contredisent sans cesse." —Leroy-Beaulieu, "De la Colonisation chez les peuples modernes," Paris, 1891 p. 557, note.

remained for nearly a year virtually a prisoner in the citadel
of Hanoi. At last the French Government, under the famous
ministry of Jules Ferry, voted credits and reinforcements, and
as soon as these arrived Rivière attacked and was killed in the
sortie of May 19, 1883, under circumstances which I have previously described. When this news reached France, a wave of
colonial and military enthusiasm broke over the country, and
the Chamber and the Senate unanimously voted a credit o
5,300,000 francs, and a powerful expedition was despatched
under General Bouët and Admiral Courbet.

At this moment, therefore, the history of Tongking may be
said to begin, and the calculation of its cost accordingly
commences here, although of course not a little money had
been previously spent in the country. For the next four years
French treasure and French lives were spent with so lavish a
hand that at last France became thoroughly alarmed at the
outlook; and after General Négrier had attacked and captured
Langson in defiance of orders, had been driven out by the Chinese
and mortally wounded, and Colonel Herbinger had lost control
of himself and retreated precipitately in the most discreditable
manner, public opinion turned against Tongking, and the Ferry
Ministry succumbed to an onslaught by M. Clémenceau on
March 30, 1885. This first chapter of the financial history of
Tongking presents the following figures :—

	Francs.*
1883	14,858,900
1884	73,250,868
1885	115,604,415†
1886	65,998,696
	269,302,879

In four years, therefore, France had spent, at the most
moderate computation that could be made, nearly two hundred

* These figures are taken from M. Jules Ferry, "Le Tonkin et la Mère-Patrie,"
1890, p. 306, a source in which they are not likely to be found exaggerated.
† In 1885 and 1886 the credits voted were 164,385,513 and 75,203,901 francs
respectively, but I have taken the sums described as actually spent.

and seventy millions of francs. The preliminaries of peace with China were signed at Paris on April 4, 1885.

For the second chapter, from 1887 to the estimated Budget of 1894, I have collected the figures from the national Budget of each year. They present the following results :—

	From France.*	From Cochin-China.	Totals.
	Francs.	Francs.	Francs.
1887	30,000,000†	11,000,000	41,000,000
1888	19,800,000	11,000,000‡	30,800,000
1889	15,615,000	11,000,000	26,615,000
1890	12,150,000	11,000,000	23,450,000
1891	10,450,000	11,000,000	21,450,000
1892	10,450,000	8,000,000	18,450,000
1893	24,450,000	5,000,000	29,450,000
1894	24,450,000	4,700,000	29,150,000
	147,665,000	72,700,000	220,365,000

Thus, during the eight years which have followed the establishment of peace and the final passing of Tongking under French dominion, France has spent over two hundred and twenty millions of francs. We therefore arrive at the following first estimate of the cost of Tongking :—

		Francs.
1883–1886		269,802,379
1887–1894		220,365,000
Total		490,167,379

I am prepared to show, however, that even this enormous figure is a long way short of the fact. The French official

* Inclusive of the subvention for the Tongking submarine cable.

† In round numbers—from Jules Ferry.

‡ In the Budget, "Service Colonial," for 1888, this figure appears as only 1,727,000 francs, but as M. Étienne said in the Chamber of Deputies when presenting the Budget of 1891, "Nous avons demandé, en effet, 11 millions à la Cochin-Chine en 1887, et nous avons dû, en 1888, en 1889, et en 1890, lui réclamer la même somme," I have made 1888 no exception to this regular credit. The difference probably appears in some other part of the Budget, where it has escaped my search.

figures for the Budget of the Protectorate of Annam and Tong-king, from 1887 to 1891, are the following :—

"SITUATION DES RECETTES ET DES DÉPENSES DU BUDGET DU PROTECTORAT DE L'ANNAM ET DU TONKIN." *

Budget de	Recettes.		Dépenses.	
	Francs.		Francs.	
	Ordinaires.	Extraordinaires.	Ordinaires.	Extraordinaires.
1887	11,877,104†	58,206,566	11,802,485	58,251,185
	69,643,670		69,043,670	
1888	13,572,132	37,297,210	10,292,093	40,577,249
	50,869,342		50,869,342	
1889	15,445,626	37,007,534	12,905,562	39,517,598
	52,453,160		52,453,160	
1890	15,307,415	32,269,398	17,775,176	29,791,637
	47,566,813		47,566,813	
1891	18,814,721	24,765,079	16,594,789	26,985,012
	43,579,801		43,579,801	

These budgets, it will be noticed, balance in a manner to provoke the most sceptical examination. A little investigation shows that the system of subdivision into "Recettes ordinaires," "Recettes extraordinaires," "Dépenses ordinaires," and "Dé-penses extraordinaires," is misleading in the extreme. The "ordinary receipts" mean simply and properly enough the revenue raised locally. The "ordinary expenditure" similarly

* Every figure in this table and in that which immediately follows it was very courteously furnished to me by the Ministère des Colonies, for which I beg here to return my best thanks. I have altered the arrangement of the figures, to display them more instructively, but all the sums and the theoretical form of the budgets are absolutely official. I have ventured to omit the centimes.

† These budgets appear originally in dollars. Up to and including 1892 the dollar is reckoned at 4 francs, in 1893 at 3.58 francs, and in 1894 at 3 francs. All these gold-prices of the dollar, it is perhaps needless to say, were in excess of the facts of exchange.

means the cost of the civil administration of the country. The " extraordinary receipts " mean neither more nor less than the exact sum necessary to make up the deficit in the " ordinary receipts," *plus* the cost to the mother country of the military and naval operations.* I do not say that this system was adopted for the purpose of throwing dust in the eyes of the casual inquirer, but it could not fail to have this effect. At any rate in 1891 the French statisticians no longer felt equal to presenting the annual results in this preposterous form. At this point, therefore, a change was introduced into the form of the budget of the Protectorate of Annam and Tongking. Beginning with the year 1892, the budget was reduced to the resources derived from local revenues alone, the French government having decided to include the military expenditure in the general budget of the " metropolis." Those are the words of the official explanation. For the next two years, therefore, the budgets of Annam and Tongking assume this pleasing shape :—

BUDGET DE	RECETTES.	DÉPENSES.	EXCÉDANT DES RECETTES SUR LES DÉPENSES.
	Francs.	Francs.	Francs.
1892	20,820,680	19,385,035	1,435,645
1893	18,531,450	18,040,098	491,352

The results thus became more attractive than ever : the revenues of the colony showing an actual excess over its expenditure. I need hardly point out that in these two years no account whatever is taken in the local budget of the vastly preponderating part of the expenses. To get at the facts, therefore, we must place these budgets from 1887 to 1893 in a different form. The expenditure is obviously both " ordinary "

* " Les ressources extraordinaires proviennent de subventions de la métropole et de la Cochin-Chine, et de remboursements effectués par le Ministère de la Guerre pour les dépenses normales de ses troupes."—" Organisation des Colonies françaises et des Pays de Protectorat," par E. Petit, Paris, 1894, p. 607.

and "extraordinary" added together, while the real and only
actual *revenue* is the "ordinary" one. We thus get the
following results :—

Budget of	Expenditure.	Revenue.	Deficit.
1887	60,643,670	11,377,104	58,266,566
1888	50,869,342	13,572,132	37,297,210
1889	52,453,160	15,445,626	37,007,534
1890	47,566,818	15,297,415	32,269,398
1891	43,579,801	18,814,721	24,765,080
1892	37,835,055*	20,820,680†	17,014,355
1893	47,490,098*	18,531,450†	28,958,648

Total deficit 235,578,791 frcs.

Instead of the cost of Tongking from 1887 to 1894 being
220,865,000 francs, we find, therefore, that from 1887 to 1893
it reached 235,578,791 francs. The conclusion arrived at above
therefore takes the following corrected shape :—

		Francs.
1862–1886		269,802,379
1887–1893		235,578,791
	Total	505,381,170

* These totals are arrived at, in the absence of the complete budget for these
years, which has been suppressed, by adding together the "dépenses ordinaires,"
the "subventions" from France and from Cochin-China, and the subsidy for the
cable. Theoretically they should be quite accurate, but I am convinced they are
under the mark, though I cannot trace any other figures.

† These official figures are obviously based upon the revenues as they were
reckoned in 1893 to have been. But in the official *Annuaire de l'Indo-Chine* for
1894 the revenues are revised to be for 1892, 4,792,502 dols., and for 1893, 5,509,543
dols. These sums, multiplied respectively by 4 and by 3·38, the official (though
incorrect) rates of exchange into francs, give 19,170,008 and 18,346,778 francs.
These are therefore the latest figures. I have, however, adhered to those
furnished me officially. As in the case of Singapore (see p. 46), the revenue of
Tongking for these years, when given in dollars, shows an increase, and when
given in francs a decrease. But it is important to bear in mind that the same
injustice does not arise in the French as in the British colony, for all the customs
duties of Tongking are collected in francs, and have therefore to be translated
into dollars for the purposes of the budget, whereas in Singapore they are alike
collected and expressed in dollars. In Tongking, accordingly, every fall in the
price of the dollar tends *pro tanto* to inflate the revenue as expressed in terms of
silver dollars; in Singapore it makes no difference.

To this must be added the subsidies to Tongking from France and Cochin-China for 1894, namely, 29,150,000 francs—as shown above. The conclusion, therefore, at which I have finally arrived is that from 1883, when the history of Tongking began, down to the latest accessible official statistics, the cost of Tongking to France has reached the colossal figure of 534,531,170 francs, or £21,881,247, a yearly average of 41,544,264 francs, or £1,781,770.[*] Or, to put the fact in a popular form, the satisfaction of including "le Tonkin" among the possessions of his country *has cost the French taxpayer 122,039 francs— £4,881—a day, Sundays included, for every day that he has had it.* It may safely be foretold that when at length he comes to realise this fact he will be surprised, and his surprise will manifest itself in a striking manner.

So much for the debit side of the account. Let us now compare it as briefly as possible with what Tongking has to show on the other side of the ledger. This is, after all, the point of real importance. It does not matter what France has spent upon Tongking, if she has thereby secured an adequate return in trade. At the present moment, too, the balance-sheet of Tongking is of more interest than ever as an example of French colonisation, since France has just voted 65,000,000 francs to repeat the experiment in Madagascar, under similar conditions of native opposition and problematical results. The following table exhibits the foreign trade of Tongking from 1888 to 1892, inclusive, the figures for 1893 not having yet been published.

* I am aware, for reasons unnecessary to give at length, that a number of items have escaped me. Though I cannot trace them with sufficient uniformity to include them, the following extracts will show I am not wrong in asserting that the above falls short of the actual total :—

" Le budget du service colonial est donc une portion du budget métropolitain, ou budget général de l'État, appliquée aux colonies, mais il ne correspond pas à la totalité des dépenses des services compris dans le budget de l'État et exécutés aux colonies ; les dépenses du ' service marine ' relèvent, en effet, du budget des dépenses de la marine." " Le budget de la guerre [1893] participe pour 1 million aux dépenses militaires du Tonkin."—" Organisation des Colonies françaises et des Pays de Protectorat," par E. Petit, Paris, 1894, pp. 490 and 531.

FOREIGN TRADE OF TONGKING, 1883–1892.*

	Imports.		Exports.	
	From France and French Colonies.	From Foreign Countries.	To France and French Colonies.	To Foreign Countries.
	Francs.	Francs.	Francs.	Francs.
1883	405,606	2,922,601	649,987	8,440,359
1884	2,015,762	7,126,304	79,483	541,147
1885	3,421,610	14,667,087	49,718	593,287
1886	4,654,829	18,290,173	65,206	605,879
1887	7,328,137	20,824,664	82,175	835,476
1888	6,521,408	17,479,240	164,228	6,546,848
1889	6,574,572	17,170,812	477,444	10,161,564
1890	8,907,668	11,830,984	1,700,052	5,321,564
1891	9,004,491	15,554,409	583,518	11,146,254
1892	9,504,926	18,927,846	420,221	10,315,639

The figures of the above table present the following summarised totals :—

TOTAL FOREIGN TRADE OF TONGKING, 1883–1892.

	France and French Colonies.	Foreign Countries.	Totals.
	Francs.	Francs.	Francs.
Imports from ...	58,939,020	144,780,600	203,728,620
Exports to ...	4,272,027	49,048,007	53,320,034
Totals ...	63,211,047	193,837,607	257,048,654

* The figures for 1883 are taken from "Le Régime Commercial de l'Indo-Chine française," Paris, 1894. Those for the following years from the "Rapport général sur les statistiques des douanes pour 1892," Hanoi, 1893. There is good reason to believe the latter to be inaccurate in the direction of exaggeration, and indeed in one or two cases I have proved them to be so. But after many vain attempts to secure a set of accurate and uniform figures I have been obliged to fall back upon these as they stand. The variations of figures in different French official and semi-official publications would be incredible to any one who has not attempted to reconcile them. In the above table the figures of coasting trade, and the trade between the different members of the Union of French Indo-China, are, of course, not included.

From this it may be seen at a glance what effect the "tarif général" has had upon the development of trade between France and French Colonies on the one hand, and Tongking on the other. This tariff was forced upon Indo-China in spite, as I have already said, of her vehement and unceasing protests, and in defiance of the prophecies of every enlightened French economist. Its intention was, of course, to exclude foreign products from Tongking, and to make of the colony a great market for French domestic and colonial products. Its result has been that French imports were comparatively little more in 1892 than they were in 1887; while foreign imports are more than in 1886 and comparatively little below 1887. And that the total trade between France and her other colonies, and Tongking, has amounted in ten years to the pitiful sum of 63 millions of francs, or £2,520,000; while the total foreign trade during the same time has been nearly 194 millions of francs, or £7,760,000. That is to say, the high protective system has been the most disastrous failure, or, as M. Leroy-Beaulieu says, "the application to Indo-China of a general Customs tariff is a colossal error."

In the debate in the Chamber of Deputies, to which I have already frequently referred, M. Armand Porteu said: "The French Colonies together contain a population of 20 to 24 millions of inhabitants. Now let us see what they cost and what they bring in. Our French Colonies cost us yearly 70 millions of francs: 58 millions inscribed in the colonial budget, 12 millions in the budget of the navy, and 5 millions in the budget of post and telegraphs. . . . Their total commerce is 410 millions per annum. Of that sum the share of France by sale and purchase is 170 millions, and our importations into the Colonies reach only 70 millions. You thus spend 70 millions in order to dispose of 70 millions' worth of goods. That is the result of your Colonial system. I ask you if it is not grievous." From the figures I have here given with reference to one colony, I can leave the statement of M.

Porteu far behind. Excluding the deficit of 1893, namely, 28,958,648 francs, the total cost of this colony to the mother country to 1892 inclusive has been 476,422,522 francs, and the total French trade with it during the same period has only amounted to 63,211,047 francs. Or, to afford a complete parallel to the figures given by M. Porteu, France has spent 476 millions of francs upon Tongking in order to dispose of 59 million francs' worth of French products.[*]

One final lesson remains to be drawn. Regarded from the ordinary point of view of the political economist, the above figures present the following result :—

		Francs.
TOTAL IMPORTS		203,728,620
TOTAL EXPORTS		53,320,034
Balance of Trade against Tongking ...		150,408,586

A blacker result than this from the conventional point of view could hardly be imagined; but these last figures point another moral even more unmistakable. To quote M. Leroy-Beaulieu again: "We are practising a systematic exploitation of the public funds for the profit of a thousand or so persons. . . . What is needed is the suppression of a Colonial Council which only represents a handful of furnishers and functionaries." That remark hits the last nail upon the head.

As a matter of sober fact, in conclusion, the French colonisation of Tongking — and Tongking is only one example of a truth which every other French colony would illustrate to a greater or less degree—has amounted to this: France has taken possession of a country; she has despatched to it an army of soldiers and a second army of

---

[*] This general statement, as I wish to make quite clear, is not an absolutely accurate one, since the details of expenditure given in the above tables refer for the most part to Annam and Tongking, while the figures of trade refer almost exclusively to Tongking alone. But the share of Annam in both cost and returns is of course a very minor factor in comparison with that of Tongking.

functionaries; a handful of dealers has followed to supply
those with the necessaries and luxuries of life; the dealers
have purchased those necessaries and luxuries from France
(the foreign imports being chiefly for native consumption),
as the Customs tariff prevents them from buying cheaper
elsewhere; these purchases have practically constituted the
trade of France with the Colony. *Castra faciunt; coloniam
appellant.*

RUSSIA IN THE FAR EAST.

CHAPTER VIII.

VLADIVOSTOK: "THE POSSESSION OF THE EAST."

THE Russian Government and the geographical situation of Russian Tartary have succeeded between them in keeping their Pacific stronghold well out of the world, and ten thousand miles nearer to it in body bring you little or no nearer to it in knowledge. "Going to Vladivostok? Dear me!" people said just as naturally at Nagasaki, a hundred yards from the vessel which was getting up steam to go there, as they did in London on the other side of the world. But the journey is easy enough to make. From Yokohama the magnificent steamers of the great Japanese steamship line, the Nippon Yusen Kaisha, take you southward along the coast to Kobe, the pleasantest foreign settlement in Japan; then to Shimonoseki, famous for its foreign bombardment in 1865, and now strongly and skilfully fortified with coast batteries of the latest design, armed with heavy howitzers of Japanese manufacture—most efficient weapons; then through the Inland Sea, ranking high among the "show scenery" of the East, and drop you at Nagasaki. From Yokohama to Nagasaki is 692 miles; from Nagasaki to Vladivostok is 659 more. At noon next day the *Takachiho* steams out into the Korean Straits; during the night she passes Port Hamilton a long way off, those bare islands of which the world talked for a year, and about which, too, opinions are as divided in the East as at home, the truth probably being that England did very well to give them up, since they would have been quite untenable in the event of a bombardment; and on the follow-

141

ing afternoon she drops anchor at Fusan, the treaty port and
Japanese settlement on the south coast of Korea. Then came
a revelation of head-gear among the white-robed Koreans, a
chat with the Commissioner of Customs, and an afternoon
with a hammerless companion, resulting in three brace of
pheasants, a snipe, and a small deer; and off again. For
twenty-four hours we steamed along a rocky, desolate, and
forbidding coast, and next morning the anchor dropped again
in the splendid harbour of Wönsan (Gensan), the western
Treaty Port, alongside the big white French ironclad, the
flagship *Turenne*. Soon a smart petty officer came up the
gangway bearing a courteous invitation to Captain Walker
and myself to dine with "M. le Contre-Amiral Layrle, commandant en chef la division navale de l'extrôme Orient," and
that night on board the *Turenne* a dozen merry guests, all very
far from home, the flashing of many wax candles over silver
plate and glittering glass, the skill of a decorated French cook,
the witchery of old Burgundy, and the strains of Offenbach
and Suppé, all combined to dispel the thought that we were
lying off the uninhabited Port Lazareff, in the wild and lonely
seas of the Hermit Kingdom. But at midnight our anchor
was heaved again, and at daylight next day but one the helm
was suddenly put over to starboard opposite a break in the
high wall of cliffs, the man in the chains took up his
monotonous cry, and we swept round into the harbour of
Vladivostok—the proudly-named " Possession of the East."

An old-fashioned theologian would say that Providence had
intended this place to be made impregnable. The harbour is
shaped, speaking roughly, like the Greek capital Γ. It has two
entrances, one at the south-east corner, the other in the middle
of the west side, both narrow deep-water channels, the latter,
indeed, being only a few hundred feet wide. The Eastern
entrance is the one used for traffic, the other being dangerous
on account of currents and sandbanks. As you steam straight
north up the long leg of the Γ, you notice first an ex-

tensive beach on the right, then several large bays open out in
succession, and you pass through a narrow opening between
Capes Novosilsky and Nazimoff, and leave the western entrance
on the left. The hills around are densely wooded, and all
the defences visible so far have been extensive earthworks
building on your right, and loads of bricks for them lying on the
shores below. Now, however, as the ship passes Cape Goldobin
you discover a large two-storied battery from which six black
muzzles look down. What may be behind the earthworks of the
upper storey you cannot tell, but the guns below are visibly
6-inch breech-loaders. They constitute only an inner line of
defence for the interior of the harbour, but they would, of
course, make it very hot for a ship in the harbour with their
plunging fire at short range, but Vladivostok is defended by
altogether different weapons, however dreadful these may look
to the captain of peaceful merchant vessels. Soon after passing Fort Goldobin, a sharp turn to the right, almost at a
right angle, brings you into the harbour, which then stretches
out due east in a straight line, upwards of two miles long
and half a mile wide. This is the Eastern Bosphorus, and the
"Golden Horn" of the Pacific.

The town of Vladivostok extends nearly the entire length of
the north side of the harbour, and in configuration it rather
resembles St. John's, Newfoundland, the houses beginning at
the water's edge and gradually thinning out as the hills behind
get steeper. They are of all sorts, from the log-cabin and
Chinese shanty to the neat wooden cottage in its little garden
and the handsome brick business house of several storeys. Over
all rises the cathedral—the one thing in Vladivostok that
remains unfinished for want of money. The anchorage is
so admirable that the *Takachiho* (now, alas! at the bottom of
the sea, off Tsushima), a vessel 327 feet long, lies within
a stone's throw of the wharves, and the same anchorage exists
all round. Directly in front are three little parallel streets
constituting the Chinese bazaar. On the west is the Chinese

and Korean town of wooden shanties; behind are five or six blocks of fine brick buildings forming the winter barracks, while straight away ahead is a broad street soon disappearing over the dusty hill, to become two miles away the great Siberian post-road. The main street runs parallel with the harbour, and on this are the chief stores and many of the private houses. A quarter of a mile along it to the east is the Governor's residence, buried in a square mass of foliage—the gardens where a first-rate band plays regularly and the society of Vladivostok comes to walk and to gossip. Further on, always between the water and the street, is the "Staff," the Governor's official head-quarters, a large handsome building, and further still, a mile or more from where we lie, a tall chimney marks the situation of the "Port," as the Russians call it, a score or more of storehouses and machine shops forming the Navy Yard or Arsenal. This extends along the shore for a quarter of a mile, and the torpedo boats and small ships of the Siberian Squadron lie alongside, with a confiscated American fishing-sloop, while the ironclads and gunboats are anchored a little further off. On the opposite shore of the harbour there are no buildings of any kind, except an iron storehouse deep in the woods here and there, isolated presumably on account of inflammable or explosive contents. On the summits of the two high hills behind the town are two stations for the fire-watch.

The streets of Vladivostok are gay enough. Civilian costume is the exception, almost every figure being either a soldier or a Chinaman. The rank and file have none of the smartness of European troops. Their uniforms are rough and simple —white blouse and cap, long black boots and belt—they are evidently expected to last a long time, and their wearers do a lot of hard manual work. If not exactly dirty, therefore, the soldiers look very unkempt. The officers also, and their clothes, have the hardened appearance of active service, but their flowing cloaks make them picturesque. Blue and white Chinamen, sombre-suited Japanese, and shrouded Koreans, with marvellous hats of cardboard and bamboo fibre, variegate the scene. An element of picturesqueness and noise is added by the droschky-drivers in their long scarlet blouses and black "zouave" waistcoats their long unpolished boots, and their flowing hair. They congregate at the corners, and dash up and down the main street at a gallop, their whips cracking like pistol-shots.

The chief hotel of Vladivostok is at a pastrycook's shop, so I remained in my comfortable quarters on board, and after breakfast I went on shore to present my semi-official introduction—an imposing-looking document, a foot square, with the Russian Eagle on the back—to the Military Governor, Rear-Admiral Ermolaiew. His Excellency received me with the utmost courtesy, but his efforts to conceal his vast surprise at my visit were in vain. He read the letter—a long one—then he looked at me; then he read it again and looked again. "Yes," he said, finally, "anything I can do for you, of course, but what on earth do you want to see at Vladivostok?" I modestly replied that, with His Excellency's permission, I wanted to see everything. "But what?" As I had only been an hour in the place, however, I was not in a position to specify my desires in detail. "But what shall I do?" To dictate to a Russian Military Governor was naturally repugnant to me, and as Admiral Ermolaiew's French—the only language in which we could communicate—was of a rudimentary character, the conversation was rapidly approaching an embarrassing dead-lock. Suddenly, with an explosive "Ah!" the Governor sprang from his chair and disappeared, returning in a minute with his wife, a most attractive and energetic lady, charming even at that early hour of the morning. Madame Ermolaiew spoke French perfectly: with the native tact of a Russian she straightened matters in a moment, and five minutes later I was bowed out between the salutes of a bluejacket and a sentry, with the Governor's card in my pocket bearing a written permission to go almost anywhere and see almost anything,

11

and with an appointment to meet an officer the next morning at eleven, who would act as *cicerone*. I was slightly out of breath, it is true, at the speed of the interview, but naturally very grateful for the distinguished courtesy.

Vladivostok is a purely military town — technically, a "fortress." That is, not only does it owe its existence to strategic and military considerations, but even after it has been thus created no other interests or enterprises have grown up around it. In this case trade has not followed the flag: the place is just Russia's one stronghold and naval base on the Pacific, and nothing else. Its imports consist of the supplies for the military and naval population and those who minister to them; its only export at present is a little sea-weed. Two other industries might be developed here, how-ever, and these are well worth the attention of energetic men with some capital. Siberia contains vast forests of the finest and largest timber, and a very important export trade in this could easily be cultivated. And the authorities find great difficulty in supplying themselves with fresh meat. Cattle are imported regularly from Korea, but the supply is poor and uncertain, while Siberia is probably as well suited in many parts for cattle-raising as Western Canada. I believe, moreover, that the Russian authorities would materially help the right man to introduce this. At present, however, all its commerce is a tribute to the God of Battles. A Russian store has just closed, and the two great stores, magnificent stone and brick buildings, employing scores of clerks and sales-men, where you can buy absolutely everything, from a pound of butter to a piano—are owned by Germans, the one by Messrs. Kunst and Albers, the other by Mr. Langelütje. There is also the smaller general store of Mr. Hagemann, almost the only English resident. The population of the place when I was there was about 15,000, of whom 5,000 were Chinese, 2,000 Russian civilians, and 6,000 troops and blue-jackets ashore. But the strength of the troops has no doubt been considerably raised lately.

The Chinese and Koreans are under very strict regulations, being only allowed to reside in their own quarter, and any found in the street after nine o'clock at night are arrested and locked up. This was found necessary to prevent disturbance. The Koreans, I should add, have an intense hatred for the Russians, due largely, no doubt, to the harshness with which they are treated. There are large numbers of them in the immediate neighbourhood, and they are always in a state of discontent bordering upon revolt. Whenever they can get hold of a Russian by himself, they are very apt to murder him out of hand. Of course, their power is but that of the mosquito on the elephant, but if Russia were engaged in hostilities they might well prove an annoying thorn in her side. Probably 2,000 Chinese labourers are employed in the arsenal alone, and they fill the streets when they come streaming out from work, and all the harbour-front population, boatmen, cargo-handlers, &c., are Chinese or Koreans. The stores employ many Chinese; they are patrolled all night by Chinese watchmen, and the only domestic servants are Chinamen or Japanese women. Many of the Chinese come in the spring, when the harbour opens, and leave again, mostly for Chefoo, in the late autumn when it closes. There has been some talk about putting a prohibitory tax upon poor John Chinaman here too, but it will come to nothing; he is indispensable.

Life in this corner of Russian Tartary is lively enough, especially in winter. Communication with the outside world is easy by mail and telegraph. Letters come by sea (very few go overland) from San Francisco in four weeks, and telegrams to European Russia are ridiculously cheap. During the summer there are the constant festivities attending the arrival of foreign men-of-war. All the Russian officers, too, are fond of society, and there is a first-rate band. In winter it is of course dreadfully cold, and a frozen stick of milk is left at the door in the morning, and the beef is kept frozen in a tub, and chopped out as wanted. But from Christmas onwards for

a couple of months there is a ceaseless round of social gaiety.
Excellent pheasant and duck-shooting is to be had over the
surrounding bays and hills, and large deer abound in an
island a day's sail to the south. This, however, is strictly
preserved as an Imperial reserve, and Russian game-keepers
are stationed there, and periodically murdered by Korean
marauders. The famous thick-coated Northern tigers are
sometimes to be found by seeking. One of the traditions of
Vladivostok, and a true one, too, tells how a young fellow
named Chudjakow was out shooting one day, when a tiger
met him. He fired and killed it. Scarcely had it fallen,
however, when a second walked out of the woods. He fired
again, hitting this one, which turned tail and disappeared. A
moment later a tiger appeared again from the same place.
He fired for the third time, supposing this to be the same
animal, and wounded it slightly. Before he could reload,
however, it was upon him, and he was fighting it for his life.
His rifle was useless, and he had only a long hunting-knife.
As he did not return at night his father and friends organised
a search-party, and at last found him unconscious between the
paws of the dead tiger. A little way off lay the body of the
first, and just inside the wood they found the second, which
had died of its wounds. The days are gone by when the
houses at Vladivostok were barricaded against the great cats,
which used to come into the back yards at night to revel in the
family slops put for them, and when men did not venture out
after dark except five or six together, all armed; but I have
seen one of the tigers thus shot by Chudjakow, and a photograph
of the young man himself and the three skins.

Everything in Vladivostok is made subservient to military
interests, and there is no pretence to the contrary. As is
the case in all "fortresses" no civil rights exist, and the
merchants can be required to leave at twenty-four hours'
notice, without any explanation being given. The Mayor is
merely the vehicle of the Governor's will. The neighbourhood

of every fortified point is strictly guarded by sentries, whom no
civilian ever passes. The local weekly newspaper, the *Vladivostok*,
with a circulation of 450 copies, is edited (excellently so far as
geographical, ethnological, and other non-contentious information is concerned) by a member of the Staff, and the Governor
himself is the Censor. In return for this, however, it receives
an official subsidy of 2,000 roubles a year. The police, who
are supposed to know everything that passes and the movements of every one, resident or stranger, are of course the
Governor's pawns, under the command of a military officer.
No foreign consuls are allowed to reside at Vladivostok, the
only foreign representative being a Japanese called Commissioner of Trade, or some such non-political title. Most
foreign newspapers and books are forbidden, as in European
Russia, and at the only bookseller's in town I could not
buy a single volume in any foreign language, except a few
French works of world-famous innocence, used everywhere
as school reading-books ; and inquisitiveness or gossip on the
part of the foreign population about local naval or military
affairs is sternly discouraged, and trespassers against this
unwritten law soon learn very distinctly that they will be more
comfortable if they obey it. I ran up against this before I had
been in Vladivostok four hours. My first day there I was lunch-
ing at a foreign house, and happened, naturally and quite inno-
cently, to put some question or other about the batteries. "That
is a matter," I was immediately told by my host, "that we make
a point of knowing nothing about. We find that ignorance on
such subjects is the only way to get along pleasantly with our
Russian friends. Besides, it is none of our business, any way.
We are here as traders, not as possible combatahts." So I
put no more questions of that kind. The regulations against
publicity have recently been made much more severe. It is
now forbidden to ascend the neighbouring hills, and patrol
parties are frequently sent to scour the surrounding country,
their orders being to deal promptly with any investigator,

The many Russian officers that I met and talked with, told
me of course just as little as they liked, and the sources
of information were therefore distressingly conspicuous by
their absence. I must add, however, that the authorities put
no ridiculous restrictions or professions of violent secrecy in
my way. I was immediately told that I could not inspect
the batteries or fortifications from within—a permission I
should never have dreamed of asking; but several places
where no Englishman had ever been before—the whole of the
Navy Yard and Arsenal, for instance—were thrown open to me;
the Governor's card took me almost everywhere; I had a written
permission to take photographs, with certain specified exceptions
—a permission unfortunately nullified to a great extent by
rain; I was immediately introduced at the Naval Club; and
finally the Governor's Adjutant lent me his own boat. As
I thus sped across the harbour of this Russian stronghold, in
a Russian official's barge, pulled by six lusty Russian blue-
jackets, with a Russian rear-admiral's flag trailing behind
me, it struck me as a decidedly unique position for an English
journalist, and as an interesting commentary upon the suspicion
and unfriendliness that are so freely attributed to the Russians
in some quarters.

CHAPTER IX.

THE POSITION OF RUSSIA ON THE PACIFIC.

VLADIVOSTOK is of great interest to the rest of the civilised world, and chiefly, of course, to England, the United States, and Japan, as the Powers with most at stake in the Pacific, for exactly the same reasons that it is of importance to Russia, namely, as the one great naval stronghold and base from which Russian ironclads could issue in time of war to fall upon their enemies in the Pacific, and to which they could return for supplies, for repairs, or for refuge. Is it a great stronghold? Could it defy a hostile fleet? Is it provided with the necessaries of an efficient naval base? Does it, as its name declares, confer upon those who hold it "the possession of the East"?

The last so-called "scare" showed exactly what would be done at Vladivostok in case of war. The lights on Skrypleff Island in the east entrance and near Pospaloff Point to guide ships through the west entrance were extinguished; the west entrance was completely blocked from Larioneff Point to Cape Tokaroffski with contact mines (one of these got adrift and blew up a Russian fishing-vessel some time afterwards); the narrow passage from Cape Novosilsky to Cape Nazimoff was blocked with contact and electric mines, except a channel fifty feet wide under the former, and a gunboat lay near by to stop merchant vessels and send an officer on board to pilot them through; while preparations were made to remove all the civilian inhabitants to a sheltered valley some distance

inland. Supposing now that these precautions were all
carried out to-day, could a fairly powerful fleet reduce the
place? We will say for the sake of argument, to begin
with, that the Russian fleet is out of the way. Until a few
years ago, what were the defences of Vladivostok? The inner
ends of both channels were commanded and their mine-fields
protected by Fort Goldobin, and this was armed with a
number of 6-inch breechloading guns of Russian manufacture.
Its upper part was only, I believe, a battery of mortars. In the
centre of the long narrow strip of land forming the western side
of the harbour were two powerful batteries, each containing, I
believe, two breechloading Krupp guns, probably about 27-ton
guns, throwing a shell of 516 lb., and these were the heaviest
guns with which Vladivostok was armed. Further to the north
was another battery, formed, I believe, of two 8-inch breechloading cannon, two more of the same Krupps, and four rifled
mortars. These two batteries are designed to protect the weak
point of Vladivostok—the shelling of the town and arsenal over
the land. That was all. The answer was therefore easy.
Vladivostok, in the absence of men-of-war to protect it, could
undoubtedly have been taken, and if the last "scare" had
become a struggle, there can be little doubt that the British
fleet would have first shelled the town and then forced an
entrance to the harbour. For the town could have been shelled
easily at 8,000 yards, while the bombarding ships constantly
moving would present a poor target for the Krupp guns at
nearly 4,000 yards; the men fighting the inner forts would have
been terribly exposed; while removing or exploding mines which
are not well protected by batteries is a comparatively easy matter
nowadays. If defending ships had been present they would
have added to the difficulty by exactly their own strength.
But after an attack made a few years ago, Vladivostok would
certainly not be the "possession of the East"—it would be
the possession of the enemy.

The truth of the foregoing assertion can be almost proved, as you prove a sum in division by another in multiplication, by the fact, hardly yet appreciated, that the Russian Government has been adding to the defences of Vladivostok in every respect and on the most lavish scale. An estimate was passed by the

THE HARBOUR OF VLADIVOSTOK.*

Governor-General of Eastern Siberia, and submitted to St. Petersburg for approval, for strengthening Vladivostok by engineering work alone at an expense of no less than 6,000,000 roubles. The Arsenal is being greatly enlarged by both new

* It should hardly be necessary to explain that I do not present this sketch-map as anything even remotely resembling a map for naval or military purposes. It is merely a reduction from the Admiralty chart, with such additions as are of general interest and mv eyes and information enabled me to add. Nor is my account of the place intended to serve naval or military ends in the slightest degree. The British authorities, at any rate, as is well known by experts, stand in no need of information about Vladivostok. They have plenty of it from a very different source.

buildings and new machinery; an addition to the great floating
Stanfield dock is just finishing; all along the harbour side
of the west arm are rows of fine new barracks; and several
new forts were already half finished when I was there, of a
size and arrangement far in advance of anything existing
previously. One of these forts, just to the north of Cape
Tokareffski, will command both entrances to the harbour and
ships in position to shell the town; another of great size will
command the mine-field with which Novik Bay, from which
Fort Goldobin and part of the town could be bombarded, is
to be protected; and two or three others, including one on
Skrypleff Island, will command the harbour and its approaches
from the east. It is only reasonable to suppose that these,
which should all be complete by this time, are armed with guns
of the latest pattern and great power. If the Government
sanctions the engineers' estimate recently submitted, batteries
will also be placed on some of the large islands south of the
harbour, an extremely important situation. By this time,
therefore, it is not too much to say that Vladivostok is impregnable from the sea. The Russians admit that the Chinese
town can always be destroyed from the sea, but I believe
they estimate that they can burn this and rebuild it for
24,000 roubles. They deny, however, that the town proper and
the Arsenal are open to shell fire from beyond the west
batteries, but I cannot agree to this, as with my field-glass I
have distinctly seen the church over the southernmost of the
two west land batteries, within bombarding distance. This,
however, is of comparatively small moment, for all war stores
would of course be removed to a place of perfect security,
and Vladivostok would be little weaker as a naval stronghold
after the town had been destroyed than before. Moreover, it
is an accepted military and naval maxim that under modern
conditions ships stand practically no chance whatever against
well-equipped and well-handled coast batteries, and that it is
little short of suicidal for a fleet to attempt to reduce a fortress

by bombardment alone. In case of war an enemy would probably try to find the Russian Fleet and blockade it somewhere, for if the ships were once destroyed or captured, Vladivostok would cease to be worth attacking. It should be clear, however, from the foregoing, that the Russian authorities are determined on no half measures. They have got Vladivostok and they mean to keep it, and it is doubtful if there is at present any army and fleet in the whole East strong enough even to try to take it away from them.

The new restrictive regulations so much discussed and so severely criticised in naval circles, by which only two ships of any foreign fleet are allowed to anchor in Vladivostok Harbour at one time, were officially stated to have been made in accordance with similar regulations by other Powers. But they were really the result of one particular incident. On August 21. 1886, the British squadron on its summer cruise north reached Vladivostok while all the Russian vessels happened to be away, and our eight ships entered in a thick fog, and were not discovered by the Russians on shore until they were dropping anchor in faultless order in the inner harbour. It was a most brilliant piece of seamanship—the Russians themselves would never have attempted it—but it was surely most indiscreet, as the consequences soon showed. For naturally enough the Russian authorities were thrown into a panic, and said to themselves that an enemy might do this very thing a short time before war was suddenly declared, when Russia on the Pacific would be at his mercy. Therefore, rather than risk multiplying unpleasantness by prohibiting the entry of foreign vessels from time to time as circumstances might seem to require, they decided to cut off the danger once for all. It was natural and explicable enough on the part of the Russians, but it is an innovation far from welcome to the greater part of any foreign fleet, which must remain knocking about outside at gun practice or steam tactics, while the flagship and one other vessel are comfortably anchored and politely entertained within. The

Russians, by the way, do not seem to navigate their own waters very well, for a gunboat had gone aground near Vladivostok just before my visit; a foreign merchant-captain told me that he had once steamed after two other gunboats on the coast to warn them they were running into shallow water; and the *Vitiaz* was totally lost a short time ago and actually in Port Lazareff —the very harbour which Russia is supposed to have selected for her base on the Korean coast.

The impression made by the rank and file of the land forces at Vladivostok is that of soldiers who have been on active service for six months, long enough to have grown careless about the polishing of leather and steel and the details of personal care which go to make up the much admired "smartness" of crack regiments. Their clothes are solid and coarse, their boots are unblacked, and their weapons look as if they had seen several campaigns. The men themselves are hardy enough, but they appear to be extremely poor and far from happy. It is certainly very astonishing to see soldiers in uniform hawking wild flowers at street-corners, as I did in Vladivostok itself. They are mostly much younger than troops with us, and they are evidently drawn from the lower classes of a farming population. Their winter barracks are spacious and handsome buildings, but their summer barracks, several miles inland by the shore of a beautiful part of the Amur Bay, are rather ramshackle, and if the truth is to be told, much dirtier than Tommy Atkins would be satisfied to live in. But I spent a jolly evening with them when I rode out with my military guide, and shared their palatable if frugal supper of black bread, potato soup, and *kvass*—a kind of thin bitter beer. The detachment I visited was under the command of a lieutenant who looked fifteen, and was certainly not twenty. They would make good rough fighting material—*Kanonen-futter* as the Germans cynically call it—all the better for war work in this far-off hard country because they do not know what it is to be petted or pampered in time of peace. In fact, peace means perhaps more hard work for them than war, for they are employed on building fortifications, making bricks, and several other occupations that are not included in the military curriculum elsewhere, very much like common labourers. The following estimate of their numbers at Vladivostok is not far from the mark: two battalions of infantry, 2,000; artillery, 850; sappers, 250; total, on peace footing, 2,600 men. This is doubtless much smaller than is generally supposed, but the tendency is to distribute the forces all over this part of Eastern Siberia, and only to collect a large number at Vladivostok in times of danger. Probably 80,000 men could be concentrated here in a short time.

The officers, on the whole, struck me as a fine body of men, dignified, devoted, and intelligent. But they must suffer intellectually from being cut off by the strict Russian censorship laws from the information which circulates so freely elsewhere. The growing importance, by the way, of this stronghold in Russian Tartary, is shown by the fact that officers are no longer liberally pensioned for short service here and elsewhere on the Siberian coast. Officers used to elect to serve in Siberia, and after ten years' service were entitled to retire upon half-pay, and after twenty years' service upon full-pay. For service in European Russia, on the other hand, retirement upon full-pay comes only after thirty-five years' service. Full-pay in Russia, however, does not mean the same as elsewhere. A Russian officer's total military income is made up of three parts, pay proper, lodging allowance, and table-money, in the proportion that a total income of say over 3,000 roubles a year, a lieutenant's pay, would mean only 1,400 roubles of pay proper. Half-pay for him, therefore, after ten years in Siberia would be 700 roubles, and full pay 1,400 roubles. These liberal terms of pension naturally made service in Siberia popular, but the whole system of naval pension was altered a year ago, and the above only applies now to officers who entered the navy before 1887. An occasional officer there speaks a little English,

several speak French, and almost all speak more or less German.
To Lieutenant Vladimir Maximoff, "flag-officer to the Commander of the port," in whose charge I was placed, and who
combined the maximum of courtesy and hospitality with an
irreducible minimum of information, I owe very hearty thanks.
As for the naval and military hospitality of Vladivostok, it was
generous and constant, and as everybody was familiar with the
Biercomment of German student-life, it was also both formal and
hilarious.

I made one peculiarly interesting discovery. It is universally
believed that Vladivostok is a closed port for four months out
of the twelve—isolated by impassable ice from about December
17th to April 17th. And this is regarded as the sole explanation of Russia's *Drang nach Süden*, her necessity to
press gradually southward for an open port in Korea or
below it. Such is not the case. A man-of-war — and therefore a dozen—can be got in or out of Vladivostok Harbour
in case of urgent need at any time of year. There is an
American ice-breaking machine, which on a trial trip broke
a channel through the thickest part of the ice, one hundred feet
long and six fathoms wide, at a pace which would take it out
beyond Goldobin Point, where the ice is naturally more or less
broken, in three or four days. Moreover Patroclus Bay, and
especially the bay further to the south-east, are practicable bays
all the year round. At any rate two American ships came up
there unaided a few winters ago. Indeed the authorities are
considering whether they will not make this the mercantile
terminus of the railway.

In conclusion, I may add that the Amur peninsula is fine
wooded country for at least thirty miles, with small rivers
running east and west, and one or two good roads. The west
side presents to the eye a succession of sandy beaches, whilst
the east side ends abruptly for the most part in precipitous
cliffs.

CHAPTER X.

THE TRANS-SIBERIAN RAILWAY AND ITS RESULTS.

IN the relations of Russia and the Far East, one matter far outweighs in importance all others put together—the Trans-Siberian Railway. It is my conviction that this colossal enterprise is destined to alter the map of that part of the world at no very distant date. To Englishmen it is therefore of the first interest, for if I am right they will shortly be called upon to decide one point of the utmost moment in connection with it.

The absorption of " Siberia "—that is, the whole of Russia's Asiatic possessions with the exception of Transcaucasia, the Transcaspian territory, and Turkestan—occupying an area of not far from 5,000,000 square miles, has proceeded, now quickly, now slowly, but without interruption, ever since the traders of Novgorod began to raid the Finnish Yugra tribe in the twelfth century, for the valuable furs they secured. For centuries the conquest proceeded, through the efforts of hunters and fishermen, the ransackers of mounds, and the mere raiders, their advances being gradually recognised from time to time by the Government. After a while, expedition after expedition added huge territories in a more formal manner. An important date is 1581, when Yermak, a Don Cossack, entering the service of the immensely wealthy Stroganov family, who ruled and practically owned the Ural district, defeated the Tartar Khan, Kuchum, and sent his lieutenant, loaded with furs, back to Moscow to " humbly salute the

Lord Ivan Vaselivich the Terrible, with the acquisition of a new Siberian Kingdom." Slowly but surely Russian settlers and soldiers pressed eastwards, and the eighteenth century was distinguished by a number of remarkable exploring expeditions. One by one, every territory was absorbed, the final great achievement, the annexation of the whole Amur district, coming in 1854. All the territory on the American Continent was ceded to the United States in 1867, and the Kurile Islands were exchanged with Japan for Sakhalin in 1875. At that date Siberia practically took its present shape.

It is an interesting fact that the first person to lay before the Russian Government a proposal for the Trans-Siberian railway was an Englishman. He was an engineer named Dull, and his plan was to construct a tramway, on which horses should supply the motive power, from Nishni-Novgorod, through Kazan and Perm to one of the Siberian ports. It is not surprising that the Russian Government passed over in silence so fantastic a scheme, unsupported by any estimates. Simultaneously with this proposal, Count Mouraviev, afterwards Governor-General of Siberia, proposed to unite De Castries Bay in the Tartar Straits with Sofisk on the Amur by a carriage road which could be afterwards converted into a railway.* The surveys for this road were actually made in 1857, but nothing came of the proposal. In the same year an American named Collins petitioned the Government for a concession to found a company to unite Irkutsk and Chita. Next, three more Englishmen, Messrs. Morrison, Horn, and Sleigh offered to build a railway from Moscow to the Pacific shore of Siberia, but asked for such privileges in connection with it, as in the opinion of the Russian Government would have led to the concentration of the whole trade of Siberia in the hands of foreigners for a long period. In the same year, 1858, a Russian named Sofronov proposed a line

* Most of the facts here given are taken from a volume published last year by the Russian Department of Trade and Manufactures. I have also drawn slightly from an interesting article by Mr. Frederic Hobart, in the *Engineering Magazine* for June, 1898.

through the Kirghiz steppes to Peking, and four years later
another Russian named Kokorev conceived the idea (based
upon the schemes of a Government mining official named
Rashet) of uniting the basins of the Volga and the Obi. His
scheme, however, although favourably received, was soon afterwards abandoned for that of Colonel Bogdanovich, who was
despatched in 1866 to inquire into the famine of two years
before. He sent the following telegram to the Minister of the
Interior : "After removing all difficulties in the provisioning of
the governments of Perm and Viatka, and investigating the
local conditions, I am of opinion that the only sure means of
preventing famine in the Ural country in the future, is the
building of a railway from the governments of the interior to
Ekaterinburg and thence to Tiumen. Such a line, being subsequently continued through Siberia to the Chinese frontier, would
acquire a great importance both strategical and for international
trade." Two years later many surveys were carried out in connection with this plan. A third scheme starting, like the two
previous ones, from Perm, but ending near Kurgan on the river
Tobol, was planned by a trader named Liubimov in 1869.
These three schemes were carefully investigated, and it was
decided to build a line 463 miles long to join Kama and the
Tobol. A Special Commission decided that it was impossible to
make the line serve as a link in the chain of the great Siberian
railway of the future without sacrificing the mining interests of
the Ural district. The idea of the through route was therefore
relegated to the future. Surveys, however, continued, and in
1875 it was at length decided to build the first section of a line
to approach the Pacific from Nishni-Novgorod, but *viâ* Kazan
and Ekaterinburg to Tiumen. In 1878, the Ural railway was
opened, and two years later the Imperial order was given to
continue it to Tiumen.

For some time afterwards preference was given to the plan of
crossing Siberia by a route which should utilise the vast stretches
of water-communication, joining these by means of railways.

12

The obvious advantage of this scheme was the enormous saving of cost. In detail it was to proceed from Tiumen, by the Tura, Tobol, Irtish and Obi rivers, to Tomsk; then by rail to Irkutsk; thence by the Angara river, and across Lake Baikal; thence by rail to the head of the Amur and down it for 1,600 miles; thence by rail to Vladivostok. One fatal objection caused the abandonment of this scheme—namely, that in winter the eleven hundred miles of railway from Tomsk to Irkutsk would be isolated, for it would begin at one frozen river and end at another. Therefore, after much discussion, and in spite of the greatly increased cost, an all-rail line was decided upon in 1891 at the instigation of the Tsar himself. The railway from Samara to Cheliabinsk had been completed in the meantime, and the Siberian railway was to begin at the latter place. On May 17, 1891, the Tsarevich, being at Vladivostok at the conclusion of his tour in the Far East, formally announced by the will of the Tsar that the Grand Siberian Railway should be built, and inaugurated the Usuri section. To take charge of the enterprise the "Siberian Railway Committee" was formed at St. Petersburg, and the Tsarevich appointed president.

The entire railway is divided into seven sections. First, the Western Siberian Section, from Cheliabinsk to the river Obi, an easy section, through an agricultural country, ending at Pochitanka, whence a branch line of 82 miles will connect it with Tomsk; 1,328 versts, at an estimated cost of 47,861,479 roubles. Second, the Central Siberian Section, from Obi to Irkutsk, a difficult and tortuous section, through a mountainous and mineral country and across many rivers; 1,754 versts, at a cost of 78,272,898 roubles. Third, the Baikal Circuit, round the southern end of the "Lake of Death," from Irkutsk to Mysovsk pier, the shortest and most difficult section, with the heaviest grades and the sharpest curves, and a tunnel 12,500 feet long at the height of 770 feet above the lake; 292 versts, at a cost of 22,310,820 roubles, which is likely to be much exceeded. Fourth, the Trans-Baikal Section, from Mysovsk to Stretensk, the most rich in minerals and containing the highest point of the whole line, the Shoidak Pass, 8,700 feet; 1,009 versts, at a cost of 53,309,817 roubles. Fifth, the Amur Section, from Stretensk to Khabarovka, the longest, easiest, and most promising section, through the " Garden of Siberia," the valleys being fertile and well-watered, and abounding in timber, and the climate milder than elsewhere ; 2,000 versts, at a cost of 117,555,835 roubles. Sixth, the North Usuri Section, from Khabarovka to Grafsk, 347 versts, cost 18,738,682 roubles. Seventh, the South Usuri Section, from Grafsk to Vladivostok, along the valley of the Usuri, through coal-bearing and mineral country ; 382 versts, cost 17,661,051 roubles. Total length, 7,112 versts ; total estimated cost, 350,210,482 roubles. The Grand Siberian Railway may therefore be thus summarised :—

	SECTION.	ROUTE.	MILES.	COST.
				£
1	Western Siberian	Cheliabinsk—Obi	880	5,120,159
2	Central Siberian	Obi—Irkutsk	1,162	7,921,394
3	Baikal Circuit	Irkutsk—Mysovsk	193	2,111,980
4	Trans-Baikal	Mysovsk—Stretensk	668	5,763,223
5	Amur	Stretensk—Khabarovka	1,325	12,708,748
6	North Usuri	Khabarovka—Grafsk	229	2,025,803
7	South Usuri	Grafsk—Vladivostok	253	1,909,302
			Total...4,713	£37,860,592*

According to the latest news, progress is being made on all the sections. From Vladivostok to Spasskoye 150 miles of railway have been open to traffic since last June, and 41 miles from Grafsk station are ready. The second telegraph line is ready for a distance of 30 miles, and 36 station-houses and other buildings have been erected. Between Cheliabinsk and Omsk 6½ miles of line are ready, and 116 station-houses and buildings completed. Nearly 9,650 tons of rails have been supplied, 270,000 sleepers, 587 tons of fastenings, 190 tons of water-pipes, and two reservoirs. The survey has been

* The discrepancies in the additions are due to the fact that the decimals are omitted from the separate items. Exchange : £10 = 92½ roubles.

completed between Omsk and the Obi for 94 miles, and over
21,000 cubic fathoms of earthworks have been made. On the
Central Section between the Obi and Krassnoyarsk much
forest has been cut down, 25,000 cubic fathoms of earthworks
made, and five stations built. The manufacturers have
supplied 260 tons of iron for the bridge across the Tom,
2,200 tons of rails and 700 tons of fastenings, 200,000 sleepers
have been laid, and 6,000 telegraph poles erected. Thirteen
miles of the line and 25 of the telegraph are ready.[*] All
this amounts, of course, to but a small fraction of the whole,
but it shows that the work is actively proceeding. The great
trial of strength will not come until the line is finished and
the Russian government is face to face with the financial
problem of maintaining it and the army of men it will require.

It is likely enough that the Siberian Railway may not be
finished either for the money or by the date calculated upon,
which is 1904. Nothing, however, unless the Russian Empire
should be plunged into war, will prevent its completion early in
the next century. When Moscow and the Pacific are in railway
connection, and to some extent even before that, the effect upon
Russia's domestic and foreign relations must be enormous. The
vast extent of Siberia thus opened up, its agricultural possibilities, its mineral certainties, the great variety of its other natural
products, and the opportunities it will offer to colonisation, will
inaugurate a new epoch in the history of Russia. But the rest
of the world is more concerned with the alteration it will bring
into the relations of Russia with other countries. This will be
startling. The railway will not be built as a commercial, but
as a political enterprise. It will not pay its expenses for a long
time to come, and the through traffic will be insignificant for a
century. Portions of it will soon be paying for themselves, but
as a whole the Siberian Railway is to be regarded as a long step
forward politically. The interesting question therefore is, in
what direction? The Transcaspian Railway is at Samarcand,

[*] The Times, October 15, 1894, Vienna correspondence.

and will soon be at Tashkend and Khokand, approaching the western frontier of China. The Siberian Railway skirts the northern and eastern frontiers of China practically from Irkutsk all the way to Vladivostok. A branch line will at once be built along the Selenga river, 75 miles, from Verkhne-Udinsk to Kiakhta, thus securing the whole Russo-Chinese trade at once. Before long, therefore, speaking in general terms, the entire northern half of China will be completely surrounded by Russian railways. Given the supineness of China and the energy of Russia, and it is not difficult to forecast the results. In the second place, the ability of Russia to convey any number of European troops to a port on the Pacific, will give her an enormous advantage over any of her European rivals there. With a powerful Pacific fleet and a sufficient number of transports she will be able to descend almost irresistibly upon any part of the Far East except Japan, which has little to fear from any invader. Unless England secures a further and firmer foothold, at least a thousand miles north of Hongkong, she will not be in a position to dispute with Russia any step that the latter may choose to take. China is threatened territorially, Great Britain is menaced commercially, but— always excepting Japan—the Siberian Railway will place the whole of the Far East almost at the mercy of Russia, unless England casts off her confidence and indifference.

Finally, there is the question of the Russian port on the Pacific. Can anybody believe for a moment that Russia will build the longest railway in the world, stretching five thousand miles from the furthest edge of her European possessions, and will spend upwards of forty millions sterling upon it, for it to end in a harbour that is frozen solid during five months of the year? Nothing could be more unlikely. Except for some European cataclysm which will set back all Russian schemes for a century, it is certain (except in the case of one possible eventuality which I describe later) that the terminus of the Siberian Railway will be in Korea. And in Korea it will be at

Wŏn-san, or Port Lazareff, as she prefers to call it. This is a splendid harbour, easily fortifiable, open all the year, surrounded by a country offering many facilities for development. Such a port is absolutely essential to Russia, and who shall blame her for trying to secure it? At any rate, as soon as the South Usuri Section is joined to the rest of the finished Siberian Railway, Russia's moment will have come. First the piece of Manchuria which projects like a wedge into her territory will become hers by one means or another, enabling her greatly to shorten and straighten the railway, and then she will simply take such part of Korea as may suit her. If this be only the district of Wŏn-san, to begin with, the subsequent absorption of the whole of the Korean peninsula may follow. She will then be in possession of a good land route, across the Yalu river, straight to the heart of China at all seasons of the year, and her position in the Far East will be unassailable. Whatever else may be thought of the prospects of the Far East, however, let the fact that Russia intends to go to Korea be regarded as certain. My own views of the international question springing out of the Siberian Railway and this fact, particularly in so far as it concerns the future of Great Britain, will be found in subsequent chapters upon the question of Korea and the future of Japan.

SPAIN IN THE FAR EAST.

CHAPTER XI.

MANILA: THE CITY OF CIGARS, HEMP, EARTHQUAKES AND INTOLERANCE.

THE passage from Hongkong to the two thousand islands which constitute the Philippine group is usually accounted the worst in the China seas. It is a sort of sailing sideways, through cross-currents of very deep seas, and into the favourite hatching-place and haunt of the dreadful typhoon. Moreover, Manila is not the easiest place in the world to find. Its position is wrong on the charts, so my skipper assured me, and he would not find it unless he knew better himself. It is, too, one of the most earthquaky places in the world. When a British scientific and surveying expedition came some years ago to the Philippines, and wished among other things to determine the precise latitude and longitude once for all, although it waited for a couple of weeks the islands were never steady enough to afford a satisfactory base for the instruments. The earthquake season was on, and they were wobbling about the whole time! This may be a "yarn," but it is a fact that the seismographs of the Observatory are in a state of perpetual motion. For myself, however, Manila will always be remembered as the place where for the first time I had my pockets publicly and officially searched. As soon as we anchored, a guard of soldiers came on board and assisted the custom-house officials in minutely examining everything in our baggage. When this was over I was stopped at the head of the gangway by the lieutenant in command and courteously informed that before I could land he

must be permitted to see what I had in my pockets. When it
came to my pocket-book he turned it over, separating every
piece of paper in it. A bystander informed me that all this was
to prevent the introduction of Mexican dollars, on which there is
a premium, and which are prohibited of a date later than 1877,
and a pamphlet attacking the priests, recently published in
Hongkong. I tried to square accounts with this officer by
hinting that I had copies of the forbidden pamphlet in my
boots, but like the Prig, he only "answered with a silent
smile."

In the most conspicuous spot in Manila stands a statue to
Magellan, who discovered the Philippine Islands in his famous
first circumnavigation of the globe in 1521, and whose lieutenant,
Legaspi, founded the city fifty years later. Then came Manila's
golden days. It was the goal of the galleon—imagination-stirring
name—that made its romantic voyages from Spain, deep loaded
with treasure; that named the coast California—fit godfather
for the golden harvest of '49—before even a foot was set on it;
whose captain earned forty thousand dollars by his trip, and
pilot twenty thousand; whose treasure-chests yielded up a total
of a million dollars to Drake alone; out of whose overflowing
stores one victorious British cruiser sailed into the port of
London with damask sails and silken rigging. The galleons are
gone, the wars of which they were the constant prey are as
forgotten as the men who fought them, and "the most fortunately situated city in the world," as La Pérouse called it, is
far off in its lonely ocean, days distant from any of the great
routes of commerce, almost unheeded by the world in which it
was once so renowned, unvisited even by the ubiquitous globe-
trotter. Yet there is something in the aspect of Manila sugges-
tive of romance—something more picturesque than other places
show. The first thing I saw was a native drifting down the
river fast asleep on a heap of coconuts. Then the streets are
dazzling with their "flowers of fire"—large trees ablaze with
scarlet blossoms. The olive-skinned mestizas, half-caste descen-

dants of emigrated Spaniard and native Indian, step daintily along on bare feet encased in *chinelas*, embroidered heel-less slippers, with gay fluttering garments of *jusi*, a woven mixture of silk and pine-fibre, their loose jet-black hair reaching sometimes almost to the ground—one woman was pointed out to me whose hair was said to be eighty inches long—and their deep dark eyes passing over you in languid surprise. The native men are a community which has forgotten to tuck its shirt into its trousers. Their costume consists of a pair of white trousers and an elaborately pleated and starched shirt, with the tails left flying about. Every one is smoking a cheroot, and every other one has a game-cock under his arm, a constant companion and chief treasure, and sometimes chief source of income too, until the deadly spur on the heel of the stronger or pluckier rival turns all its pride and brilliance into a shapeless heap of blood and feathers in the dust, while a thousand voices execrate its memory.

The City of Manila consists of two parts : the Spanish walled city, called the parish of *Intra Muros*, and the general settlement outside. The former is crowded with Spanish houses, the streets being so narrow that in many of them two carriages cannot pass each other; their overhanging upper storeys make a perpetual twilight; the inhabitants go out but little, and the whole place leaves upon you an impression of darkness, of silence, of semi-stagnation. Outside the walls are the wharves, all the warehouses and business offices, the hotels, many large residences of the wealthy half-caste population, and as the city gradually merges in the country, the charming river-side bungalows of the foreign residents, the Club, the racecourse, and so on, till you reach the squalid but picturesque outlying native villages. Inside the city you cannot take a hundred steps without coming upon striking evidence of the earthquakes. Here is a church half broken down by the convulsion of such a year; there are the grass-grown ruins of the Government Palace destroyed by another historic outburst; in the great Cathedral itself the lofty roof of the transept is split and cracked in an alarming fashion. On the shore of the bay there is an extensive and well laid-out boulevard or embankment, called the Luneta, where all fashionable Manila walks or drives in the evening to the music of the military band. Behind this are the forts, moss-covered antiquities of masonry, armed with rusty and harmless pieces which might have come from the gun-deck of some old galleon. The military authorities, however, make up in strictness of regulation what they lack in effectiveness of armament, for the foreign tennis-club was refused permission to play upon a piece of land within hypothetical range of these guns on the ground that it was "within the military zone," and I myself was told, though with great courtesy, by H. E. the Captain-General, that he must refuse me permission to take any photographs in which a part of the fortifications appeared. It was, of course, only for their ancient picturesqueness that I wished to photograph them—a mop vigorously twirled would be as effective for defence. In one fort at another place there are two decent modern guns, nearly surrounded by brittle masonry, and of these I purchased a large and excellent photograph taken from inside and showing every detail! Manila, however, if the information is of interest to anybody, could be reduced with ease by a couple of gunboats.

The history of Manila has been well divided * into four epochs: 1. The Chinese period ; 2. The Spanish and Mexican period of monopoly before the introduction of steam traffic ; 3. The period of open commerce with British predominance, which commences simultaneously with the age of steam ; 4. The period from the opening of the Suez Canal until the present time. The Chinese were the original traders with the Philippine Islands, doing business always from their junks to the shore. They were persecuted and massacred, but returned in ever increasing numbers. Legaspi encouraged them, and their numbers at the beginning of the seventeenth

* By Mr. Consul Stilgand, in a very interesting Report, F. O., No. 1201.

century have been estimated at thirty thousand. When the British occupied Manila in the course of one of the wars with Spain, the Chinese revenged themselves by joining the invaders, in return for which, as soon as our ships had left, a general massacre of Chinese was ordered and carried out, and so late as 1820, says Mr. Stigand, another massacre of Chinese and foreigners took place. At the present day there are one hundred thousand Chinese in the Archipelago, of whom forty thousand are settled in Manila, where they occupy the chief shops and do almost all the artisans' work. The second period was that of purely Spanish commerce, from 1571 to the beginning of this century. The Philippines were a dependence of Mexico, communication was forbidden except through Acapulco, from which port the State galleons, termed *Naos de Acapulco*, made their annual voyages, laden with the treasure which has rendered their name one of the most picturesque words in history. They were four-deckers, of about 1,500 tons, and strongly armed. In times of war they were, as everybody knows, the easy and greatly-sought prey of the enemy's ships. One of them, the *Pilar*, captured by Anson, was a prize worth a million and half dollars. At last foreign enemies pressed them so hard that after the Philippines had been without a State galleon for six years, they were discarded, and a commercial company, largely financed by the King of Spain himself, was formed in 1765, and to it was conceded the exclusive privilege of trading between Spain and the Archipelago, except for the direct traffic between Manila and Acapulco. This monopoly in its turn came to an end in 1834, and from that time the Philippines have been, according to Spanish ideas, open to commerce. The opening of the Suez Canal brought Manila within thirty-two days' steam of Barcelona, and, as Mr. Stigand avers, doubled the importance of the commerce of the Philippine Islands, which now reaches the yearly sum of fifty million dollars. The two principal banks, and the principal firms in Manila, are all British, and of the ships that entered and

cleared from the port during 1898, amounting to 240 in all, 189
were British and 58 Spanish. But for the excessive port dues and
the bad harbour accommodation which compels cargoes to be
carried in lighters to ships lying off the Bay, foreign trade with
Manila would undoubtedly be greater than it is. The one
railway in the islands, from Manila to Dagupan, which has just
been completed by the building of a bridge over the Rio Grande
river, has also been constructed chiefly with British capital, on
which it promises ultimately to pay a good return. The fall of
silver has hit it very hard, however, since the Government
subsidy which, at par of exchange, would be £85,000, is only
£53,000 at the present rate. Japanese enterprise is likely to
make itself felt before long here as elsewhere, since Mr.
Nakamura, formerly Japanese Consul, is announced to be on
the point of establishing a trading company in Manila, with
a capital of half a million dollars.

Considered as a contemporary community, Manila is an
interesting example of the social product of the Roman Catholic
Church when unrestrained by any outside influence. Here the
Church has free sway, uninterrupted by alien faith, undeterred
by secular criticism. All is in the hands of the priests. The
great monasteries, with their high barred windows, shelter the
power, the wealth, the knowledge of the community. The
Dominicans, with their Archbishop, the Augustinians, the
Recoletanos, and the Franciscans, divide the people among them,
their influence being in the order I have named them. Wise in
the knowledge of that which they have created, their own wealth
is invested in foreign banks, chiefly in Hongkong, though that of
the Dominicans, richest of all, is entrusted to the Agra Bank.
The people are plunged in superstition, and their principal
professed interest in life (after cock-fighting) is the elaborate
religious procession for which every feast-day offers a pretext.
The two newspapers are parodies of the modern press, ignorant
of news, devoid of opinion save the priests', devoted in equal
parts to homily and twaddle. The port, for its exasperating

restrictions and obstructions, is said by agents and captains to be the most disagreeable in the world to enter or leave. The civil authority itself is in many respects subject to the religious: during the chief religious festivals nobody but the Archbishop is permitted to ride in a carriage. A large part of the real estate of the city is in the possession of the religious orders. If you would prosper, it is absolutely indispensable that you should be on good terms with the priests. Their suspicion and disfavour mean ruin. The personal liberty of the common man may almost be said to be in their keeping. It is hardly necessary to add that the people as a whole are idle and dissipated, and that most of the trade is in the hands of the foreign houses. Altogether, Manila, distant as it is from other communities, with little intercourse to enlighten it, and few visitors to criticise or report, is a remarkable and instructive example of the free natural development of " age-reared priestcraft and its shapes of woe."

Of the six characteristics of Manila—tobacco, hemp, earthquakes, cock-fighting, priestcraft and orchids—the first two are known to all the world. Manila cigars and Manila hemp are household words, the yearly product of the former reaching the colossal total of nearly 140,000,000, besides tobacco, and of the latter 80,000 tons, of which Great Britain takes considerably more than half. Orchid-hunters come here year after year, travel far into the virgin forests of the interior, and emerge again after months of absence, if fever and the native Tagalos spare them, with a few baskets full of strange flowers which they carry home with infinite precaution and sell for a king's ransom. I was told of one collector who sold a plant for £500. Tobacco is of course the staple industry, and a morning spent in a tobacco factory is extremely interesting. Through the kindness of Messrs. Smith, Bell & Co., the leading business-house in Manila, I visited the most important of these, " La Flor de la Isabella," and followed the tobacco from its arrival in the bale, through the seasoning-room, to the wetting and

sorting-tubs, on the benches where it is rolled into cigars, past
the selecting-table where its colour and quality are decided by
a lightning expert, through the drying-room, and at last into
the gaily-labelled cedar box.   Manila tobacco is considered here
to be superior to any in the world, except the famous "Vuelta
Abajo" of Cuba, and millions of Manila cigars are sold as
Havanas.   In fact, the two styles, Manila and Cuban, the
former with the end cut blunt off and parallel sides, are
turned out in almost equal quantities.   Five colours are distinguished for sale, Maduro, Colorado Maduro, Colorado,
Colorado claro, and Claro, although the expert at the selecting-
table divides his heap into thirty different colours.   The filling
of a cigar is called *tripa*, or tripe, the wrapper *capa*, or overcoat.
London takes assorted colours, while the dark brands are sent
to Spain, the light ones to New York, and the straight cheroots
to India.   From this factory a million and a half cigars are
shipped every month to one London firm alone.   The figures of
tobacco-making are astounding.   At "La Flor de la Isabella,"
and this is only one of a score of factories in Manila, 4,000
people are employed, their hours of labour being eight, from
7 to 12 and from 2 to 5 o'clock.   And from the huge "Im-
periales" to the tiny "Coquetas" and the twisted "Culebras,"
4,000,000 in Manila style and 1,500,000 in Cuban style are
made monthly.   But cigarette-making caps the climax.   The
tobacco leaves are cut into *hebra* or thread, which we call
"long-cut," and the whole process of making is done by a
single machine.   I saw nine of these hard at work, and each
turns out twelve thousand in a day.   It is a simple sum:
9 × 12,000 × 30 × 12, say 38,000,000 cigarettes a year from
one factory.   And yet—

> "There is poison, they say, in thy kisses,
>   O pale cigarette!"

Or, from the other point of view, what an altar for Mr. Lowell's
worship of—

"the kind nymph to Bacchus born
By Morpheus' daughter, she that seems
Gifted upon her natal morn
By him with fire, by her with dreams."

The great cockpit of Manila at the "Fiesta del Pueblo" is one of the most remarkable spectacles in the world. Imagine a huge circus with an arena raised to the height of the faces of those standing; behind them tier upon tier gradually rising; above the arena, which is enclosed with fine wire netting, the red draped box of the farmer—the leading Chinaman of Manila, named Señor Palanca; and a packed audience of four thousand people. Squatting on the earthen floor of the ring, inside the wire netting, are the *habitués*, half Chinese and half *Mestizos*, while the officials walk about—the *juez de justicia* or referee, the *sentenciador* or umpire, the *casador*, "go-between" or betting-master, and several others. Then two men enter the ring, each carrying a bird whose spur is shielded for the moment in a leather scabbard. One wears his hat—he is the owner of the challenging bird—called *llamado;* the other, hatless, is the outsider or *dejado*, who takes up the challenge. An official calls out the sum for which the challenger's owner backs it, and how much is still lacking to make up the sum. Then comes the most extraordinary scene of all. The moment the words are out of his mouth, it rains dollars in the ring From those inside, from those who are within throwing distance, apparently from everywhere, dollars pour in, without method, without ownership, without a bargain, so far as one can judge amid the deafening clamour. When the sums on the birds are equal the betting master shouts *Casada!* "matched," literally "married," the farmer from his box on high yells *Larga!*— "loose them," and the fight begins. Sometimes it lasts ten minutes, sometimes only a second, the first shock leaving one bird a mangled corpse. No need to describe it—every one knows how a cock fights, and that it is the very gamest and pluckiest thing that lives. The fight over, the betting-master goes round

18

handing money back recklessly, so it seems, to anybody who
holds out a hand. I asked Señor Palanca how betting could
possibly be carried on like this. He replied that each one asks
for or takes the sum that belongs to him. But if anybody
should put out his hand for another's money? He gave me to
understand that it was never done, and that if anybody were
detected doing so he would probably have a dozen knives in his
body on the spot. In a short time I had witnessed 105 cock-
fights, and I shall never willingly see another. The entry of
the two brilliant birds; the final adjustment of the long razor-
edged spurs; the frantic betting; the rain of silver; the irrita-
tion of the birds, held up to pull a few feathers out of each
other in turn; their stealthy approach; the dead silence; the
sudden double spring and mad beating of wings; the fall of
one or perhaps both, the gay plumage drenched in blood, and
perhaps a wing half-severed and hanging down; the mad yells;
the winning bird carried carefully away, the loser pick·d up
like carrion and flung away with a curse; the distribution of
money; the instant appearance of another pair—the ceaseless
spectacle was an obsession of horror. The authorities make
a large revenue from the cockpit. For this and one other,
Señor Palanca pays 68,600 dollars a year, and there are five
other farmers.

Two other reminiscences may conclude my sketch of Manila.
One is that a hundred people were dying every day of cholera
while I was there, and several times my guide pushed me
hastily back against the wall as we threaded our way along the
narrow streets, and stuffed his camphorated handkerchief in
his mouth, muttering "*Colerico!*" as a couple of men passed
bearing on their shoulders a long object wrapped in a sheet
and slung between two poles—the latest case going to the
hospital. One of the Chinese firemen died of cholera on board
the steamer three hours before we sailed. The other reminiscence is that the thermometer stood at 105° in the shade, as I
saw, and at 160° in the sun, as I was told.

The Philippine Islands are the only Spanish possession in the Far East. Indeed, only a part of them can properly be said to be in Spanish possession at all, as the natives of many of the islands have never been brought under Spanish rule. At this moment hostilities are proceeding in the almost unknown island of Mindanao, with uncertain results as yet. Although mining has always been a failure, there is undoubtedly vast wealth in the tropical forests of the Philippines, but it will hardly be developed under the present *régime*. In spite of her growing fleet of first-class cruisers at home, Spain is without influence in the Far East outside her own immediate territories, and she will play little or no part in shaping its destinies.

PORTUGAL IN THE FAR EAST.

CHAPTER XII.

MACAO: THE LUSITANIAN THULE.

WHERE the carcase is, there also will the eagles be gathered together." China is the great carcase of Asia, and round her the eagles of Europe and America press and jostle one another. England is entrenched at Hongkong, and many a fat slice has she carried away. And now she is stretching out another claw through Thibet. America has half of Shanghai, and to and from San Francisco the bird of prey passes regularly in his flight. France is trying hard to carry off her share of the carcase through Tongking, and Port Arthur in the north brought huge sums to a French syndicate. Herr Krupp has secured Germany's chief plunder, and the Yamên of Li Hung-chang at Tientsin is a nest of commercial intrigue on behalf of the Fatherland. And Russia is laying a heavy paw upon China from the north. All this is natural enough, and so far as England and America are concerned it is the inevitable flow of trade in the channels of least resistance. But among the birds around this Asiatic carcase there is a beetle; among the birds of prey there is a parasite. The extreme south-east corner of China is the scene of the dying struggles of a mongrel fragment of a once intrepid and famous race—a fragment drawing its meagre sustenance with more difficulty every day. The hand of Vasco da Gama would have wavered upon the helm as he rounded the Cape of Good Hope, of all the men in Europe "the first that ever burst into the silent seas" of the East, if he could have foreseen to what a wretched pass and laughing-stock

his countrymen there would come after less than four hundred
years. The daughter of a King of Portugal was at Hongkong a
few years ago. She went, of course, to visit her own people
and stand under her own flag at Macao. But a glimpse was
too much for her, and she left within twelve hours.

Yet Macao (what is the relation of its name, one wonders, to
the Piccadilly game over which Beau Brummel used to preside,
doubtless with much profit to himself, at Watier's ?) is not such
a bad place, at first sight. Its bay is a perfect crescent. Around
this runs a broad boulevard, called the Praya Grande, shadowed
with fine old arching banyan trees. At each horn the Portuguese
flag waves over a little fort. Behind the town, green wooded
hills rise like an amphitheatre, and among the houses a
picturesque old building sticks up here and there — the
cathedral, the barracks, the military hospital, the older Fort
Monte. The whitewashed houses with their green blinds and
wide shady porticoes and verandas, from which dark eyes look
idly down upon you as you pass, recall many a little Italian and
Spanish town. A couple of yacht-like Portuguese gunboats lie
at anchor in the river beyond the bay. On Sundays and
Thursdays the band plays in the public gardens, and surely
nowhere in the world do the buglers linger so long over the
reveille and the retreat as they do here every day. To the busy
broker or merchant of Hongkong, who runs over here in the
summer from Saturday to Monday, after a week of hard work
and perspiration, coining dollars in a Turkish bath, Macao is a
tiny haven of rest, where the street is free from the detestable
ceaseless chatter of Chinamen, where the air is fresh and the
hills green, and where a little " flutter " at *fan-tan* is a miniature
and amusing substitute for the daily struggle with exchanges
and settlements and short sales.

And Macao has its glorious past, too. After they had
rounded the Cape the Portuguese occupied a great part of the
coast of India, sent an Embassy to the Emperor of China, and
occupied Ningpo. There one night 1,200 of them were

murdered. So they resettled a place called Chinchew, where
the same fate overtook them. Nothing daunted, they came
further south, and after helping the Chinese to destroy hordes
of pirates were permitted to settle in peace on a small peninsula
near the mouth of one of the two river approaches to Canton.
Here Macao was founded in 1557, and up to 1848 the Portuguese
paid a yearly rental of 500 dollars in presents or money. In
1582 when the Crown of Portugal passed to Spain, Macao
followed suit. When it went back again in 1640 in the person
of John IV. of Portugal, Macao again changed its flag and made
"a great donation" to the new king. At this time it was
described as "a melhor è mas prospero columna que os Portu-
gueyes tem em todo o Oriente"—the best and most prosperous
colony that the Portuguese possess in all the East. Then its
population was 19,500. By 1830 it had dwindled to 4,628, of
so mixed a blood that only 90 persons were registered as of pure
Portuguese descent. To-day it holds 63,500 Chinese, 4,476 so-
called Portuguese, and 78 others—in all 68,086. What is the
explanation of this sudden enormous multiplication of its
population? Like Satan, Macao was "by merit raised to
that bad eminence." It won back its ancient prosperity by
offering its houses and its traders as the last refuge in the East
to that hell upon earth, the legalised coolie traffic. When
Hongkong stopped this for ever under the British flag by the
Chinese Passengers Act of 1854, Macao opened eager and
unscrupulous arms to the "labour agents," and for nearly
twenty years, when public opinion became too strong for
even this mongrel and far-away community, the little city
flourished, its inhabitants made fortunes, the Praya Grande
was crowded every evening by a gay and gaudy throng, the
streets were beautified, the cathedral was rebuilt, and the
Portuguese colony became famous throughout the East for
its elaborate religious processions and its eloquent priests.
And during these twenty years uncounted thousands of coolies
were decoyed, entrapped, stolen, and pirated to Macao, kept

prisoners in the gloomy "barracoons," whose grated windows
are still everywhere visible, theoretically certified as voluntary
contract labourers by an infamous profit-sharing *procurador*, and
then shipped to toil, and starve, and rot, and die in mines and
fields and plantations everywhere, literally "from China to
Peru." As a single specimen of the traffic it is commonly
affirmed that of 4,000 coolies sent to the foul guano-pits of
the Chincha Islands, not a single soul returned. Altogether
500,000 Chinese were exported *via* Macao, before the traffic
was finally extinguished in 1875. There has been lately a
semi-surreptitious attempt to revive the trade. A company
was formed to supply a million Chinese to South America,
and a ship called the *Tetartos* actually carried 800 "free
labourers" to Brazil in October of last year, concerning
whose destination and fate there is still great uncertainty.
And it has been rumoured that a new and influential coolie
emigration "ring" is being planned, but fortunately public
opinion and Chinese official opposition may be counted upon
to thwart its efforts.

A retribution has fallen upon Macao—it seems as though the
curses of the murdered coolies have come back to it. Not a soul
walks the beautiful Praya; the harbour is silting up so fast, from
the detritus brought down by the Pearl and West rivers, between
which Macao is situated, that in a few years there will not be as
many feet of water in it; even the Chinese are leaving it—the
last of rats to quit a sinking ship; its miserable inhabitants,
interbred from Chinese, Portuguese, Malay, Indian, and unknown
human jetsam to such an extent that the few Portuguese troops
here regard the Chinaman as socially superior to the "Mestiços,"
have fallen into utter apathy; they hardly show themselves out
of doors, they subsist on monies furnished to them by their
pluckier relatives in foreign employ in Hongkong and elsewhere,
and the military band in the public gardens plays to a score of
loafers. There is no manufacture, no social life, and almost no
trade since the smuggling of opium has been stopped by Sir

.Robert Hart's recent treaty, giving Macao in perpetuity to the Portuguese on the condition that its Customs should be virtually controlled by his staff.

Another illegitimate source of income was lost to Macao in 1885. The most intense interest is taken in China—an interest comparable only to that of the great sporting events of the year with us—in the official literary and military examinations in Peking, and upon the results of these every other man in China desires to have a wager. A lottery to this end, called the Wei-sing Lottery, has existed for a long time. The Chinese Government have made more or less sincere efforts to put it down ; indeed, in 1874 the Emperor went so far as to cashier the Governor-General Ying Han for sanctioning its establishment in Canton. The authorities of Macao, of course, saw the possibilities of an enormous profit herein. They therefore farmed out the lottery to a Chinaman, who smuggled the tickets from Portuguese into Chinese territory, and who paid them 853,000 dollars a year for the privilege. Against this the Chinese were powerless, so in 1885, in self-defence, they consented to the Wei-sing in China, with the result that the sum the monopolist was able to pay the government of Macao fell . instantly to 86,000 dollars. Trade is going the way of the coolie traffic, the opium-smuggling and the lottery revenue, but the peculiar genius of Macao is not yet at an end. According to the British Vice-Consul, a new source of income has been invented in what is called "lie" tea, the legitimate tea trade having almost completely fallen off. Mr. Joly writes : "This term sufficiently explains its quality, for there is no doubt that the mixture could only be called tea in its correct acceptation through a considerable sacrifice of truth. These teas are manufactured from exhausted tea-leaves, which are dried, re-fired, and mixed with a certain proportion of genuine tea and of seeds and dust. Most of this preparation proceeds to Hamburg, where no 'Adulteration Act' is in force; but a good deal of mystery enshrouds its ultimate fate, for there are

various versions as to its disposal, some parties averring that
it is consumed by the lower classes, others that it is sold to
ships, and others that a quantity of it probably leaks into
England as well. From what I can gather, some of this 'lie'
tea is often packed in chests labelled 'best Congou,' and
shipped to India for the lower classes. But tastes differ, just
as the tea sent to France and the Continent generally is a
mere conglomeration of stalks and twigs, and to all appearances
no tea at all." Macao, however, is practically being wiped out
of existence by Hongkong, with its enormously greater capital,
enterprise and freedom of trade. So far from attempting to
meet this competition, the Macanese authorities go blindly
along the old road of commercial restriction, the port dues at
Macao being exactly three times what they are at Hongkong.
In 1854 the Abbé Huc wrote as follows: "Aujourd'hui Macao
n'est guère plus qu'un souvenir; l'établissement anglais de
Hongkong lui a donné le coup mortel; il ne lui reste de son
antique prospérité que de belles maisons sans locataires, et dans
quelques années, peut-être, les navires européens, en passant
devant la presqu'île où fut cette fière et riche colonie portugaise,
ne verront plus qu'un rocher nu, désolé, tristement battu par
les vagues, et où le pêcheur chinois viendra faire sécher ses
noirs filets." Although this prophecy is not yet wholly fulfilled,
each year brings its realisation nearer. One peculiar source of
revenue, however, remains—the sale of postage-stamps. Whenever Macao desires a lift for its treasury it is able to secure it
by abandoning one set of stamps and issuing another, when
philatelists from all over the world eagerly add it to their
inflated collections. Our consul declares that he has " endless
applications from different countries for stamps of this colony."

Portugal doles out to Macao a yearly pittance, and its other
chief source of revenue is the 150,000 dollars it draws annually
from its gaming-tables. For, as I have said, whenever one
wickedness was stopped in Macao it was quick to find another,
and to-day it is the only place in the Far East where you can

play *fan-tan* under a foreign flag. But its history is almost closed, the days of its disappearing trade and its decomposing population are numbered, and unless a Cement Company which has been started on a small island leased from the bishop, or the establishment of bonded warehouses, as suggested by the Chinese Customs, should bring back a semblance of prosperity, this "gem of the orient earth and open sea" will have disappeared like other places and peoples which were, sinned too much, and are not.

One classic memory, however, may save Macao from oblivion. It was here that the exiled Camoens composed the greater part of his *Lusiads*. On one of the hillsides overlooking the bay is an extensive old shrubbery, where narrow paths twist in and out among gnarled and ancient trees, and where half-a-dozen enormous boulders heaped together form a natural archway or grotto—the *Gruta de Camoës*. Camoens was appointed *Provedor dos defuntos e ausentes*—Commissary for the Defunct and the Absent—in Macao, and is supposed to have come here every day to work at his great task. The place, which is now known as "Camoens' Garden," belongs to a family named Marques, and by them a remarkably fine bronze bust of the half-blind poet, inscribed "Luiz de Camoës, Nasceo 1524, Morreo 1580," was placed in the arch in 1840, upon a pedestal bearing six cantos of the *Lusiads*, while tributes to him in half-a-dozen languages are engraved upon stone tablets placed around. There is a fine sonnet of Tasso's and various verses in Portuguese and Spanish, while Sir John Bowring's exaggeration is unfortunately conspicuous :—

> "Gem of the orient earth and open sea,
> Macao, that in thy lap and on thy breast
> Has gathered beauties all the loveliest
> On which the sun smiles in his majesty ; "

and so on. One degree worse in style, though a thousand times truer are some wonderful Latin verses perpetrated by a Mr. David, who laments—

> " Sed jam vetustas aut manus impia
> Prostravit, eheu !   Triste silentium
> Regnare nunc solum videtur
> Per scopulos, viridos et umbras ! "

Among all, however, the sincerest seems to me to be some
quaint lines in French, said to have been written by the commander of a French man-of-war which visited Macao in 1827,
and ingeniously dedicated as follows :—

> " Au Grand Luis de Camoens, Portugais d'origine Castillane,
>   Soldat religieux, voyageur et poète exilé,
>   L'humble Louis de Biensi, Français d'origine Romaine,
>   Voyageur religieux, soldat et poète expatrié."

This poet too was doleful, for apostrophising Camoens he
says :—

> " Agité plus que toi, je fuyai dans les champs,
>   Et le monde, et mon cœur, l'envie et les tyrans."

What the Macanese of to-day think of Camoens may be
judged from the fact that I tried in vain to borrow or buy in
Macao a copy of the *Lusiads*, to see what are the stanzas
engraved on the pedestal, the chiselling having become illegible.
Camoens himself was shipwrecked off Malacca on his way home
when pardoned, and swam ashore with the manuscript of the
Lusiads, losing everything else.   Curiously enough, by the way,
on leaving the grotto and turning into the old half-deserted
cemetery I came across an old-fashioned granite monument,
with this inscription : " Sacred to the Memory of the Right
Hon. Lord Henry John Spencer Churchill, 4th son of George
5th Duke of Marlborough, Captain of H.B.M.S. *Druid*, and
Senior Officer in the China Seas.   Departed this life in Macao
roads, 2nd June, 1840.   This monument is erected by His
Officers and Petty Officers in testimony of their Esteem and
Affection."

Finally, Macao, as I have said, is the Monaco of the East,

and from its gaming-tables its impecunious government reaps
150,000 dollars a year, the price said to be paid by the syndicate of Chinese proprietors for the monopoly. The game is a
peculiarly Chinese one, well fitted to afford full scope to the
multitude of refinements and hypothetical elaborations with
which the Chinaman, the greatest gambler on earth, loves to
surround his favourite vice. It is played on a mat-covered
table, with a small square of sheet lead and a heap of artificial
gilded " cash." On one side stands the croupier, on the adjoining side sits the dealer, and between them, a little to the rear, is
the desk and treasury of the cashier. The sides of the leaden
square are called one, two, three, and four. The dealer takes
up from the heap as many "cash" as he can grasp with both
hands and places them apart upon the table. Then the
players, who sit and stand round the other two sides of the
table, make their bets, that is, they place at either side of the
square any sum from 50 cents to 500 dollars, or at either
corner any sum up to 1,500 dollars. When all have done,
the dealer slowly counts the heap out in fours, and the last
remaining four or three or two or one, as the case may be, is
the winning number. Those who have placed their money at
the corresponding side of the square, which is called playing *fan*,
are paid three to one; those who have staked at the corner,
covering two numbers or playing *tan*, are paid even money if
either number wins. From all winnings the bank deducts eight
per cent. Besides the above ways, there are many other of
infinite complication, scored with buttons and cards and ivory
counters, which nobody except a Celestial can possibly understand. But they play with the greatest eagerness, the coolie
who works a week to save his dollar, the shopkeeper who
calmly stakes his watch and chain if he is short of ready money
and the well-to-do merchant, who watches the game for half an
hour to judge of the chances and then lays down his hundred
dollar bill and walks imperturbably away whatever the result may
be. Of course everybody asks, cannot the dealer after years of

practice take up a fixed number of "cash" according to the
sums staked upon the table? It seems probable, but I have
watched him for a long time and I am convinced that if he could
it would in nearly all cases be impracticable, for many sufficient
reasons. A few years ago it was common enough to see a
thousand dollars on the table for a single deal, when the
Hongkong brokers were rich, and came over on Saturday nights.

Conspicuous in Macao are the following lines by S. de Passos,
chiselled in marble over an arch :—

> " Nacão que dormes, do sepulchro a borda,
>   Ergue-te, surge, como outr' ora, ovante !
> Teu genio antigo, teu valor recorda,
>   E aprende n'elle a caminhar avante ! "

But the appeal comes too late. Portugal had her Eastern
glory, as she had also what Richard Burton called her "mani-
fold villainies." Her share in the politics of the Far East is gone
for ever, and Macao is not even an inspiring monument to its
memory.

CHINA.

CHAPTER XIII.

PEKING AND ITS INHABITANTS.

A S soon as you are safely on Chinese soil at Tientsin you begin to ask how far it is to Peking and how you can get there. You are told eighty miles by road, and a hundred and twenty by river, and that there are three methods of travel open to you—cart, horseback, and boat. I chose the second, hired a couple of ponies and a *mafoo* (groom), and thankfully left the noisy, narrow, and nasty streets of the native city of Tientsin behind me at seven o'clock one bright Sunday morning. Then forty miles of jog-trot and canter along a narrow path across a landscape of dry mud, and a night at a Chinese inn—a series of small cold, bare guest-rooms surrounded by a hollow square of stalls. To bed at eight, up again at three in order that the cart which carries the baggage and bedding and food might start and reach Peking before the gates are closed at five o'clock.

A trip to Peking is good for two moments of interest and satisfaction—two real sensations of traveller's delight. The first is at first sight of the walls of the great city, after the second dull ride of forty miles. You enter through a gate of no proportions or pretensions, you ride for a quarter of an hour among hovels and pigs, and then suddenly on climbing a bank a striking sight bursts upon you. A great tower of many storeys forms the corner of a mighty wall; from each of its storeys a score cannon-mouths yawn; for a mile or more the wall stretches in a perfectly straight line, pierced with a thousand embrasures, supported by a hundred buttresses. Then you halt

your pony and sit and try to realise that another of the desires
of your life is gratified; that you are at last really and truly
before the walls of the city that was old centuries before the
wolf and the woodpecker found Romulus and Remus; in the
wonderland of Marco Polo, father of travellers; on the eve
of exploring the very capital and heart of the Celestial Empire.
This is the first of your two precious moments. When you ride
on you discover that the cannon-mouths are just black and
white rings painted on boards, and the swindle—fortunately you
do not know it then—is your whole visit to Peking in a nutshell.
The place is a gigantic disappointment.

Although the temptation is great to write marvels about a
place one has come so far to see—to play Polo, so to speak,
on one's own account—the truth is that Peking is not worth the
trip. It is worth coming to study, but not to see. The nose
is the only sense appealed to by the capital of China. It is not
half as picturesque a place as Seoul, nor a quarter as interesting as San Francisco. Moreover, you cannot see nearly as
much of it to-day as you could a few years ago. One by one
the show-places have been closed to foreigners, and the Marble
Bridge, the Summer Palace, the Temple of Heaven—to mention
only the first that come to mind—are now hermetically closed
against the barbarian, and neither rank nor money nor impu-
dence can force an entrance. Even the ascents to the top of
the wall—the only place where a foreigner can walk in comfort
and decency—are now barred, and you must find a bribable
sentry. And if by reason of strength or luck you do get into
one of the forbidden spots you are very likely to have a narrow
escape—as I had at the Great Llama Temple—of never getting
out again.

The history of Peking is to be read in the walls which
surround it in ruin or in preservation, and if you trace them
within and without the city (I did not) they will show you
where lay the "Nanking" of the Khitan Tartars in 986; how
the famous "Golden Horde" of Kin Tartars laid out their

capital of Chung-tu in 1151; what Genghiz Khan and his Mongols thought a great city should be in 1215; how the immortal Khublai Khan constructed Khanbalik, "the city of the Khan," a century later—Polo calls it Cambaluc; and much more interesting history down to the advent of the present Manchus in 1644. And it is the walls, in excellent preservation, that mark the divisions of the Peking of to-day—first, the so-called "Chinese" or Outer City, more properly the Southern City; adjoining it the Inner or "Tartar City," properly called Northern; inside this the "Imperial City," and inside this again, like the inmost pill-box in a nest, the "Forbidden City," the actual Imperial residence itself. The ethnological distinctions of Chinese and Tartar are practically effaced; the only distinction for the flying visitor is that the shops are in the Chinese City, while most of the temples, public buildings, and "sights," together with all the foreign residences, are in the Tartar City, and that the wall of the latter is much the larger and more massive structure. The ground-plan of Peking is supposed to represent a human body, the palace being the heart, but it is better described as being laid out on the chess-board plan of American cities west of Chicago. There are two great streets which intersect at a central point, and from all parts of these other streets, lanes and alleys run in straight lines. Every corner in Peking seems to be a right angle; there are no winding thoroughfares. The houses are all very low with flat roofs, and I did not see a single first-class Chinese dwelling-house in the whole city. But it is the streets of Peking that strike the observer first, and fade last from his recollection. Whether wide or narrow, dark alley or main artery, they are entirely unpaved—the native alluvial soil and the native sewage form every Pekingese pathway. From this state of things spring several curious consequences. The roads are so uneven, the holes in them so numerous and deep, the ridges so high and steep, that no vehicle with springs can navigate half a mile. The only conveyance, therefore, is the famous Peking cart, an

enormously strong and heavy square two-wheeled, covered
vehicle, drawn by a mule, the passenger squatting tailor-fashion
inside and the driver sitting on the shaft. If you go out to
dinner or your wife goes to church, this is practically your
only vehicle, as there are very few chairs in Peking. But to
be rolled about and jolted in one of these is simple torture,
and if you do not hold on closely to the hand-rails inside you
run no little risk of having your brains dashed out. After a
good shower of rain in Peking you cannot set foot out of doors;
the mud is often three feet deep, and the centre of the street
sometimes a couple of feet higher than the sides. But on the
other hand, if no rain comes there is the dust, and a Peking
dust-storm, once experienced, is a dreadful memory for ever.
After a drought the dust is ankle-deep, every night at sunset it
is watered with the liquid sewage of the city, and so it has come
to be composed of dried pulverised earth and dried pulverised
filth in about equal proportions. And when the storm comes
you are blinded and choked by it; it penetrates your clothing
to the skin; windows and doors and curtains and covers do not
stop it for an instant; people say it even finds its way into
air-tight boxes. So whether the barometer indicates "rain"
or "fair," you are equally badly off. The Secretary of the
British Legation says in his latest Report: "The foreign community started a roads' committee with the praiseworthy desire
of cleansing and levelling the foul streets immediately around
the legations and Customs residences. A water-cart was purchased and created no small sensation among the populace on
its first appearance; but only a torrent of rain suffices to lay
the deep dust of Peking, and the efforts to remove the filth of
the roads have proved inadequate and almost abortive." Few
European travellers, he adds, have visited Peking during the
past three years.

To learn what the Chinaman really thinks about the foreigner,
you must go to Peking: no other city in China will serve so
well. And the discovery will be far from flattering to your

national pride. Peking is the only place I have ever visited where the mere fact of being a foreigner, a stranger in speech, dress, and manners, did not of itself secure one a certain amount of consideration, or at any rate make one the object of useful interest. Here the precise opposite is the case. The "foreign devil" is despised at sight—not merely hated, but regarded with sincere and profound contempt. "If the Tsungli Yamèn were abolished," said a Peking diplomat to me, "our lives would not be safe here for twenty-four hours. The people just refrain from actually molesting us because they have learned that they will be very severely punished if they do." At home we cherish the belief that we are welcome in China, that the Chinese are pleased to learn of our Western civilisation, that they are gradually and gladly assimilating our habits and views, and that the wall of prejudice is slowly breaking down. It would hardly be possible to be more grossly and painfully mistaken. The people to a man detest and despise us (I am speaking, of course, of the real Chinese, not of the anglicised Chinese of Hongkong and elsewhere, who are but a drop in the ocean of Celestial humanity); and as for the rulers, it will not be far from the truth to say that the better they know us, the less they like us.

Let us say that you start out in the morning for a prowl in Peking. What are your relations with the people you meet? First of all, of course, they crowd round you whenever you stop, and in a minute you are the centre of a mass of solid humanity, which is eating horrible stuff, which is covered with vermin, which smells worse than words can tell, and which is quite likely to have small-pox about it. As for taking a photograph in the streets, it is out of the question. The only way I could manage this was to place my camera on the edge of a bridge, where they could not get in front of the lens, and then I was in imminent danger of being pushed into the canal, as the bridges have no rail or parapet. The crowd jostles you, feels your clothes with its dirty hands, pokes its nose in your face, keeping up all the time (I was generally with a friend who understood Chinese) a string of insulting and obscene remarks, with accompanying roars of laughter. By and by the novelty and fun of this wear off, and you get first impatient and then infuriated. But beware, above all things, of striking or even laying a finger on one of these dirty wretches. That would be probably a fatal mistake. They will do nothing but talk and push; but if you should hit one of them, you would be more than likely not to get away alive, or at least without bad injuries. But suppose that you walk steadily and imperturbably on? The pedestrian you meet treats you with much less consideration than one of his own countrymen; the children run to the door to cry "*Kueidsu !*"—"devil!"—at you. They have other indescribable and worse ways of insulting you. When a member of a foreign legation was riding underneath the wall, a brick was dropped upon him from the top. It just missed his head and struck the horse behind the saddle. The Chinese children, again, have an original way of amusing themselves at the expense of the foreign devils. A child will provide itself with a big fire-cracker, and then sit patiently at the door till he sees you in the distance coming along on your pony. Then he will run out, drop the cracker in the road, light the slow-match with a fire-stick, and retire to a safe place to watch events. With devilish precocity he generally manages to cause it to explode just under your pony's nose; and if you are lucky enough to keep your seat and pull up a mile or so in the direction you do not wish to go, he doubtless considers that his experiment has only been a moderate success. If you should break your neck and be left there dead in the road, that would confer imperishable lustre upon his family and neighbourhood. When this has happened to you once or twice, you learn to jog about the Celestial City with short reins and your knees stuck well into your saddle, ready for developments at any moment. I was told that Lady Walsham's chair was actually stopped in the open street and she herself grossly insulted, that a member of our Consular service was nearly killed outside the Llama temple,

and that there are few foreigners who have not had some unpleasant experience or other. No doubt it is sometimes the
foreigner's own fault, but a life-member of the Aborigines
Protection Society would fail to get on smoothly at all times.

The foreign legations in Peking are in a street near the chief
gate of the Tartar City, known among the foreigners as
" Legation Street." It is half a mile long, either mud or dust,
as level as a chopping sea, with here and there its monotony of
blank walls or dirty native houses broken by a strong gateway
with a couple of stone lions in front. These are the legations ;
and inside the gate you find pleasant gardens and generally
spacious and comfortable foreign houses, sometimes built *ad hoc*
and sometimes converted to their present use from Chinese
temples. So long as you are the stranger within the gates, you
are extremely well off; but as soon as the porter shuts them
behind you—well, the residents in Peking say it is a charming
place, but for my part I can only believe in their veracity at the
expense of their taste. I would rather live in Seven Dials or
Five Points. When your guide says, "This is Legation Street,"
you laugh, it is so dirty, so miserable, with its horrible crowd of
dogs and pigs and filthy children. But when you have lived in
it for a few days you laugh no more : you count the hours till
you can get away.

What, however, about the " sights " of Peking ? To
be truthful is to declare frankly that there are almost
none. Much the finest building that I saw—indeed, the only
one not in positive dirt and decay—is the entrance pavilion
in the grounds of the British Legation, shown in my illustration. That is a massive wooden roof, richly carved and
gorgeously coloured, supported upon many columns correspondingly decorated. One day I was riding with a member
of the Russian Legation, and he said, " By the way, wouldn't
you like to see the Imperial Chinese War Office ? " " Very
much indeed," I replied enthusiastically, supposing it to be
something splendid. So we turned into a wretched by-street,

and steered our ponies round the mud-holes and the heaps of gar-
bage till we reached it—a broken-down, weather-stained, rotting
structure, with a waving field of weeds on the roof, and a guard
lounging at the door one degree more dirty and dilapidated than
the place itself.   And all the other offices of State—the Board
of Rites, the Board of Punishments, the Astronomical Board,
and the rest—are facsimiles of the Board of War.   Professor
Douglas says, in the *Encyclopædia Britannica*, that the halls of
the palace, " for the magnificence of their proportions and bar-
baric splendour, are probably not to be surpassed anywhere."
Whatever may be his authority for this statement—I thought no
foreigner had ever had an opportunity of examining them—nothing
else in Peking suggests any magnificence and splendour.   The
yellow-roofed buildings of the palace are closely walled in, and
no foreign foot passes the threshold of the " Forbidden
City "; but I have looked at them through my glass from the
top of the highest building in the neighbourhood, and they
appear commonplace enough.   And when the Emperor recently
quitted the palace in great pomp, and after him came the
solemn procession of the Records, an experienced eye-witness
said of the latter, " Like everything Chinese, it was disappointing, tawdry, and sordid," and added, " It is safe to conjecture
that the Emperor's own retinue, could it be seen, would reveal a
similar state of affairs."   The Temple of Heaven, with its semi-
circular marble altar and bright blue dome, as you look down
upon it from the wall, seems to be in good preservation, and a
really impressive and beautiful structure ; but not a single other
place or thing did I see that suggested the " gorgeous East " in
the remotest degree.

Of interesting places, however, there are certainly a few
in Peking.   First among these comes the wall itself.   It is built
of large bricks, filled in with sand, and is fifty feet high, sixty
feet wide at the base, and forty feet at the top.   Peking, seen
from the wall, is a stretch of flat roofs, more than half hidden in
foliage, from which here and there a tower or a pagoda or high-

roofed temple projects. Not a trace of the actual dirt and discomfort and squalor is visible; the air is fresh, the smells are absent, and the Celestial capital is at its best. A walk of a mile along the top brings you to the famous Observatory, and the marvellous bronzes of the Jesuit Father Verbiest, who made and erected them in 1668. Below the wall, in a shady garden, are the much older ones which Marco Polo saw, less accurate astronomically, but even more beautiful for their grace and delicacy, and linking one's imagination closely with the romantic past; for this great globe and sextant and armillary zodiacal sphere were constructed in 1279 by the astronomer of Khublai Khan. Either the climate or their own intrinsic excellence has preserved them so well that every line and bit of tracery is as perfect to our eyes as it was to those of the great Khan himself.

Then there is the Examination Hall. The Government of China is a vast system of competitive examination tempered by bribery, and this *Kao Ch'ang* is its focus. It is a miniature city, with one wide artery down the middle, hundreds of parallel streets running from this on both sides, each street mathematically subdivided into houses, a big semblance of a palace at one end of the main street, and little elevated watch-towers here and there. But the palace is merely the examiners' hall, the streets are three feet wide, and one side of them is a blank wall, the towers are for the "proctors" to spy upon cribbing, and the houses are perfectly plain brick cells measuring 38 inches by 50. In the enclosure there are no fewer than fourteen thousand of these. After emerging successfully from a competitive examination in the capital of his own province, the Chinese aspirant comes to Peking to compete for the second degree. He is put into one of these cells, two boards are given him for a seat and a table, and there he remains day and night for fourteen days. Every cell is full, an army of cooks and coolies waits upon the scholars, and any one caught cribbing or communicating with his neighbour is visited with the severest punishment. The

condition of the place when all these would-be *literati* are thus
cooped up for a fortnight, with Chinese ideas of sanitation, may
be imagined, and it is not surprising to learn that many die.
But what joy for the successful ones! They are received in
procession at the gates of their native town, and everybody
hastens to congratulate their parents upon having given such a
son to the world. By and by there is another examination in
which the already twice successful compete against each other,
thousands again flock to Peking, and the winners are honoured
by the Son of Heaven himself, and their names inscribed for ever
upon marble tablets. Better still, they are provided with Government posts, and this is the reward of their efforts. But the
subject-matter of their examination is simply and solely the
letter-perfect knowledge of the works of Confucius, the history
of China, and the art of composition and character-forming as
practised by the great masters of old. In the works of the
masters, argue the Chinese, is all wisdom; he who knows these
works best is therefore the wisest man; whatever needs doing,
the wisest man can do it best. So the successful *literati* are sent
all over the country to be magistrates and generals and commanders of ships and engineers and everything else haphazard,
without the slightest acquaintance of any kind with their subject,
densely and marvellously ignorant and impenetrably conceited.
An idea of the part this Examination Hall plays in the contemporary life of China may be gained from the fact that in
June, 1894, no fewer than 6,896 candidates presented themselves
in Peking, of whom 820 were successful, including the son of a
well-known Formosa millionaire, who was promptly made
Assistant Imperial High Commissioner of Agriculture in
Formosa. The Marquis Tsêng was one of the great Chinamen
of the present day who did not enter public life by this triple
portal to invincible incompetence.

The shrine of the Master himself is really an impressive spot.
The great hall and its columns are of bare wood, the floor is of
plain stone, and no adornment mars the supreme solemnity of

the place. In the middle, upon a square altar, stands a small tablet of red lacquer, upon which is written in Chinese and Manchu, "The tablet of the soul of the most holy ancestral teacher Confucius." Up the marble terrace to this hall the Emperor comes to worship twice a year, and the Chinese do really hold this place in some veneration, for when I offered its miserable guardian five dollars to let me photograph it, he repulsed the offer with much scorn. Yet five dollars would have been a small fortune for him.

One experience of Celestial sight-seeing I am not likely to forget, and should be very unwilling to repeat. Among the places of interest in Peking the *Yung Ho Kung*, the Great Llamaserai or Llama Temple, ranks very high. It is a monastery of Mongol Buddhism or Shamanism, and contains over a thousand Mongol and Thibetan monks ruled over by a "Living Buddha." No foreigner, however, had been in it for several years, as the inmates are a rough and lawless lot, practically beyond the control of the Chinese authorities, and the last party that entered it was rudely handled. It is regarded as all the more sacred, too, because an Emperor was born in one of its temples before they were given to the Llamas. When I spoke of going there both my *mafoo* and "boy" told me that strangers could no longer get in, the former adding that he had accompanied different employers there six times without success. A friend in Peking, however, told me that one of the priests, called the Pai Llama, whatever that may mean, had come to him a few weeks before to borrow five dollars, and had said as an inducement that if he or any of his friends wanted to see the Llamaserai he would take them over it himself without a fee. So my friend gave me his big red Chinese card with the Pai Llama's name on it as an introduction, and a member of the Legation, who spoke Chinese, was good enough to go with me, as he was equally anxious to see the place. It is on the out skirts of Peking, nearly an hour's ride from Legation Street, and we passed in through two or three gates from the street without

any difficulty. Then some boy-neophytes or acolytes—we knew
them from their shaven heads—ran ahead of us and warned the
priests, who shut the doors. After a quarter of an hour's
colloquy we bribed the doorkeeper to tell the Pai Llama, and
by and by the latter appeared, a small dirty individual, who
succeeded with much difficulty in persuading the others to open
the gates and let us step just inside. Then he immediately
disappeared and we saw him no more. After another half-hour
of bargaining we agreed to pay them a certain moderate sum to
show us the four chief sights of the Temple. The first of these
was the great Buddha, a wooden image 70 feet high, richly
ornamented and clothed, holding an enormous lotus in each
hand, and with the traditional jewel on his breast. In each
section of his huge gold crown sat a small Buddha, as perfect
and as much ornamented as the great one. His toe measured
21 inches. On each side of him hung a huge scroll 75 feet
long, bearing Chinese characters, and a series of galleries,
reached by several flights of stairs, surrounded him. The
expression of his great bronze face was singularly lofty, and I
was seized with a great desire to photograph him. The crowd
of monks was outside the locked door, one only entering with
us, so I hinted to him that if he permitted me to take a photograph a dollar might be forthcoming. The dollar interested
him, but he had no idea what a photograph was. After a while
my companion succeeded in explaining what the Chinese call
the "shadow-picture," and then he would not hear of it, declaring that the whole temple would instantly fall down if such a
thing were attempted. I offered two dollars, three, four, five,
ten, and then, my eagerness increasing with the difficulty,
twenty. At last he said that for twenty dollars he would agree
to smuggle me in next morning to do it, as if any of the other
priests knew, there would be trouble. So we passed on to the
other sights—two magnificent bronze lions, and a wonderful
bronze urn: many temples filled with strange idols, hung with
thousands of silk hangings, and laid with Thibetan carpets; all

sorts of bronze and enamel altar utensils, presented by different emperors, among them two elephants in *cloisonné*, said to be the best specimens of such work in China; and the great hall, with its prayer-benches for all the monks, where they worship every afternoon at five. In a couple of hours we had seen everything, and came out again into the central courtyard. Here were already a hundred or more monks waiting for us, all with their heads shaven like billiard-balls, and on the whole a set of as thorough-paced blackguards as could be imagined; filthy, vermin-covered, bloated, scrofulous, and with the marks of nameless vices stamped clearly on many of their faces. "I shall be glad when we are out of this," I remarked, and my companion heartily assented. But easier said than done. They crowded round us with brutal inquisitiveness, pulled us about, shouted to us, and laughed grossly as half-rational gorillas might do. My companion said to them that we were very much pleased with our visit, and we slowly edged toward the door. But there seemed to be a sort of tacit conspiracy to crowd us in any other direction. They did not actually oppose us, but somehow we could not get there. It was as though they did not like to let us get away, yet were conscious that they had no excuse for detaining us. After a quarter of an hour of this we began to get annoyed. Just then we all came to a sort of tunnel gate in a wall, leading from one court to another, my companion and one crowd first, I and another crowd afterwards, and my "boy" and a third crowd last. As I was passing, a man whom I took from his dress to be a sort of doorkeeper sprang out and addressed me volubly. Not understanding him I took no notice, when he grasped my arm to detain me. I shook him off and was passing on when suddenly he seized me by the collar with both hands and flung me violently back against the wall. At such a moment one does not reflect upon consequences, and I did what anybody else would have done. The moment his grasp quitted my collar I struck him. He recovered himself, and the misunderstanding was about to be prolonged vigorously on both sides when a very old priest in a fine yellow robe emerged from a doorway and began to play the peacemaker with many smiles, holding us each by the hand. A second's reflection showed me the extreme folly of getting into a quarrel in such a place, so I responded effusively to the venerable Llama's overtures, and, calling my "boy," bade him explain that if the priest had anything to say to us we should be very glad to hear it, but that if he laid a finger on us he would get into trouble. As we were two, and they were upwards of two hundred by this time, I have wondered since that the ludicrous side of this did not strike them. However, as I followed up the remark with a few small coins, nobody cared to impugn the logic.

As soon as I overtook my companion I saw from the movement of the crowd that something was wrong, and when I forced my way into the middle it was evidently a much more serious affair than mine. A young brute of a monk had approached him from behind and suddenly and violently kicked him. In return he had received a good cut across the face from a riding-whip. The monk was foaming with rage, and rapidly stripping off all his upper clothing with a most unmistakable intention. Already he was nearly half-naked, and although perhaps a trifle fat, still an ugly customer to handle. "He struck me with his whip!" he exclaimed, pointing to the mark on his face, and then followed a string of remarks levelled at us. "What does he say?" I asked. "He says we sha'n't get out alive." Just then a monk shouted something which the others eagerly echoed, and a dozen of them instantly ran and shut the great gates of the courtyard.

There was no doubt whatever that we were in a very tight place. We were in the centre of probably the most dangerous place in Peking, on the outskirts of the city, a quarter of a mile from the street, with half a dozen closed gates between us and it, and completely at the mercy of two hundred savage Mongols and Thibetans, who had vowed to have our lives. There were a thousand of them within call, they acknowledge no Chinese authority whatever, the Chinese Government would be extremely loath to interfere with them for fear of provoking trouble in Thibet, and if they had just knocked us on the head and hid our bodies in one of their temple dens, we should very probably never have been heard of again. Clearly the only thing to do was to get out of the place at any cost. Then I called my "boy," who was yelling and struggling to keep possession of my two cameras, and told him to ask quietly the best-looking of the monks for how much they would consent to let us go out. All this took but half a minute to do, and as soon as the crowd heard the question the pugilistic gentleman was squelched by common consent. "Fifty dollars" was the conclusion arrived at after several minutes' discussion. "Tell them we have not so much money with us, but they can come and get it from my house to-morrow morning." But they were much too wary to fall into such a palpable trap. To bring the story to an end, however, at last my "boy" made a bargain with them, and we were fleeced of several dollars at each gate that they could manage to lead us through before we reached the street and our horses. I got through the gate all right, and my "boy" was following when several of the monks precipitated themselves on him and sent him flying head first into the middle of the street, while the broken camera, tripod, and bag of double-backs landed each in a separate mud-hole.

That afternoon as I was mending my camera the "boy" came in with the tea. "Master?" "Well?" "I no go Llama Temple any more—belong velly bad man!" And I did not keep my appointment next morning to photograph the big Buddha furtively.

Above all other characteristics of Peking one thing stands out in horrible prominence. Not to mention it would be wilfully to omit the most striking feature of the place. I mean its filth. It is the most horribly and indescribably filthy place that can be imagined. Indeed imagination must fall far short of the fact. Some of the daily sights of the pedestrian in Peking could hardly be more than hinted at by one man to another in the disinfecting atmosphere of a smoking-room. There is no sewer or cesspool, public or private, but the street; the dog, the pig, and the fowl—in a sickening succession—are the scavengers; every now and then you pass a man who goes along tossing the most loathsome of the refuse into an open-work basket on his back; the smells are simply awful; the city is one colossal and uncleansed *cloaca*. As I have said above, the first of the two moments of delight vouchsafed to every visitor to the Celestial capital is at his first sight of it. The second is when he turns his back, hoping it may be for ever, upon " the body and soul-stinking town" (the words are Coleridge's) of Peking.

CHAPTER XIV.

TO THE GREAT WALL OF CHINA.

THE first time I met a camel-train near Peking I reined up my pony and feasted my eyes upon it. And although I saw hundreds afterwards, I found them just as amusing as ever. The two-humped or Bactrian camels of Northern China are much bigger than those we know at home, and I have seen few sights so picturesque as a string of them approaching over these brown plains. A score are fastened together by a cord attaching the nose of one to the tail of the other; a bell, a couple of feet long, is hung round the neck of the last, to warn the driver in front by its ceasing if the line breaks anywhere; a medley of bales and boxes and clothing is slung on their backs; ruddy-faced Mongols, dressed in scarlet and yellow, with ornaments of gold and silver in profusion, sit up aloft and smile at you as you pass; the great shaggy beasts step softly along, ingeniously out of step, lifting their sponge-like feet and dropping them again with perfect and unvarying deliberation, the whole train moving with the silence of a dream, broken only by the *jang-jang* of the solitary bell. Their big brown eyes look you straight in the face, and there is something pathetic and reproachful in their glance. All day long, one street of Peking is filled with these picturesque processions, gaunt, wretched creatures with worn-out coats and covered with coal-dust, carrying sacks of coal from the Western Hills into Peking; and far finer and better-kept animals bearing tea away up into the North. During all my stay in Peking I longed for the moment when I

211

too should ride away at dawn toward Mongolia, in the worn
tracks of these strange beasts and their merry masters.

My pony was a little creature not much bigger than a dog,
with a white coat as long and thick as a Polar bear's. The
mafoo had bought him a few days before from a Mongol for
twenty taels, and he had never had a foreign saddle and bridle
on till I mounted him. Therefore the all-day ride was not so
monotonous as usual, and for the first five miles it was even
exciting. We started at daybreak and the sun was well above
us before we got outside the two gates of Peking. Then the
mafoo took the lead. Once in the open country we were on a
great alluvial plain, dotted with mud houses, broken up by
irregular patches of verdure and cultivation, laced in all directions by dozens of bridle-paths, and ending on our left in the
dim outline of the Western Hills, the summer sanitarium of
Peking. We plunged into the labyrinth of roads, and the mafoo
threaded his way among them without a moment's hesitation.
Afterwards I found that he had been over them forty-six times
before, but for my own part I could see hardly any signs by
which to distinguish one from another. Till eleven o'clock we
trotted steadily on, reaching then a small town called Sha-ho,
where we stopped an hour for rest and tiffin. Here already
foreigners are scarce and I was the centre of much curiosity,
keen and inquisitive, but quite good-natured. Crossing a river
over two very old broad flat bridges of white marble, built
curiously at an obtuse angle to each other, we emerged again
into the plain. This grew more and more uneven as we
advanced, till at last we were riding along a narrow path on the
sloping stony bank of a dry water-course. The stones grew
bigger and more numerous, till they could no longer be safely
negociated, and then my guide struck up to the right, and an
hour's detour across country, with half a mile of such bad going
at the end that I got off and led my pony, brought us at three
o'clock to the fortified city of Nan-k'ou, thirty miles from
Peking, our resting-place for the night.

Nan-k'ou is a very interesting little place. Its wall is in ruins, but that only makes it the more picturesque. On the hills right and left of the entrance to the pass which the city is supposed to guard, are two sprightly little towers; a dozen others are just visible dotted about the chain of hills around it. Its one broad street, paved once with great blocks of stone, now worn away and upset till a pony can hardly make his way at all over their slippery rolling surface, is crowded with traffic of men and beasts, and every fifty yards a wide arched doorway leads into a spacious inn-yard. This street is part of the great commercial highway between China and all her neighbours of the North. Through it a constant stream of camels and ponies and donkeys and even laden coolies passes, bringing Mongol produce to Peking, and taking brick-tea back from Tientsin to Kiakhta on the Russian frontier. And through this street this stream has passed for who knows how many years—thousands, at any rate.

I strolled along it and turned into one of the gateways. But I had only just time to step aside when a drove of at least a hundred ponies suddenly stampeded through it and galloped headlong through the street, whinnying and kicking up their heels in delight at being free. Just outside the city they drank greedily at a little stream, and then rolled over and over each other in the dirt. But such a spectacle of cruelty to animals as was afforded by the state of their backs I have never seen. Not one of them was without a large raw wound on each side, and half of them had horrible, deep, bleeding, festering sores bigger than two hands. The sight was sickening, and nothing whatever was done for them except that afterwards I saw a coolie beating the insides of the rough pack-saddles with a stick to keep the blood-soaked places from getting quite hard. Each pony had carried two bales of tea, as hard as blocks of granite. I tried the weight of one and found I could just raise it off the ground. Therefore the ponies were shockingly overloaded.

The camels require so much space for themselves and their

burdens that they have special caravanserais. Their saddles,
with the loads deposited on each side, are arranged in regular
rows, like game after a battue, and the animals betake themselves to a trough which runs all round the yard, squeezing close
together.   The yard of a caravanserai at feeding-time therefore
exhibits a complete circular horizon of camels' tails.   When
they have eaten they sink down and very deliberately chew the
cud.   It is just as well to keep on good terms with a camel, for
when he is standing up he can swing his hind leg like a pendulum
in an arc of about twenty feet and therefore deliver a kick which
would break in the door of a San Francisco gambling-den;
while when he is lying down he can always spare a couple of
gallons of cud to spit at an enemy.   I saw a Mongol driver to
whom this had happened, and the sight was unpleasant and
instructive.   Several hundred camels shared the hospitality of
Nan-k'ou with me that night.

Next morning we embarked upon little white donkeys, the pass
being impracticable for ponies.   This road in its glory is said to
have been paved with great smooth granite blocks; now in the
valley it is a broken mass of rough stones in a river bed, through
which a shallow stream runs; while during the ascent and at
the height of the pass it is a bad mountain road obstructed by
great masses of rock.   A couple of hours' riding and walking
brought us to another walled town called Chu-yung-kuan, famous
for a heavy arched stone gateway, the whole inside of which is
covered with sculptures in low relief and a Buddhist inscription
in six languages—Chinese, Thibetan, Mongol, Sanscrit, and two
others that I could not get any one to identify.   From the other
side of this gateway the pass of Nan-k'ou is spread out before
you, a brown, barren, rock-strewn, gloomy valley, rising and
narrowing till it disappears in the hills, through which an endless
file of brown camels is slowly passing, filling the air with the
dust of their feet and the clangour of their bells.   For an hour or
more we jogged on.   Then when the pass had become wearisome
and I was thousands of miles away in thought, my *mafoo* rode

up beside me and silently pointed to the hill-top on the right. I strained my eyes, and there, sure enough, the sky-line far away was broken by the crenellated outline of the Great Wall itself. "This," said Marco Polo when he saw it, "is the country of Gog and Magog."

The Great Wall of China is, after all, only a wall. And it was built with the same object as every other wall—to keep people from coming where they were not wanted. Mr. Toole's famous account of it is as historically accurate as any. "The most important building in China," he is accustomed to say, "is the Chinese Wall, built to keep the Tartars out. It was built at such an enormous expense that the Chinese never got over it. But the Tartars did. And the way they accomplished this feat was as follows: one went first and t'other went arter." It differs from other walls in only two respects, its age and its size. It was built by the great Emperor Chi Hwang-ti, who came to the throne in B.C. 221, to keep back the Mongolian hordes, and was called by him the "Red Fort." The origina wall is 1,400 miles long and stretches from far Kansu to Shan-hai-kwan on the gulf of Pe-chih-li, the present terminus of China's solitary railway—from Tientsin. This wall, however, is neither so well built nor so large as that which I am describing, the latter being a five-hundred mile erection, dating from several hundred years later. It is, however, an integral part—and the most impressive—of the "Great Wall." Besides its age it enjoys the reputation of being the only work of human hands on the globe visible from the moon. The Chinese name for it is *Wan-li-ch'ang-ch'êng*, "the rampart ten thousand *li* long." And the gate on this highway is called *Pa-ta-ling* and is about fifty miles north-west of Peking and 2,000 feet above the sea. Beyond it lies Mongolia.

Half an hour after this first glimpse I stood upon the wall itself. The gateway is a large double one, with a square tower upon it, pierced with oblong openings for cannon, of which a dozen old ones lie in a heap, showing that at one time the road

was seriously defended at this point. A rough stairway leads to
the top, which is about twenty feet wide, with a crenollated
parapet on each side, and you can walk along it as far as you
can see, with here and there a scramble where it has fallen in a
little. On the whole it is in excellent repair, having of course
been mended and rebuilt many times. Every half-mile or so is
a little square tower of two storeys. The wall itself varies a
good deal in height according to the nature of the ground,
averaging probably about forty feet. On one side Mongolia, as
you see it, is a vast undulating brown plain ; on the other side
China is a perfect sea of brown hills in all directions, and across
these stretches the Great Wall. On the hill-top, through the
valleys, up and down the sides it twists in an unbroken line,
exactly like a huge earth-worm suddenly turned to stone. For
many miles it is visible in both directions, and when you can no
longer trace its entire length you can still discover it topping
the hills one after another into the remote distance. And as
you reflect that it is built of bricks, in almost inaccessible
places, through uninhabited countries ; that each brick must
have been transported on a man's shoulders enormous distances ;
and that it extends for 2,000 miles, or one-twelfth of the circumference of the globe, you begin to realise that you are looking
upon the most colossal achievement of human hands. The
bricks are so big and heavy that I had to hire a little donkey to
carry off two of them. This is the only piece of vandalism
to which I plead guilty during years of tempting Eastern
travel, but the temptation was irresistible and " they never will
be missed " Nowadays, of course, the wall serves no defensive
purpose whatever, and is not guarded in any way. Not a soul
lives within miles of it at most points, and it is but a landmark
for the Mongols' camel-trains, a stupendous monument to the
past of China, and an evidence of Celestial greatness and
enterprise gone never to return.

After taking a dozen photographs, several of which are
here reproduced, and reflecting how comical now were the

learned arguments produced in England a few years ago to prove that there was no such thing as a Great Wall of China, I turned back to Nan-k'ou, reaching there at night-fall. Next morning before daylight we started for the tombs of the great Ming dynasty, thirteen miles away, and as famous in China as the wall itself. These lie in a pleasant green valley surrounded with an almost complete circle of high wooded hills—an ideal spot for an emperor's grave. There are thirteen of them, called the *Shih-san-ling*, disposed in the shape of a crescent, but the crescent is so extensive that only four or five of them can be seen at once. I visited the largest, the tomb of Yung-le, who brought his court hither in 1411. A square of perhaps two hundred yards across the face is surrounded with a high wall of plain red brick. The side of the hill forms the fourth side, and the entrance is through a pair of ordinary wooden doors. When you enter, the spectacle is not at all striking. There are a few little pavilions on either side of you, each covering a carved stone tortoise or an inscribed tablet, and in front a long low temple-shaped building with an approach of steps and balustrades in carved white marble. Inside is gloom, through which you faintly discern the magnificent outlines of thirty-two enormous wooden columns, each a solid log of hewn and polished teak twelve feet round and thirty-two feet high. Where they came from—unless it was from Burmah—or how they were conveyed hither, nobody knows, but their grandeur is indisputable. In the centre, upon a sort of stone table, stands a plain tablet of red lacquer, a couple of feet high and a foot wide, bearing the posthumous title of Yung-le, "The perfect ancestor and literary Emperor." But the ancestor him-self is not here. Passing out behind the great columns and again crossing the garden, at the edge of the hillside there is a solid square tower of brick and granite, supporting a kind of obelisk. The sarcophagus itself is deep in the hill, and upon the obelisk a long inscription narrates the deeds and extols the virtues of the long-departed Ming. On the whole, however,

China disappoints you here once more, as everywhere and always. The situation is finely chosen for the last resting-place of immortal emperors, but man's handiwork rather weakens than enhances the effects of nature. There is no suggestion, for instance, of the solemnity of that cathedral aisle—

> " Where the warriors in the gloom
> Watch o'er Maximilian's tomb ; "

and there is nothing to arrest the hasty footstep lest even " the hushed tread "—

> " Should burst the bands of the dreamless sleep
> That holds the mighty dead."

As you ride away you pass through an avenue of stone carvings, where pairs of knights and courtiers, with camels and elephants —beasts fit to follow their master into the shadow-world— glare at you from each side. They are enormous, being some fifteen feet high and carved out of a solid block of stone ; and wonderful, for you cannot imagine how they were transported. But they are utterly dwarfed by the hills around them, and soon your only recollection of them is that your pony positively refused to pass between them and ended by bolting with you. And I may as well give my little Polar bear of a pony credit for the way in which he trotted back to Peking so as to get there before the gates closed, in all forty miles in four hours, with three-quarters of an hour for rest and food. I have known costlier horseflesh make poorer progress. And when we got back again at last to Tientsin my mafoo sold him to the inn-keeper for twice what he had paid for him.

TO understand contemporary China it is absolutely necessary to undergo, either personally or by proxy, some very unpleasant experiences. This must be my excuse for the following chapter. China is claiming her place among the nations of the world. The question, What shall that place be? can only be answered by those who know what China is. I have looked upon men being cruelly tortured; I have stood in the shambles where human beings are slaughtered like pigs; my boots have dripped with the blood of my fellow-creatures;—repulsive as all this is, it is one of the most significant and instructive aspects of the real China, as opposed to the China of native professions and foreign imagination, and therefore it must be frankly described.

It was in Canton, a colossal human ant-hill, an endless labyrinth of streets a dozen feet wide and a score high, crowded from daylight to dark with a double stream of men and women, exactly like the double stream between an ant-hill and a carcase. All this mass of humanity was presided over for years by H.E. Chang Chi-tung, now Viceroy of the Hu Kuang provinces, the most independent and foreigner-hating Viceroy in China, and therefore it may be imagined what is the temper of the populace, especially as the Cantonese are the most turbulent people of the Flowery Kingdom.

During the day the streets of Canton are in semi-obscurity, as they are closed in at the top by broad strips of cloth and long advertising streamers; but at night they are as black as Tartarus. Public safety and order are supposed to be preserved by occasional posts of soldiers, with a collection of weapons and instruments of torture hung up outside to strike terror into the evilly-disposed. But, as may be imagined, crime of every kind is rife in Canton, and so bad is the reputation of the place that very often a servant from another part of China, travelling with his master, will rather forfeit his situation than accompany him there. And where the crime is, there is the punishment too. It by no means follows in China that the person punished is the criminal, but there is enough legal cruelty in Canton to glut an Alva. Respect for the presence of an occasional foreigner causes a good deal of it to be hid, and the spectacle of a man hung up in a cage to starve to death in public is therefore not seen there as it is in other parts.

The magistrate sat in his Yamên dispensing justice. He was a benevolent-looking man of perhaps forty, with an intellectual forehead and the conventional enormous pair of spectacles. He glanced up at us as we entered, visibly annoyed at the intrusion and hardly returning our salutation. But as we were under the wing of a consul for whom Chinese officialism has no terrors whatever, a fact of which the Cantonese authorities have had repeated experience, we made ourselves quite at home. There was little of the pomp of Western law in the scene before us. The magistrate's own chair, draped with red cloth covered with inscriptions in large characters, was almost the only piece of official apparatus, and behind it were grouped half-a-dozen of the big red presentation umbrellas of which every Chinese official is so proud. Before him was a large open space and a motley crowd, in which the most conspicuous figures were the filthy ruffians in red hats, known as " Yamên-runners," whose business is to clear a way before their master in the streets and do anything else that he wishes, down to the administration of torture. The magistrate himself sat perfectly silent, writing busily, while several persons before him gabbled all at the same time. These were presumably the plaintiff, the defendant, and the policemen. After a while the magistrate interrupted one of the speakers with a monosyllable spoken in a low tone without even raising his head, but its effect was magical. The crowd fell back, and one of the little group in front of the chair wrung his hands and heaved a theatrical sigh. Before we could realise what had happened, several pairs of very willing hands were helping him to let down his trousers, and when this was accomplished to the satisfaction of everybody he laid himself face downwards on the floor. Then one of the "runners" stepped forward with the bamboo, a strip of this toughest of plants three feet long, two inches wide, and half an inch thick. Squatting by the side of the victim and holding the bamboo perfectly horizontal close to the flesh, he began to rain light blows on the man's buttocks. At first the performance looked like a farce, the blows were so light and the receiver of them so indifferent. But as the shower of taps continued with monotonous persistence I bethought me of the old torture of driving a man mad by letting a drop of water fall every minute on his shaved head. After a few more minutes of the dactylic rap-tap-tap, rap-tap-tap, a deep groan broke from the prisoner's lips. I walked over to look at him and saw that his flesh was blue under the flogging. Then it became congested with blood, and whereas at first he had lain quiet of his own accord, now a dozen men were holding him tight. The crowd gazed at him with broad grins on their faces, breaking out from time to time into a suppressed "Hi-yah," as he writhed in special pain or cried out in agony. And all this time the ceaseless shower of blows continued, the man who wielded the bamboo putting not a particle more or less force into the last stroke than into the first. At length the magistrate dropped another word and the torture stopped as suddenly as it had begun, the prisoner was lifted to his foot and led across the court to lean against the wall. For obvious reasons he could not be "accommodated with a chair."

The next person to be called up was a policeman. The magistrate put a question or two to him and listened patiently for a while to his rambling and effusive replies. Then as before the fatal monosyllable dropped from his lips. With the greatest promptitude the policeman prepared himself, assumed the regulation attitude, and the flagellation began again. But I. noticed that the blows sounded altogether different from before, much sharper and shriller, like wood falling upon wood, rather than wood falling upon flesh. So I drew near to examine. Sure enough, there was a vital difference. The policeman had attached a small piece of wood to his leg by means of wax, and on this the blows fell, taking no more effect upon his person than if they had been delivered on the sole of his boot. The fraud was perfectly transparent — everybody in the room, including the magistrate himself, must have known what was happening. Thus another peculiarity of Chinese justice is evidently that the punishment of an ordinary offender is one thing, while that of an erring official is quite another. I learned that the policeman was ordered to be bambooed for not bringing in a prisoner whom the magistrate had ordered him to produce. When the sham punishment was over he jumped briskly to his feet, adjusted his clothing, and resumed his duties about the court.

While we had been watching the process of "eating bamboo," far different punishments were going on in another part of the court-room unnoticed by us. The bamboo is not so very far removed from still existent civilised deterrent methods, but what was now before us recalled the most brutal ages. In one corner a man had been tied hand and foot on a small bench the length of his back, in such a manner that his body was bent as far back as it could possibly be stretched in the form of a circle, his back resting on the flat seat of the bench, and his arms and legs fastened to the four legs. Then the whole affair, man and bench, had been tilted forward till it rested upon two feet and upon the man's two knees, almost falling over—almost, but not quite. This, as well as the bambooing and other tortures, is illustrated in the native drawings here produced. The position of the miserable wretch was as grotesque as it was exquisitely painful; his hands and feet were blue, his eyes protruded, his mouth gasped convulsively like that of a dying fish, and he had evidently been in that position so long that he was on the eve of losing consciousness. And he was apparently forgotten. A few boys stood gazing at him open-mouthed, but nobody else paid any more attention to him than if he had been a piece of furniture. This was enough for my companions, and they left the room. But how is the Western world to know what the Celestial Empire really is unless people are willing to see and hear of its innumerable horrors? The utterly mistaken notion of China which is so wide-spread at home is due in great part to this very unwillingness to look straight in the face what a French writer has so well called the "rotten East."

In another corner an unfortunate creature was undergoing the punishment called "kneeling on chains." A thin strong cord had been fastened to his thumbs and great toes and passed over a hook in an upright post. Then by pulling it sufficiently he was of course lifted off the ground, his knees being the lowest part of his body. Under them a small chain, with sharp-edged links, had next been coiled in a circle as a natty sailor coils a rope on the deck. The cord had then been slackened till the whole weight of the man rested upon his knees, and his knees rested upon the chain. The process seems simple, but the result is awful. And this man had been undergoing a prolonged course of torture. Amongst other things, his ankle-bones had been battered with a piece of wood shaped like a child's cricket bat. His tortures ended for the moment while we were looking at him. Two attendants loosened the cord, and he fell in a heap. They rolled him off the chain and set him on his feet. The moment they let go he sank like a half-filled sack. So they stretched him out on the floor and each one of them rubbed one of his knees vigorously for a couple of minutes. But it was no use, he was utterly incapable of even standing, and had to be dragged away. As we passed out, a woman was before the magistrate, giving evidence. Her testimony, however, was either not true enough or not prompt enough, in the official's opinion, for he had recourse to the "truth-compeller." This is a little instrument reserved exclusively for the fair sex, shaped exactly like the thick sole of a slipper, split at the sole part and fastened at the heel. With this the witness received a slap across the mouth which rang out like a pistol-shot. A glance at the frontispiece of this volume, which is a facsimile of a native drawing professing to be a perfectly truthful representation of a common method of torturing women, will show that this woman was more fortunate than many of her sex in China.

It is only fair to add that the Chinese have a sort of rational theory of torture, although they are far from adhering to it. By Chinese law no prisoner can be punished until he has confessed his guilt. Therefore they first prove him guilty and then torture him until he confesses the accuracy of their verdict. The more you reflect on this logic the more surprising it becomes. To assist in its comprehension I procured, by the aid of the Consul and a few dollars, a complete set of instruments of torture—light bamboo, heavy bamboo, ankle-smasher, mouth-slapper, thumb-squeezer, and sundry others. "Mandarins," says Professor Douglas, "whose minds have grown callous to the sufferings of their fellow-creatures, are always ready to believe that the instruments of torture at their disposal are insufficient for their purposes. Unhappily, it is always easy to inflict pain; and in almost every yamun throughout the Empire an infinite variety of instruments of torture is in constant use."

One Chinese punishment, of which I am fortunately able to give a striking picture, deserves particular attention. This is ling-chi, or death by the "thousand cuts." It is otherwise known as death by the "slow process" or by the "slicing process." It is supposed to be reserved for culprits who commit triple murder and for parricides, but the penal code is no doubt as elastic in this as in other respects. Here is a specimen announcement of *ling-chi*, from the official *Pekin Gazette :—*

"Ma Pei-yao, Governor of Kuangsi, reports a triple poisoning case in his province. A woman having been beaten by her husband on account of her slovenly habits, took counsel with an old herb woman, and by her direction picked some poisonous herb on the mountain, with which she successively poisoned her husband, father-in-law, and brother-in-law. She has been executed by the slow process.— *Rescript : Let the Board of Punishments take note."*

The criminal is fastened to a rough cross, and the executioner, armed with a sharp knife, begins by grasping handfuls from the fleshy parts of the body, such as the thighs and the breasts, and slicing them off. After this he removes the joints and the excrescences of the body one by one—the nose and ears, fingers and toes. Then the limbs are cut off piecemeal at the wrists and the ankles, the elbows and knees, the shoulders and hips. Finally, the victim is stabbed to the heart and his head cut off. Of course, unless the process is very rapidly carried out, the man is dead before it is completed, but if he has any friends who are able to bribe the executioner he is either drugged beforehand with opium, or else the stab to the heart is surreptitiously given after the first few strokes. It would be easy to quote from the *Pekin Gazette* dozens of instances of the infliction of this penalty, and these would probably be but a fraction of the occasions on which it is practised. I believe it has only been witnessed once by a foreigner, as the Chinese have a great and not unnatural objection to the presence of foreigners on such occasions. The photograph here produced is no doubt the only one ever taken. A few words of explanation concerning it are therefore desirable. The British captain of a river steamer plying between Hongkong and Canton strolled one day into the native city with a small hand-camera which he had just purchased. Observing a crowd in the street, he made his way through it and discovered the remains of a man who had been

executed by the *ling-chi*. As his camera was a very small one,
he was able to point it at the spectacle and snap the shutter
without attracting attention, as the bystanders would never
have allowed a formal photograph to be taken. On his return
to Hongkong he placed his camera in the hands of an
experienced photographer, who developed the negative and
made from it an enlargement of which this illustration is a
copy. It is thus a unique and absolutely genuine illustration
of contemporary Chinese life. The susceptible reader will
doubtless be grateful to me for having caused the edge of
this picture to be perforated.

It is, however, the last act of the drama of Chinese justice
that is the great revelation. I am inclined to think that nobody
can claim to have an adequate and accurate appreciation of
Chinese character who has not witnessed a Chinese execution.
This is not difficult to do at Canton, or even at Kowloon, on the
other side of Hongkong harbour, for the Canton river swarms
with pirates, and when these gentry are caught they generally
get short shrift. A few bambooings to begin with, then several
months in prison—and it is not necessary to explain what a
Chinese prison is—with little to eat and a stiff course of torture,
and then one fine morning a " short sharp shock " at the execu-
tion-ground. If the reader cares to accompany me further I
will try to place the scene before him.

The execution is fixed for half-past four, so at four the guide
comes for us at Shameen, the foreign quarter of Canton, and
our chairs carry us rapidly through the noisy alleys of the native
city. Until we get close to the spot there is no sign of anything
unusual. There suddenly we run into a jammed crowd at the
end of a long and particularly narrow street. The chair coolies,
however, plunge straight into it and it gives way before us till
we are brought up by a huge pair of wooden gates guarded by a
little group of soldiers. To hear these men talk you would
suppose that they would die then and there rather than let you
pass, but the production of a couple of ten-cent pieces works a

miracle and they open the gates for us, vainly trying to stop the
rush of natives that follows and carries us before it right into
the middle of the open space. It is a bare piece of ground, fifty
yards long by a dozen wide, between two houses, whose blank
walls hem it in on three sides. To-day it is the execution
ground; yesterday and to-morrow the drying-ground of a potter
who lives there. There is no platform, no roped-off space,
nothing but this bare bit of dirty ground so crowded with
Chinese that we are forced into the middle, not more than four
feet from whatever is to take place. It is useless to try to get
further off—here we are and here we must stop.

Suddenly the gates are thrown open again, and welcomed by
a howl of delight from the crowd, a strange and ghastly procession comes tumbling in. First a few ragamuffin soldiers,
making a fine pretence of clearing the way. Then a file of
coolies carrying the victims in small shallow baskets slung to
bamboo poles. As soon as each pair reaches the middle of the
space they stoop and pitch their living burden out and run off.
The prisoners are chained hand and foot and are perfectly helpless. The executioner stands by and points out where each load is
to be dumped. He is dressed exactly like any other coolie
present, without any badge of office whatever. The condemned
men have each a long folded piece of paper in a slit bamboo
stuck into his pigtail; upon this is written his crime and
the warrant of execution. One after another they arrive and
are slung out. Will the procession never end? how many can
there be? this is perhaps more than we bargained for. At last
over the heads of the crowd we see the hats of two petty mandarins, and behind them the gates are shut. The tale of men is
fifteen, and the executioner has arranged them in two rows,
about two yards apart and all facing one way. All except one
seem perfectly callous, and he had probably been drugged with
opium, a last privilege which a prisoner's friends can always
obtain by bribery. They exchange remarks, some of them
evidently chaff, with the spectators, and one man was carried in

singing and kept up his strain almost to the last. The executioners—there are now two of them—step forward. The younger tucks up his trousers and sleeves and deliberately selects a sword from several lying close by, while the other, an older man, collects the strips of paper into a sheaf and lays them on one side. Then he places himself behind the front man of the nearest row and takes him by the shoulders. The younger man walks forward and stands at the left of the kneeling man. The fatal moment has come. There is an instant's hush and every man in the two rows of condemned men behind twists his head up and cranes his neck to see. I will not attempt to describe the emotions of such a moment—the horror, the awful repulsion, the wish that you had never come, the sickening fear that you will be splashed with the blood, and yet the helpless fascination that keeps your eyes glued to every detail. The knife is raised. It is a short broad-bladed, two-handed sword, widest at the point, weighted at the back and evidently as sharp as a razor.

For a second it is poised in the air, as the executioner takes aim. Then it falls. There is no great apparent effort. It simply falls, and moreover seems to fall slowly. But when it comes to the man's neck it does not stop, it keeps falling. With ghastly slowness it passes right through the flesh and you are only recalled from your momentary stupor when the head springs forward and rolls over and over, while for a fraction of a second two dazzling jets of scarlet blood burst out and fall in a graceful curve to the ground. Then the great rush of blood comes and floods the spot. As soon as the blow has fallen the second executioner pitches the body forward with a "Hough!" It tumbles in a shapeless heap, and from every throat goes up a loud "Ho!" expressive of pleasure and approval of the stroke.

But there is no pause, the executioner steps over the corpse to the front man in the second rank, the knife rises again, it falls, another head rolls away, another double burst of blood follows, the headless body is shoved forward, the assistant shouts

"Hough!" and the crowd shouts "Ho!" Two men are dead. Then the headsman steps back to the second man of the front row and the operation is repeated.

Two things strike you: the brutal matter-of-factness of the whole performance, and the extraordinary ease with which a human head can be chopped off. As a whole it is precisely like a drove of pigs driven into the shambles and stuck; and in detail it is—or seems—no more difficult·than splitting a turnip with a hoe or lopping off a thistle with a cane. Chop, chop, chop—the heads roll off one after the other in as many seconds. When the seventh man is reached, either because the knife is blunted or the executioner misses his blow, the neck is only cut half through. But still he does not stop. He comes quickly back, takes another knife, passes on to the next man, and only comes back to finish the wretched seventh when all the other heads are lying in bloody pools in front of the shoulders which carried them a few moments before. And every man has watched the death of all those in front of him with a horrid animal-like curiosity, and then bent his own neck to the knife. The place is ankle-deep in blood, the spectators are yelling with delight and frenzy, the heads are like bowls on a green, the horrible headless bodies are lying all about in ghastly grotesque attitudes, the executioner is scarlet to the knees and his hands are dripping. Take my word for it that by this time you are feeling very sick.

Fortunately you are not detained long. The moment the last head is off, the crowd is gone with a rush, except a score of urchins who begin skylarking with the bodies and pushing each other into the blood. The bodies are thrown into a pond and the heads are plastered up in big earthenware jars and stacked up with those already round the wall of this potter's field. I had a few minutes' conversation with the executioner afterwards. Decapitation, he told me, was not the occupation of his family; it was only a perquisite. But the business is not what it was. Formerly he used to get two dollars a head for all he cut off;

now he only gets fifty cents. It is hardly worth while chopping men's heads off at that rate. But then it doesn't take very long. Would I buy his sword? Certainly. Nine dollars. It hangs on my wall to-day, a valuable antidote to much that I read about the advancing civilisation of China.

CHAPTER XVI.

THE IMPERIAL MARITIME CUSTOMS: SIR ROBERT HART AND HIS WORK.

THE "I. G." These letters, meaningless at home, call up instantly in the mind of every foreigner in China a very distinct and striking image—they are as familiar in the Far East as "H.R.H." is at home. For the image is that of the benevolent despot whose outstretched hand unites or severs the Celestial Kingdom and the outside barbarian world; through whose fingers five hundred millions of dollars have run into the coffers of the Son of Heaven, and never one of them stuck; to whom the proudest Chinamen turn for advice in difficulty or danger when other helpers fail; who has staved off a war by writing a telegram; who has declined with thanks the proffered dignity of Envoy Extraordinary and Minister Plenipotentiary of Her Britannic Majesty; who has ringed China round with an administrative commercial organisation the whole world cannot surpass; who, finally, born to struggle for the poet's bays, has laboured late and early all his life over dollars and duties, with a diplomatic nut, which other people have failed to crack, thrown to him now and then for relaxation. The "I. G." signifies a person and a post: the former is Sir Robert Hart, Bart., G.C.M.G., the latter is Inspector-General of the Imperial Chinese Maritime Customs. And the transcendence of the Customs Service in China may possibly be judged from the story that a Commissioner once took personal affront and quitted the sacred edifice when a missionary implored the Almighty to "deliver this people from their wicked customs."

After the above, it is hardly necessary to say that Sir Robert Hart is by far the most interesting and influential foreigner in China. To begin with, his power is enormous. The Chinese language, so far as his own field is concerned, is much the same as English to him, and with the Tsungli Yamên he has the influence which thirty years of close dealing with Chinese officials gives him, backed by the proud boast that they have never had reason to regret taking his advice. Then he handles the service he has created from nothing, to one which employs over 3,500 people, presides over an annual foreign trade of £44,000,000, collects £3,600,000 a year, clears 30,000,000 tons of shipping annually, and lights 1,800 miles of coast, exactly as an engineer handles a machine he has constructed—just as tenderly and just as firmly. And yet very few of the men whose livelihood and prospects are absolutely and at every moment in his hands, without the possibility of appeal, would willingly see anybody else in his place. The mere irresponsibility of the "I. G." would ruin most men. Yet Sir Robert owes all his success to his free hand. Does he learn of an old friend or schoolmate fallen upon evil times? "Send your boy to me," he telegraphs, and the youngster's future depends then only upon his own ability and industry. When there was a particularly bad piece of work to be done by one of his subordinates in delimiting the new Tongking-Chinese frontier— months of lonely labour, in savagery and solitude, with never a breath to draw that might not bring fever with it—whom did he send? His brother. Yet his avowal of nepotism is refreshingly frank. "I have never," he says, "advanced a worse man over a better, yet if promotion is due to one of two men of equal deserts, and one of them is of my own flesh and blood, it would be simply unnatural to pass him over." More than once already he has brought out the son of some companion of his boyhood, seen him grow up in the service from student to

Commissioner, save his competency and retire, leaving his benefactor and chief still working the same number of hours every day at his desk. But he rules with a despotism that a Tsar might envy. Any subordinate proved to have discredited the service in any way, is instantly dismissed. His secretary and representative in England, Mr. James Duncan Campbell, C.M.G., who has already distinguished himself in diplomacy on behalf of China and his chief at Paris and Lisbon, is absolutely impersonal in putting all applicants through their preliminary examination; but recognising how often even a limited competition of the broad and practical kind established for the Customs fails to "place" the man who will really be fittest for the work, it is part of Sir Robert's plan to allow Mr. Campbell occasionally to select from the unplaced competitors an individual who seems to him a desirable recruit, as promising and possessing qualities that indicate all-round fitness. So the benevolent despotism works.

Sir Robert Hart left the Consular Service for the Customs—it was barely in existence then—in 1859, and in 1863 he became Inspector-General. And during the thirty-five years that have intervened he has been home twice, once for twelve months and once for six—that is, he has had in his whole lifetime less holiday than one of his subordinates gets every five years. He has never been to the Western Hills, a few miles away, to which all the foreigners in Peking retreat in summer, and he has never even seen the Great Wall, two days' journey distant. But "next spring," he says, he is certainly going home. "Pooh," say people in the Customs Service, when you tell them this; "he has been 'going home in the spring' for the last fifteen years." As for the services he has rendered to China, to England, and to the world, the statesmen of Europe know them very well, and it would take a volume to tell them to others. Besides the creation of the Customs Service itself, which will be his immortality, to take the latest example, it was he alone who concluded the treaty of 1885 between France and China. All negotiations

had failed and matters looked very black and threatening.
Then, as usual, the Ministers of the Tsungli Yamên came
to Sir Robert. He agreed to take up the task on his two
invariable conditions—that he should have a free hand, and
that his connection with the affair should be kept a profound
secret till he either succeeded or failed. Then negociations
began by telegraph in cipher between his "den" in Peking
and his representative in Paris, and very awkward ones they
were. Month after month they proceeded, and at last, when
80,000 taels had been spent in telegrams, Mr. Campbell,
who conducted the negociations at the Paris end of the line,
was able to report to his chief that a settlement had been
reached, and that the Protocol was ready for signature. The
"I. G.'s" reply (March 31st) was characteristic: " Signez
sans délai, mais ne signez pas premier Avril "! The treaty
was signed on April 4th. Then Sir Robert got into his
cart and went to the Tsungli Yamên. The Ministers were
there and he sat down to a cup of tea with them. By
and by he remarked, with the apparent indifference of the
Oriental diplomat, "It is exactly nine months to-day since
you placed the negociations with France in my hands."
"And the child is born!" instantly cried one of the
Ministers, seeing the point and delighted at the truly Chinese
way of conveying the information. And the curious part of the
business was that all this time a special French envoy had been
residing at Tientsin, chafing at the slow progress he was making,
and not having the least idea that other negociations had been
on foot until he received word from home that he might return,
as all was arranged. He was so angry that he would not speak
to Sir Robert. After sending the last telegram settling the
French business, Sir Robert went to the funeral service of Sir
Harry Parkes, the British Minister, who had just died. As he
entered the chapel of the Legation, Mr. O'Connor, the British
chargé d'affaires, handed him the translation of a telegram
which had just arrived. It was a despatch from Lord

Granville offering him the post of British Minister to China. He accepted, after much hesitation, and his appointment received the Queen's signature on May 3, 1885. At his own request the matter was kept secret at home while arrangements were making for the succession to his position as head of the Customs Service. Meanwhile a Conservative Government succeeded to office in England and telegrams from the Foreign Office kept asking, "May we not publish the appointment?" Sir Robert had seen, however, by this time that the Customs Service would suffer severely if he left it at that time, and this was more to him than any other honour in the world. He therefore telegraphed, "Must I keep it?" and Lord Salisbury replying in very complimentary terms that he was free to do exactly as he thought best, he finally declined—the Empress of China, who was at that time exercising the Imperial function, as his official reply truly but perhaps inadequately explained, preferring that he should remain.

I have said that the statesmen of Europe are well aware of Sir Robert Hart's services, and the proof of this is that there are few civilians so decorated as he. In England a Conservative Government made him a C.M.G., and a Liberal one added the K.C.M.G., and later the G.C.M.G. and Baronetcy. Sweden made him a Chevalier of the Order of Gustavus Vasa; Belgium, a Commander of the Order of Leopold; France, a Grand Officer of the Legion of Honour; Italy, a Grand Officer of the Crown of Italy; Austria sent him the Grand Cross of the Order of Francis Joseph; America has presented him with several medals of Republican appreciation; Portugal has decorated him with the Military Order of Christ; the Emperor of China has conferred upon him the coveted peacock's feather and the Order of the Double Dragon, and has ennobled his ancestors; and his friends at Belfast—his native place—will no doubt be much interested to learn that he is, by direct gift from the Pope—nothing less than *sub annulo piscatoris*—a Commander of the Papal Order of Pius IX. As for

knowledge of China and the Chinese, there is no one living who
can compare with him, and I learned more of the inner working
of Celestial affairs during the fortnight that I had the honour of
being his guest, than a lifetime of simple residence could have
afforded.

The " I. G." and Sir Robert Hart, however, are two very
different people. " I was calling upon Lady Hart one day,"
said a lady to me, " and as I wished to speak with Sir Robert I
was shown into his office. I found the ' I. G.' there. Oh, it
was terrible—I covered my face and fled ! " The distinction
is indeed admitted by himself. He is not Jekyll and Hyde,
but he is certainly post and person. The secret by which he
has accomplished so much is an extraordinary devotion to
method—most extraordinary of all for an Irishman. This is a
subject on which he is far from averse to giving good advice to
men younger than himself, and on which, too, he establishes an
immediate *entente cordiale* with his guests. " Your early tea,"
he says, " will be brought to you when you ring your bell—
please ring it once only, holding the button pressed while you
can count three. Then will it be convenient to you to tiffin at
twelve sharp ? Because if not, I will tiffin myself at twelve
sharp and order your tiffin to be served at any hour you like.
I ride from three to five—there is always a mount for you if you
wish it. Dinner at half-past seven sharp, and I must ask you
always to excuse me at eleven." The consequence is that everything runs like clockwork in Sir Robert's household, and a guest
is perfectly at home from the start. But the above methodity
is nothing, in comparison. In the dining-room there is a big
wicker chair, always covered with a rug, so that you cannot sit
down in it. In that chair the master of the house has had his
tea every afternoon for thirty years. Upon a shelf stands a large
blue and white cup. Out of that he has drunk his tea for thirty
years. And by employing the odd moments that his " boy "—
who is punctuality itself—has kept him waiting each day in that
chair for that cup, he has managed during the last year or two

to read the whole of Lucan's *Pharsalia*! Of course he has kept
a diary since he could hold a pen. To test his preciseness I
made a point of standing each day behind my door, watch in
hand, till the clock struck twelve or half-past seven. Then I
walked into the central hall from my own side of the house.
Sure enough the door opened opposite me and my host walked
in from the other. It was like watching for a transit of Venus,
or waiting for the apostles to come out of the clock at Strasburg
at noon. And as I find I have not said a word of his outer man
I may conclude these personalities by saying that he is of
medium height and slight build, rather bald, with a kind,
thoughtful, and humorous face, a low voice, a shy and punc-
tilious manner; that he is a most entertaining companion, a
teller of countless good stories, fond of fun and merry company,
devoted to children, a player of the violin and 'cello, and a
host whose care and thoughtfulness for his guests are feminine
in their insight and famous in their execution. Sir Robert
Hart's remarkable personality has played, and may yet play, so
great a part in the politics of the Far East that I need hardly
apologise for giving these details in illustration of it.

And what, in a word, is this Customs Service? It is first
and foremost the collection of all their Maritime Customs at
the twenty-four trading ports, reaching nearly 22,000,000 taels
last year, their chief source of national income, which the
Chinese have confided to the hands of one foreigner, leaving
him absolutely free in his action and unhampered by any
colleague.

In passing round the coasts of China you frequently see a
smart little cruiser flying the yellow flag, with perhaps a miniature steel turret and a couple of quick-firing guns on board; or
in a swift launch.passing you will notice the Chinese crew and
foreign skipper in dapper uniforms, and a ten-barrelled Norden-
feldt projecting over the bow. These are the Customs fleet,
watching the coast for smugglers, and ready at a moment's
notice to fetch back some outgoing junk that disobeys the

waving of the red flag signal to heave-to and be examined. The
duty on opium is so high that smuggling is extremely profitable,
and therefore the Customs officers are proportionally keen in
discovering and preventing it. Along the coast, too, in the
neighbourhood of Hongkong and the Treaty Ports you will see
little stations, consisting of a house or two, a few boats, and a
look-out. These are also the Customs, and all the lighthouses
are in the same hands. Indeed, Sir Robert Hart has already
established the "Customs Post" between the Treaty Ports, and
he very nearly gave China an Imperial Post Office and an
Imperial silver coinage as well. The relations between Sir
Robert Hart and the Chinese Government exhibit the most
extraordinary example of confidence in individual integrity that
I have ever heard of. The "I. G." fixes the total cost of the
service, the Tsungli Yamên hands it over to him without a
word, and all money collected is paid directly by the merchants
into the Chinese bank. A little while ago the grant was
1,300,000 taels annually (a "Haikwan" or Customs tael is the
official monetary standard in China, a Mexican dollar and half,
in 1898 about 3s. 11¼d.), but an envious Chinaman, whom
I will not name, approached the Ministers at the Yamên with
a secret offer to do it for 500,000 taels less. The Yamên quietly
informed Sir Robert of the attempt to cut him out. His action
was characteristic He replied that the annual sum had been
inadequate for some years, and that he, on the other hand,
must ask them to raise it by 400,000 taels, which they accordingly did ! With this 1,700,000 taels a year Sir Robert does
exactly what he likes, his own remuneration being fixed, paying
to others the salaries he considers just, according to the conditions he has established. The pay of a student when he enters
the service to learn Chinese is 900 taels a year, and this rises to
3,000 taels, more or less, the pay of a full Commissioner. Instead
of a promise of pension, which Sir Robert felt that he could
not be certain the Chinese would keep when he should be gone,
he pays a bonus of one year's pay for seven years' service to the

Indoor Staff, for ten years' service to the Outdoor Staff, and for twelve years' service to the Chinese Staff. But this bonus may be withheld at his pleasure (he has never yet withheld it), and it therefore does not form part of a dead man's estate— a thoughtful provision for widows and children. The Indoor Staff get two years' leave after every seven years' service, and the Outdoor one year after every ten, both on half-pay. As may be expected, the *personnel* of so attractive a service is of a very high class, comprising all nationalities, and to be "in the Customs" confers social standing throughout the Far East. He is a fortunate father, in these days, who can see his son safely started on so pleasant, so well-paid, so assured a road of livelihood, though in exile.

The establishment of the Chinese Customs takes us back to one of the most interesting chapters in the story of the opening of China. The theoretic basis upon which the collection of duties had previously stood, left, like so many other Chinese theories, little to desire, but actual practice corresponded only remotely with it. The native tariffs were "minute and precise," the duties leviable amounting to about 10 per cent. *ad valorem*, but the rule was for each district to be assessed, so to speak, at a certain figure, which it was obliged to remit, anything over that sum remaining the personal profit of the collecting officer. This naturally resulted in a "dicker" between the merchant and the Customs, the latter demanding as much, and the former paying as little, as possible. In an official memorandum upon the subject Sir Robert Hart wrote as follows : " The paltriness of the amount to be answered for, the absence of the supervision of superiors, and the generally subordinate nature of the work to be performed, have all tended to produce such utter laxity and irregularity that the Tariff rates have become dead letters except in that they represent the maximum collectable on any one article ; the additional exemption from all question as to extra and unreported collection has encouraged, if not originated, a species of dishonesty, in which each subordinate lies to his superior, who, again, winks at such knavery, involved, as he is himself, in turn, in precisely similar transactions."

The introduction of foreign supervision resulted through the confusion that sprang up when Shanghai was held by the rebels in 1854, the Government officials expelled and their Yaméns closed, the collection of duties by the Chinese at an end, and the foreign Consuls in self-defence against future demands taking duties from merchants in the shape of promissory notes whose validity was questionable. But as Lord Clarendon wrote to Lord Elgin, it was "no part of the duty of Her Majesty's Consular authorities to take greater care of the Chinese revenue than the Chinese authorities are disposed to take." To bring the confusion to an end, it was at length agreed that the Chinese custom-house at Shanghai should be reopened under the proper authority, and that it should be placed under the supervision of foreigners to be nominated by the Consuls of the three Treaty Powers—England, France, and the United States. This, of course, was a purely foreign measure, and it met with opposition alike from the Chinese, who found their illegitimate profits threatened, and from the European merchants, who were more strictly treated and unable any longer to drive bargains for the clearing of their cargoes. Nevertheless, said Sir Robert Hart, it tended, "with unpremeditated gravitation," to become Chinese, and no serious objection was made from any quarter when the proposal was made to extend it to the whole foreign trade of China. Accordingly, by Art. 46, and Rule X. of the rules appended to the tariff, of Lord Elgin's Treaty of Tientsin, 1858, it was agreed that "one uniform system shall be enforced at every port." This was the birth of the Chinese Imperial Maritime Customs. For a time, like its immediate predecessor, it met with opposition from both natives and foreigners, since both suffered in pocket from its honesty and exactitude. But first of all, it secured for the Chinese Government funds "from a hitherto unappreciated source, and that, too, to an extent never dreamt of before." In fact, one may say without exaggeration that it has been the backbone of all Chinese finance ever since. To-day, when China hints that she desires a loan, and is prepared to offer part of the Customs revenue as a guarantee, the agents of all the great banks and financial houses of Europe tumble over one another in their anxiety to be first in the field with their offers. Yet they would look askance indeed at a loan based solely upon native administration. The service has been extended to each fresh port of China; its numbers and responsibilities have continually increased; and all sorts of duties, outside its original charter, have been laid upon the willing shoulders of its staff. To-day, as I have said, a position in the Customs gives a high social standing of its own. The Customs publications are among the most elaborate volumes of public information and statistics issued in the world, its huge volume of "Decennial Reports" just circulated being possibly the most instructive single work ever printed about China. Finally, to the Customs Service and the labours of Sir Robert Hart, the world owes the lighting and buoying of the whole coast of China. In 1863 there were only two small lights in the Canton district and a lightship at Shanghai, whereas now there are 108 lighthouses, 4 lightships, 89 buoys, and 67 beacons, employing a staff of 66 foreigners and 186 natives, all under the control of the Inspector-General of Customs, and paid for out of the tonnage dues. Although the Customs Service was established under the Treaty of Tientsin between Great Britain and China, all nations have shared equally in its advantages, and they are equitably represented upon its staff. Britishers (it would be inaccurate to say "Englishmen," where many are Scotch and Irish), Americans, Germans, French, Swedes, Danes, and now Portuguese, form the *personnel*, subjects of every nation having a treaty with China being equally eligible under the most favoured nation clause. There are doubtless more subjects of Great Britain than of any other Power, but not nearly so many as there would be if appointments were bestowed in

17

proportion to the share of each country's trade with China. The staff is at present as follows :—

	FOREIGNERS.	CHINESE.
Revenue Department	682	3,185
Marine "	81	388
Educational "	6	1
	769	3,574 TOTAL 4,343.

The value of the Foreign Trade of China, controlled by the Customs, for 1898 was 267,995,180 taels—£44,665,855 *; the duties collected amounted to 21,989,300 taels—£3,664,883 ; the number of ships entered and cleared was 37,902, and their aggregate tonnage 29,818,811. The direct trade of Great Britain with China amounted to 89,828,987 taels—£6,637,361, but the total trade with the British Empire, namely, Hong-kong, Singapore and the Straits Settlements, India, Australasia, South Africa, and Canada, reached the enormous figure of 195,710,240 taels—£32,618,373, or *over 78 per cent.* of the entire Foreign Trade of China.

The Chinese Customs Service forms, in short, an *imperium in imperio* without parallel, so far as I know, in history, and it should be a matter of great pride to us that it is built upon the genius, the devotion, and the integrity of an Englishman.

The one dark spot on the horizon of this great organisation is the question of Sir Robert Hart's successor. It is practically certain to be an Englishman—at least, the appointment of a man of any other nationality, however qualified in other respects, would be as unwelcome to the service as it would be impolitic and unfair. It has been suggested, however, that the Chinese Ministers might be tempted, when Sir Robert resigns, to replace him by a Chinaman, in the belief that the

* The tael is nominally an ounce of silver, but its value varies in China in different parts according to the quality of the metal. All the official calculations as above are in Haikwan—or Customs—taels. The average exchange value of this for 1898 was 3s. 11¼d., but at present its average exchange value has fallen to 3s. 4d., at which rate I have calculated it. It must be borne in mind, of course, that the purchasing power of silver in China has not fallen with European exchange.

service would run of itself, and that they might therefore just as well follow the usual custom of selling the post to the highest bidder. Such an event would be a calamity for the commerce of the world, and therefore the Treaty Powers would never permit it. For whatever may be thought of the statement at home, not a single voice will be raised in the East to contradict me, when I say that among her 350,000,000 people China has not one official who could be trusted to handle so much money without regarding it first of all as a means of personal enrichment. In 1864 Sir Robert wrote to the Secretary of State at home that the Inspectorate "will have finished its work when it shall have produced a native administration, as honest and as efficient, to replace it." Does the experience of thirty-five years lead him to cherish this hope of ultimate Chinese honesty and efficiency? I cannot say, of course, but I should be extremely surprised to learn it.

CHAPTER XVII.

THE GRAND SECRETARY LI.

THE Emperor of China has hitherto been practically invisible to any barbarian eye, and if he were not, he probably knows less about his country than the least of his officials. The real Emperor is the Empress—his aunt, and her proud and determined personality is known to the outside world chiefly through Li Hung-chang. Between the Empress and the Great Viceroy there has always been a close political partnership and an offensive and defensive alliance. Therefore the presence of the Viceroy, till his recent fall from power, at any rate, has been the nearest possible approach for a foreigner to the throne of China. Viceroy of the province of Chihli, hence *ex officio* guardian of the gate of China, Senior of the four Grand Secretaries of State, formerly Grand Guardian of the Heir Apparent, President of the Board of War, Superintendent of the North Sea Trade, Count Shinu-ki of the first rank, special plenipotentiary times without number; practical owner of an army and a fleet; immensely wealthy, preternaturally astute, utterly unscrupulous, having been able to laugh calmly at the dreaded Censors themselves, Li Hung-chang may be fairly looked upon as the ruler for many years of these 350,000,000 of shaven heads and plaited tails, at least so far as the outside world is concerned. If I had a chief object in my travels in the Far East, it was to have an interview with Li Hung-chang. And I talked with him at last for two hours.

Li Hung-chang was born in Anhui in 1825, and is a Metropolitan Graduate of the year 1847. In the following year we come across the first mention of him in public affairs. He was Financial Commissioner at Soochow, and there issued a proclamation of a highly dictatorial character against coiners and "smashers." He fought against the Taipings for the first time in 1853, when they were defying the Imperialists in the province of Chihli, and he was one of the principal Imperialist leaders when the Wangs again took up their arms in the valley of the Yangtze in 1858. In 1859 he was made *Futai*, or Governor, of Fuhkien, and in 1862 Governor of Kiangsu. This was the moment when Ward, the founder of the "Ever-Victorious Army," who had carried on the war against the Taipings with a handful of queer foreigners and a few thousand native troops whom he had been allowed to enlist and train, had been killed in retaking Tseki, and when his lieutenant, the traitor Burgevine, was trying to succeed him in the command. Li refused to recognise Burgevine's rights, and in spite of the fact that the latter won several battles, succeeded in getting him dismissed by the Emperor, and thus clearing the way for the military reputation of himself and his lieutenant, General Ching. In February, 1863, the British Government consented to the command of the "Ever-Victorious Army," which up to that time had experienced at least its fair share of defeats, being given to Captain Charles Gordon, R.E. Li showed signs at first of being as jealous of him as of his predecessors and the force he commanded; but he probably soon discovered that so long as Gordon was allowed to win the battles he did not care a straw who took the credit, and their relations were amicable until Li committed his great act of treachery. When it became evident to the Taiping leaders that Soochow must fall, and with it their rebellion come to an end, they decided to surrender to the Imperialists. Mow Wang alone was for fighting to the bitter end, and he was accordingly murdered by his fellow Wangs. Chung Wang, the great Taiping general, and eight others surrendered. General Ching had sworn brotherhood with Lar Wang, and Li had pro-

mised Gordon that the lives of them all should be spared. Gordon
himself had quarrelled with Li because the pay of his men had
not been paid, and had withdrawn the " Ever-Victorious Army "
to its headquarters at Quinsan.   The first thing Li did as soon as
he was left in undisturbed possession of the place was to invite Lar
Wang and eight other Wangs to a banquet on board his own
boat, and shortly afterwards their nine headless bodies were
found on the shore. Gordon's anger was so great that he is
said to have returned and sought Li for a whole day, revolver
in hand, to shoot him, but the astute *Futai* was not to be found.
Gordon, however, retired in disgust, refused to have anything
more to do with Li and his cause, and indignantly refused the
decoration and the large sum of money that the Emperor sent
him.   He came to realise, however, that he would be doing great
harm by allowing the war to drift on, instead of bringing it to a
speedy close, as he felt able to do; so he returned to his command.   Years afterwards he appears to have forgiven Li, and
at any rate the incident did not destroy his opinion of Li's
character as a whole, for I have seen a letter from him in which
he says, " Li, in spite of his cutting the Wangs' heads off, is
a man worthy the sacrifice of a life I have ceased to value."
Nevertheless, Gordon's estimate of Li's character may be judged
from his view of the future relations of China and Russia, which
was that Russia would advance, driving the Chinese forces
gradually back upon Peking, and that Li, while pretending, in
response to reiterated and imploring appeals from the Emperor
and Empress, to be making his best efforts, would do absolutely
nothing; that then, when the Russians had taken Peking, Li
would open negociations with them, grant them any terms they
desired in return for their support of him; that they would
retire and that Li would pose successfully as the saviour of
China, and possess himself of the throne. This opinion of
Gordon's was once published in Shanghai, and Li was so angry
that he succeeded in bringing enough pressure to bear to get
the paper suppressed.   "It is impossible," says the chief

historian of China, with regard to the murder of the Wangs, "to apportion the blame for this treacherous act between Li Hung-chang and General Ching. The latter was morally the more guilty, but it seems as if Li Hung-chang were the real instigator of the crime." * The facts that the fatal banquet took place on Li's boat, that Ching was directly subordinate to Li and would hardly have dared to take so irrevocable a step on his own authority, and that Gordon himself was sure who was the perpetrator of the crime, leave little doubt on the subject. All that can be urged in Li's defence is that to break one's promise and murder one's enemies in cold blood is no serious infraction of Chinese military ethics. The Wangs were fortunate that they were not tortured as well as murdered.

In 1867 Li took the field against the Shantung rebels, and in the same year he was made Governor-General of Hu Kwang. In 1870 he was elevated to his present post of Viceroy of Chihli, the most important viceroyalty in China, since that Province lies between the capital and the outside world, and this post he has held ever since, except for a period when he went into mourning. In 1876 he took the leading part in coping with the great famine, and in 1884 he was made Grand Secretary of State.

For many years the Yamèn of Li Hung-chang at Tientsin has been the centre of Chinese foreign affairs—indeed the question has been raised whether it would not be better for the foreign Ministers to reside there, instead of ruining their tempers and wasting their time by fruitless visits and endless discussions at the Tsungli Yamèn, the theoretical Board of Foreign Affairs at Peking. Whenever China has had to deal diplomatically with foreign nations, Li has been her mouthpiece. Thus at Chefoo, where Sir Thomas Wade very rightly compelled Li to meet him, he signed the Chefoo Convention (never ratified) in 1876; at Tientsin, the Li-Fournier Convention of 1884, in connection with which charges of falsification of the document were made

* D. C. Boulger, "A History of China," iii. p. 616, from which work I have also taken the allusion to the first mention of Li in public life.

by each signatory against the other, leading to Captain Fournier's subsequent duel in Paris; the Treaty with M. Patenôtre, representing France, at Tientsin in June 1885; and the Li-Ito Convention of Tientsin regarding Korea, in 1885. His career, however, has by no means been an uninterrupted success. Many times he has been reprimanded from the throne for faults small and great, and his enemies have unceasingly plotted against him. His great influence has never been sufficient to procure the restoration to office of that very able literate but unscrupulous man, Chang Pei-lun, who was disgraced and banished to the Russian frontier for having deserted his post as governor of Foochow Arsenal, and to whom Li married his daughter—in spite of her weeks of weeping and desperate opposition, according to gossip—in 1889. Much of his power—or rather, much of the failure of his enemies—must be attributed to the army with which he has surrounded himself. This has been supposed to number fifteen thousand men, but all Chinese figures on such matters are pure guess-work. These have undoubtedly been the best-armed and best-drilled troops in China, and from them have been drawn the contingents for the defence of the Taku Forts at the mouth of the Peiho River, and the fortress of Port Arthur. One of the most astonishing features of the Japanese war is the fact that this army has given no account of itself; indeed, it is not certain that it has not been kept in the neighbourhood of Tientsin all the time, in view of eventualities in which its master might have dire personal need of its services. I made many attempts while I was staying at Tientsin to see some of these much-praised battalions and their camps, but although I had the formal permission of Li himself to do so, every opportunity that I suggested was found to be quite impossible, and I never caught sight of them, except the few that were occasionally to be seen in the streets. With regard to the great Viceroy himself, however, I was more favoured.

It will easily be believed that he is not the most accessible of men, and after waiting a week at Tientsin for an answer to my request for an interview, my methods of influence being all exhausted for the moment, I had temporarily relinquished the project and ordered my ponies to be ready to start for Peking the next morning. It happened to be the Race Day at Tientsin and business was suspended, the banks closed and everybody gone to the course. At half-past two, as I had my foot in the stirrup to go too, a European-looking note was put into my hand. It was beautifully written, and read: "Dear Mr. Norman, I have the pleasure to inform you that His Excellency the Viceroy Li will be pleased to receive you this afternoon at 4.30. I hope therefore to find you in the waiting-room of His Excellency's Yamên at the hour appointed. Yours sincerely, Lo Fêng Luh." There was no time to be lost, as the Viceroy's residence is two or three miles from the hotel, and it was necessary to procure a chair, with bearers in official red hats, and a man to carry one's card, for I was informed that it would not be dignified to pay such a visit of ceremony on horseback or in a jinriksha. A friendly Chinese merchant soon procured these for me, and the four bearers carried me off in the closed chair, like a cat in a basket, at the rate of five miles an hour, while the card-man trotted alongside and objurgated anybody who got in the way. Mr. Lo Fêng Luh, I should add, is the English Secretary to the Viceroy, and an official holding several important appointments.

The Yamên (literally "official gate") of a Chinese official is his combined private and official residence, though in general use the word "Yamên" is equivalent to "office" or "bureau." It consists always of a number of buildings surrounded by a strong wall, with a wide gateway and painted doors. In the centre are the official's private living-rooms and the apartments of his wife, and of his concubines if he has any; then come his secretaries' offices, his waiting-rooms and his large official court or reception room. Around the yard into which you enter are the buildings where his servants and "runners" live, the latter being the harpy-like dependents, who shout when his distinguished visitors enter, form his train when he goes out, do all his dirty work, "squeeze" his petitioners and sell his secrets—a set of ruffians of the worst type. If he is a magistrate his Yamèn contains also a prison, and his "runners" stand by to deal with culprits condemned to "eat bamboo." An official Yamèn is also a house of refuge for anybody fleeing from popular vengeance. Half an hour's shaking through the narrow streets of the native streets of the city of Tientsin brought me to a bridge over the river, across which two dense crowds were passing both ways—coolies, beggars, mandarins in chairs, on ponies and on donkeys, and all kinds of common citizens. By the time we had jostled half-way across, the famous Yamèn was in full view—a mass of roofs enclosed in a high wall of grey brick, with a big gateway projecting at one side, over which a score flags and banners were waving, while in front a crowd of petitioners and beggars raised a ceaseless hubbub. My bearers broke into a trot as soon as they came in sight of the gate, and entering it swung rapidly round a blank wall built directly in front of it, and deposited me in the courtyard behind. This wall is set up in every Yamèn with the geomantic object of stopping evil influences, which can only proceed in a straight line. Two enormous and gaudy figures of officials or emperors or deities—I do not know which—were pasted to the doors, and opposite these, so placed as to catch the eye of the Viceroy every time he goes forth, is a similar flaming monster, the t'an or beast Avarice—a warning against the besetting sin of Chinese officialdom. While I was noticing these, and the runners loitering about were commenting in chorus upon my personal appearance in a manner evidently very entertaining to themselves, my card-man had rushed forward and two petty officials came to conduct me to the waiting-room.

This was the first surprise. The great man's anteroom resembled the out-patients' waiting-room in a charity hospital at home—a bare, dirty, whitewashed room, no bigger than an ordinary parlour, with a seat like that of a third-class railway carriage running round it, broken at intervals of a couple of feet by small tables placed upon it. Mr. Lo Fêng Luh, by contrast more resplendent in his official winter dress of silk and satin and sable and ermine, wearing of course a red-roofed hat crowned by a big button, was already there, and tea was served to us at once. Before we had time to touch it, however, the Viceroy's chamberlain came to say that the Chung Tang awaited us. I should explain that to say " Li Hung-chang," as we do, is to Chinese ears both ignorant and rude ; he should be spoken of as " Li Chung Tang," i.e., " Grand Secretary Li," or more simply, when in his own province, " the Chung Tang." The foreign community at Tientsin, at least all of them who are familiar with Chinese etiquette, invariably employ the last expression.

We followed the chamberlain, or whatever he was, for a couple of minutes, across a yard, through several doorways, around the veranda of an open court, and turned abruptly into a room and round a large screen. " The Viceroy," said Mr. Lo, with perfect European manners, as he stepped back and left me face to face with a tall and strongly-built Chinaman who put out his hand and smiled pleasantly and grunted a solitary syllable. " The Viceroy says he is very glad to see you," explained Mr. Lo, very much as a proud mother elaborately interprets the inarticulate cackle of her first-born. The great man acknowledged my bow in the Chinese manner—by bowing with his clasped hands at the height of his chin, and motioned us to be seated, myself opposite him, Mr. Lo on a foreign circular lounge between us.

Li Chung Tang is a pure Chinaman, not Manchu like the dynasty he serves. He is very tall for a Chinese, five feet eleven, I should guess, and must have been a powerful man in his youth. His face is the most strongly moulded I saw in China—not flat, as they usually are, but with all the features distinctly marked and the lines broad and deep, a face that would hold its own in comparison with any foreign face. A thin

grey moustache and "chin-beard" did not conceal his mouth
and chin at all, but what the general expression of his face may
be I have no idea, as he wore an enormous pair of round
tortoise-shell goggles.   This may be his custom, as it certainly
gives him a great advantage in diplomatic conversation, or it
may have been by a temporary order of the doctor, as he was
just recovering from a rather alarming attack of facial paralysis
which rendered him unable to speak for several days, and of
which I could see traces in the twitching and drawn lines of one
side of his face.   But at any rate he looked me straight in the
eye during nearly the whole of our interview, while I have so
slight a notion of what he really looks like, that if I were not
familiar with his photograph I doubt if I should recognise him
in the street without his glasses.

The Viceroy was dressed simply, not to say shabbily, in the
ordinary Chinese stiff round hat, a thickly-padded upper
garment of some kind of yellow silk and an undergarment of
grey silk.   His hands were tucked into his wide sleeves and only
came out twice during our conversation, once when he wished to
blow his nose, which he did in the familiar but indescribable
manner of the tramp in the street, and once when he was
startled by a little piece of news.   Yet he smoked a pipe five
feet long.   An attendant stood with pipe, smoking materials
and fire, at the back of the reception-room, and every five
minutes he walked solemnly forward, filled the pipe, blew the
fire-stick into a flame, the Viceroy opened one corner of his
mouth, the attendant inserted the stem and applied the light to
the bowl, the great man absorbed the smoke and opened his
mouth again, when the pipe-bearer withdrew as he had come.
This occurred a score times at least, and never a muscle did the
Viceroy move, except just to open the corner of his mouth wide
enough to admit the pipe-stem.   The reception-room is a small
parlour, well-furnished with modern European furniture, except
on one side where an alcove, hung with scarlet silk, contains a
cushion and table adopted for sitting and writing in the Chinese

fashion. The Chung Tang probably sits in this elevated post
on state occasions; on the present he reclined very comfortably
upon a sofa. Three or four attendants did nothing and did it well,
simply listening to the conversation, while I saw in the back-
ground that another had opened a window an inch and was
listening from outside. These attendants are always present at
official interviews, extraordinary as such a habit may seem to us,
and the natural result is that most of the foreign representatives
have one at each Yamôn in their pay, and that there are few
secrets which money will not buy. After I left the Chung Tang
I met a facetious acquaintance who inquired where I had been.
"Talking with the Viceroy," I replied. "Oh," he said, "I'll
get all you said to him for a couple of dollars to-morrow."
Naturally I offered it to him then and there at half-price.
There are two interesting pictures in this reception-room. One
represents the fable of the monkey, the cat and the chestnuts,
and I believe the Viceroy pointed to this on a recent occasion
when he was approached on behalf of British interests in Thibet.
The other puzzled me a good deal. It hung immediately over
the Viceroy's own seat and was a very large full-length portrait
in oil, representing a tall man with a long grey beard, in a frock
coat, and covered with decorations. Later I learned that it was
a portrait of Herr Krupp, presented by himself. Its position
suggests the reflection—an undoubtedly true one—that the
Chinese have always loved that foreigner best who has best
helped them to keep all foreigners away.

As soon as we were seated, an attendant brought tea and
champagne and placed them on a little table beside each of us,
and the interview began, Mr. Lo translating so perfectly and so
promptly that it was as though we were both speaking the same
language. My own idea, of course, was that I was about to
interview the Viceroy. Nothing was further from his intention,
which was clearly to interview me. Question after question fell
from his lips for a whole hour, and as Mr. Lo apparently did
not translate the feeble attempts I made from time to time to

stem the interrogatory torrent, I was as helpless as a man in a
dentist's chair. I think the best thing I can do is to repeat the
first part of the conversation *verbatim*, not that the subject-
matter is of the slightest importance, but because it throws a
flood of light on the working of the Viceroy's mind, and exhibits
a curious mixture of childishness, astuteness and Chinese
manners. After nearly an hour of it I began to feel that I must
be with Alice in Wonderland. Here it is, then, as nearly word
for word as I can recall it.

"The Viceroy hopes you are in good health and that you have
had a pleasant journey." Reply taken for granted. "Where
have you been?" and "Where are you going?" Easily
answered. "How old are you?" This, I afterward learned,
is an inquiry essential to politeness in China—I ought to have
returned the compliment. "What is your yearly income from
writing for newspapers?" I remembered that sophists hold it
to be not always imperative to speak the exact truth under
pressure, and I replied accordingly, with the natural result
that the next remark was, "His Excellency says you must
be a very skilful writer to earn so much money." I could not
observe whether he also winked under his goggles. "You
have made a long journey—have you no companion?" "None
whatever." "Are you not afraid of being stabbed?" "In
dangerous countries—not, of course, in China—I carry means of
defending myself." "The Viceroy says you must have been in
very great danger." "Not to my knowledge." "The world is
full of wicked people." "His Excellency is evidently well
acquainted with it." "Are you going to Thibet?" I took
this inquiry for a joke, as nobody knows better than the Chung
Tang that it is almost as easy to go to the moon, so I replied in
the same spirit, "Yes, and I have specially to beg from His
Excellency the favour of a safe-conduct and letter of recommendation to the Grand Llama himself." But it was no joke at
all. "Impossible!" exclaimed the Viceroy, sitting bolt upright
so suddenly that the pipe-bearer narrowly escaped prodding him

in the eye with the mouth-piece. "Impossible! Certainly not! I cannot do anything of the kind. It would be most unwise of him to think of going." I did not dare to admit that I had ventured to joke with the great man, so I said, "Then if it is impossible for me to go, perhaps His Excellency will tell me what is the truth about the recent troubles." "The people of Thibet are very foolish," was the reply, "but I have sent a Commissioner to them, who is at this moment conferring with the English, and there will be no more fighting." I tried to look like a person who believes what he is told As a matter of fact, Li Hung-chang has as much power over the Thibetans as the Sultan has over the Mahdi, but Thibet is a very sensitive spot with the Chinese authorities, and they would probably do anything, even to declaring war, to keep it out of the hands of the barbarians.

Then followed an hour during which the Viceroy questioned and cross-questioned me upon everything I had seen in the Far East, and my opinions upon every conceivable question at issue between the Powers. At last my patience gave way. I had seen Li Hung-chang, I had talked with him, I had examined his surroundings, and if he was not going to tell me anything, it was not worth while for me to sit there any longer. So to the twentieth inquiry about possible Russian action in Korea, I replied, "My opinions upon such a matter can have no value whatever for His Excellency, whereas if he would favour me with an authoritative statement concerning the relations of China, Korea and Russia, it would have the greatest possible value for the rest of the world." And I emphasized the request by taking up my hat and drinking the glass of wine; for I had been instructed previously that when either host or guest in China wishes to give the signal for departure, he empties his cup or glass. When Mr. Lo had translated my remark there was a moment's silence. Then, speaking very deliberately, the Viceroy said, "The relations referred to in your question are as follows: there is a distinct understanding between China and Russia that any action by the latter in Korea will be regarded by the former as a *casus belli*." In reply to a second question the Viceroy added, "At present the relations between China and Russia are simple. Upon the long Russian-Chinese frontier China is strong, Russia is weak. Vladivostok is very far from real Russia. It is alone. Russia and China had better be good friends." "But when the trans-Siberian railway is finished, Excellency——?" "Yes, then the relations of China and Russia will be revised. As regards Korea, it is a country unable to stand by itself, any talk of its 'independence' is waste of words, the relation of China to it is the same as it has always been, and you may be prepared shortly to see events which will make this relation quite clear to all the world."

I knew enough of China at the time not to attach much importance to all this; but recent events have shown how peculiarly fatuous it was. Did the Viceroy know, when he said these things to me and similar ones to many other persons, that China was rotten through and through, and as incapable of either attack or defence as she was of internal reform? I think he did. When our conversation was over, he took his glass at last and we all drank, Mr. Lo translating, "His Excellency wishes you a pleasant journey, and says you will please give a good account of your interview with him." Then the Viceroy was so kind as to accompany me across his private courtyard and Mr. Lo politely saw me into my chair.

He would be a presumptuous critic who should attempt an analysis of so complex and subtle a character as that of the Grand Secretary Li. Something, however, must be said, if only in correction of a popular misapprehension. It is commonly supposed that Li's intimate acquaintance with foreigners and his long experience of their diplomatic and commercial methods have led him to conceive a certain sympathy with them and a certain desire to see foreign influence stronger in China. This is far from the fact. The more Li has seen of foreigners the less he has liked them. We must not be wholly surprised at this, since in some respects foreigners have shown him an unattractive side of their character. His Yamên has been the focus of every commercial intrigue undertaken on behalf of Western nations, and most European commerce with official China has been conducted by means of intrigue. So far as merchants are concerned, British and German and French and American have occupied virtually the same position, though I like to think that our own countrymen have not descended to the methods of some of their competitors. But the difference between British and other civilised commercial dealings with the Viceroy has been this, that whereas other nations have been supported through thick and thin by their Ministers, our diplomatic agents have left our merchants to fight their battles alone. This policy has sometimes been carried to the point of indifference, and China merchants have some very well-founded grievances against at least one British Minister for his supineness, but on the whole the attitude of our representatives has been one of dignity. As regards France and Germany, every diplomatic concession Li has desired has had to be bought by a corresponding commercial concession on his part. Hence many a fat contract lost to British trade. And on countless occasions when a commercial offer has been refused by the Chinese on its merits, an irate Minister has hastened off to the Viceroy's Yamên and by means of very direct hints, if not by thinly-veiled threats, has secured a favourable consideration for it. Moreover, the great European firms have been well aware of the part that bribery plays in Chinese affairs. Whether Li has taken bribes or not, I do not know, though dozens of amusing stories on the subject are in circulation in Tientsin; but it is safe to say that if he has not, he occupies a solitary position of honour among Chinese officials. Those are the circumstances, therefore, under which Li has not always seen the best side of European civilisation. Apart from individual acts, however, he is like all his countrymen in thoroughly disliking us and all the principles of our ways.

18

Between the European and the Chinaman there is this quite
instinctive, as well as quite reasoned, aversion. He has sought
to avail himself of our abilities, especially where these might
enable him to hold us and all other foreigners at arm's length
in the future, but to him the millennium would be the final
disappearance of every "foreign devil" from China. Upon
this point there can be no doubt whatever, however much it
may suit the policy of China from time to time to let the
contrary be assumed. A recent British Minister to China said
to me himself that he believed the vast majority of Chinamen
of all classes would willingly mortgage the whole revenue of
China for the next thirty years, to see the back of the last
foreigner, and to have the certainty that he would never return ;
and that Li Hung-chang would be the leader in this step.
There can be no better example of Li's employment of Western
relations to suit the purposes of China than a remarkable letter
he wrote in 1881 to a Korean official :—" Of late years Japan has
adopted Western customs. . . . Her national liabilities having
largely increased, she is casting her eyes about in search of
some convenient acquisition which may recoup her. . . . The
fate of Loochoo is at once a warning and a regret to both China
and Korea. . . . Her aggressive designs upon Korea will be
best frustrated by the latter's alliance with Western nations." *
While this was his advice, however, the Viceroy has endeavoured
in every possible way, through his nominee and creature, Yuen,
the Chinese Resident in Seoul, to thwart foreign influence upon
Korea.

In a previous chapter I have spoken of Li Hung-chang's
commercial enterprise, the China Merchants' Steam Navigation
Company and the cotton-mills at Shanghai. These are other
examples of his attempts to beat foreigners at their own game.
He has also established a medical college at Tientsin, where
twenty youths are trained for the medical staff of the army and

* Quoted in "The Life of Sir Harry Parkes," by F. V. Dickins and S. Lane-
Poole, ii. p. 395.

navy. In view of his treatment of several young Chinese graduates in medicine, however, whom in public he complimented, and in private refused to employ, one hesitates to accord him the credit which should belong to this innovation.

The news now is that Li Hung-chang has been degraded, and that his unique position is gone for ever. We should not be too ready to believe this. It may be, of course, that his enemies have thrown him at last, but the Emperor and Empress-Dowager will hardly realise how dependent upon him they have been, until the barrier of his unique personality and experience has been removed from between themselves and the barbarian world. The decree depriving him of his Yellow Jacket and peacock's feathers must not be taken *au grand sérieux.* "Degradation" of this character is merely a Chinese method of incentive. In fact, the decree itself virtually promises restitution, and as I have not seen a translation in the English Press it is worth reproducing in full :—

The *Wo-jên* having broken faith with Korea and forcibly occupied that country, the Throne sympathised with its tributary kingdom in her distress and so raised an army to attack the common enemy. Upon Li Hung-chang, Imperial High Commissioner of the Pei-yang, having chief control of the forces there, rested the entire *onus* of being prepared for emergencies. But, instead, he has been unable to act with speed and promptness in his military preparations, so that much time has elapsed without any important results. He has indeed failed in the trust reposed in him by us. We therefore command that his decoration of the three-eyed peacock feather be plucked off from (his hat), and that he be stripped of his Yellow Riding Jacket as a slight punishment. It is necessary then, that the said Imperial High Commissioner exert himself to the utmost and decide upon what should be done ; that he direct and hasten the various armies from the various provinces to the front, in order that all may put forth their best strength to chase and root out the enemy. In this way Li Hung-chang may hope to redeem his former errors.

This is instructive not only for the light it throws upon such Chinese "degradation," but also as a contemporary example of the paternalism of the Imperial sway. It might be a great mistake, however, to conclude from this that the aged Viceroy has at length reached that third day on which there—

" comes a frost, a killing frost ;
And—when he thinks, good easy man, full surely
His greatness is a-ripening—nips his root,
And then he falls."

CHAPTER XVIII.

CHINA AMONG THE GREAT POWERS.

IN the original plan of this volume, the chapter with the above title was intended to be one of the longest and most argumentative. At that time, though it was less than a year ago, China was regarded by almost all foreign writers as one of the Great Powers. Her enormous resources in population, and her excellent credit—thanks to Sir Robert Hart's work, which made every financial house in Europe eager to lend her money—were regarded with the greatest respect by military writers. It was understood that she had taken to heart the lesson of her defeat by France, and was labouring earnestly to guard against similar misfortunes in the future. It was known that she had purchased enormous quantities of military and naval equipment in Europe, that she had built arsenals, docks, and forts up and down the country, and that a considerable number of the most capable and energetic foreign military and naval experts had been engaged for years in arranging her armaments and drilling her men. She had gained one or two distinct successes in diplomacy against European Powers, and Li Hung-chang had frequently declared that he would regard certain actions as a *casus belli*; her naval base and dockyard at Port Arthur had been built for her at enormous expense by a French syndicate; Gordon's advice to fortify Wei-hai-wei had been followed; the powerful Taku forts at the mouth of the Peiho commanding the approach to Tientsin, and the Bogue forts on the Canton River had frowned impressively upon every foreign visitor; while the famous Northern Squadron of German-built ironclads had visited the ports of the Far East and exchanged elaborate salutes. From all this, foreign writers came to the conclusion that China had shaken off her Oriental lethargy, had drawn boldly upon her vast reserve of strength, had armed herself strongly according to modern scientific fashions, and had therefore at last taken her place among the great military and naval Powers of the world. To such an extent was this believed, that probably a majority of publicists came to look upon China as the great bulwark in Asia against the Russian advance, and suggestions of an Anglo-Chinese alliance were the commonplaces of diplomatic conversation. Such was the opinion a few months ago regarding China, and it was against this view that the present chapter was to be directed. I had come to the conclusion, and had frequently expressed it in print, that so far from China being a Great Power, her land forces would not stop any foreign army for a week, and that her navy would be the prey of the first foreign fleet that attacked it; that so far from an Anglo-Chinese alliance being a reasonable ideal, in the first place China would not make an alliance with any foreign country, second, if she made one she would not adhere to it, and third, if she made it and adhered to it, it would not be worth having.

The unlooked-for outbreak of war between Japan and China, and its inevitable results, have rendered unnecessary any further exposure of the hollowness of Chinese claims. The sword of the Japanese has proved mightier in demonstration than the pen of any critic could have hoped to be. Against the French soldiers in Tongking, as brave as possible, but mere handfuls in number, exhausted by the climate, badly led, and feebly supported from home—the Chinese troops won a good many victories and were several times within a hair's breadth of winning greater ones; but against the regiments of Japan, fighting in a climate which was their own, admirably officered, perfectly armed, and enthusiastically supported, the Chinese braves have fallen back like sheep. And since in the first naval battle the European strengthening of the fleet was killed off, the Northern Squadron has done nothing but lie under the guns of the forts, or search those parts of the sea where it was certain that no Japanese ships would be found. A-san, Phyöng-yang, the Yalu River, Kinchow, and Port Arthur, have given us at last that most difficult thing to secure—the truth about China. It would be waste of time, therefore, to dwell upon matters now so familiar to the whole world, or to argue in support of truths so irresistibly taught by events. It may still be interesting, however, to describe briefly some of the ways in which China prepared herself for the defeat which has now overtaken her, especially since these are hardly less amusing than instructive.

Five years ago the Englishman who knows more of that inscrutable entity, the Chinese mind, than any man living, told me that of all her "vassals," there were only two for which China would fight—Thibet and Korea. Personally, I do not believe that anything which could happen, short of an advance upon Peking itself, would cause China to declare war against any European Power. The role of sleeping leviathan suited her perfectly, but she has well known that the first step she might take would destroy the illusion upon which her security has been based. What she has liked is to remain perfectly quiescent, while the world trembled to think what she might do if aroused—to lie still in her Confucian savagery, while such utterances as that mass of rubbish called "China: the Sleep and the Awakening," which the Marquis Tsêng signed (but did not write) in the *Asiatic Quarterly* for January, 1887, have represented her as advancing with a cautious but irresistible march. The strangest thing is that the civilised world has been deceived by these tactics, and even such keen analysts of national characteristics as the late Mr. Charles Pearson have painted a future in which China, having prepared herself by long training, should put forth her gigantic strength and overrun the world. This ethnical fable of "Jack and the Bean-stalk" has been amusing enough to anybody who really knows the first facts about China, but it is safe to conjecture that nobody has been moved by it to such hearty laughter as the Viceroy of Chihli himself. Japan has had no illusions about China, and she was quite ready to prick the bubble. But the Beanstalk is hard to cut down. At the beginning of the war a news agency solemnly announced that each province of China was called upon to furnish 20,000 men; nineteen multiplied by 20,000 is 380,000, and the astounded reader was invited to believe that this enormous force was gathering and marching to Peking like Lars Porsena's men to Rome. The newspaper reader might perhaps not be expected to know that the Emperor of China could as easily raise 20,000 men in Mars as in some of his provinces; that it would not be difficult to enlist a considerable force in one part of China to attack another part; that absolutely no organisation exists in China for the handling of such masses; that the men would find themselves without uniforms, without arms, without food, without the most rudimentary knowledge of war, without leaders of any description whatever; or that a huge army of the kind in the neighbourhood of the capital would be almost certain to seize the opportunity to upset the present alien Government. But it is hardly making too high a demand upon any reader that he should have glanced at the map of China, made a rough multiplication of the degrees of longitude he saw before him, and asked himself how 20,000 men were to march a thousand miles through a country which is always on the verge of famine. However, when one of our leading statesmen was of opinion that China must inevitably win in the end, "because of her enormous armed strength," other people might be excused for going astray. One expression of opinion, however, puzzled me extremely. Captain Lang, R.N., to whose great administrative skill and absolute devotion to her interests China owes most of whatever naval strength she has acquired—and whom, it

may be added, she characteristically rewarded by dismissing
him with insult — has been reported as saying to an
interviewer, among many other rather startling tributes to
Chinese naval prowess, that " with an officer like Admiral Ting,
whom I would not hesitate to follow anywhere, the Chinese
navy would prove a splendid force."   But this worthy
" Admiral " has had no education whatever as a seaman, owing
his appointment to the ordinary routine of compctitive examination in the Chinese classics, and being merely the nominal equal
of Admiral—as he then was—Lang, to " save the face " of the
Chinese.   In fact, he was previously a cavalry General, a
branch of the service in which he would be equally unpreju-
diced by any information.   Moreover, Admiral Ting Ju-ch'ang
was the hero of the famous story of the Chinese Admiral who
was found one day playing pitch and toss, or what corre-
sponds to it in China, with the sentry at his door, both of
them seated on the floor of the Admiral's cabin.   I had an
opportunity once of talking with a foreign instructor on board
a certain Chinese ironclad.   In reply to my inquiry when the
ship would sail, he said, " The only way we really know when
we are to sail is by the Admiral coming aboard.   He leaves the
ship as soon as we come into port, and we never see him again
until we sail.   He knows nothing at all about naval matters—
he is just the mandarin put on board by Li.   Why, when somebody comes aboard to visit him, he'll perhaps call a sampan and
see him off over the port side!   Then I have seen him gambling
here on the quarter-deck with a common seaman, and when he
has won all his money he'll tell the paymaster to advance the
seaman some more, so that he can go on playing.   Yes, sir,
that is a literal fact.   The only men on board that could really
do anything are these young fellows, the captain and lieutenants,
and they have no power at all.   They fought against the French
and got nothing at all for it—just a few dollars, and were told
to take themselves off.   The rings on the big Krupps are beginning to open out already, and if there is the least dirt or sand

you can't shut them." "Then I suppose," I said, "that no European squadron need be afraid of the Pei-yang Squadron yet?" "No fear, sir, it is only a question who will get them as prizes," was the reply.

"The truth is, that if the Japanese do not sweep the Chinese from the sea, then study, skill, devotion, and experience go for nothing, and there is no need for us to train our naval officers at all. One thing only could save the Chinese on the sea—the enlistment by large promises of money of European naval officers, in whose hands complete and unfettered control should be placed. The Chinese seamen are not wanting in courage, but naturally enough they have no confidence whatever in their leaders, and they would probably fight well enough to give their undoubtedly fine ships a chance if they were well commanded." *

The actual condition of the Chinese army and navy, while so much was believed of it abroad, cannot be understood from any descriptions in general terms. Let me therefore give a few scattered facts which came to my knowledge. I was once being shown by a Chinese naval officer over one of their two biggest ironclads, which was on a cruise at the time, and therefore presumably in first-rate condition. I noticed a gun carefully protected in a canvas cover. As we passed it, I asked casually what it was. The officer explained with pride that it was a new quick-firing gun, and called a quartermaster to remove the covering. The order was obeyed with evident reluctance, and when the gun was at length exposed it proved to be used by one of the watches as a receptacle for their "chow," and was filled with chop-sticks and littered with rice and pickles. Of course I promptly looked the other way, but it required no knowledge of Chinese to interpret the remarks of the officer to the quartermaster. No doubt the whole watch went through the process of

* To avoid the appearance of prophesying after the event I may be permitted to say that I wrote these words on August 18, 1894, and that they appeared in the *Contemporary Review* for September. The battle of the Yalu was fought on September 17.

"eating bamboo" the moment I was off the ship; but the
Chinese are incorrigible. It would be discouraging to a
European engineer who should be appointed to a Chinese ship
to find that if there were any subordinate boiler small enough
for the purpose, it had been used for stewing dog. There is
nothing inherently improbable in the story repeated by the correspondent of the *Pall Mall Gazette* that a Chinese warship went
to the Yalu without one of its guns, the commander having
pawned it and not been able to redeem it in time.

Another example of Chinese administration which came to
my knowledge may be interesting at this moment. Some years
ago the Chinese Government ordered a magnificent set of
Hotchkiss cartridge-making machinery. In due time this
arrived, but two mandarins claimed it for their respective
districts, and, failing to agree, each seized such portions of the
machinery as he could secure and carried them off to his own
place. When I was there, half the machinery was in one
arsenal and half in another several hundred miles away.
Unfortunately, Europeans are not always above taking advantage of Chinese supineness. A cargo of cocoa powder was
ordered from well-known manufacturers and landed at Port
Arthur for use in the big guns there. By-and-by it was tried
and found not to ignite, and finally the whole of it was thrown
into the sea. But both Europeans and Chinese had pocketed a
good "squeeze" out of the transaction. The superintendent of
one of the largest arsenals in China receives an allowance to buy
steel: he buys iron, and pockets the difference. It is, therefore,
fair to presume that the rifle barrels he is turning out are made
of iron. With my own eyes I saw at an important arsenal the
machinery for making rifle barrels standing idle, while hundreds
of men in the same workshop were making them by hand.

Here is another story which I know to be true. An American
agent showed a Chinese Viceroy the performance of a Hotchkiss
gun. The Viceroy promised an order, but said he should like
first to show it to some of his officers, to find out if they could

use it. So the gun was lent. The Chinese took it to pieces, worked day and night in making full-sized working drawings, put it together again, and sent it back, and the Viceroy wrote to say that he had decided not to purchase it. Again—in all these instances I have names and places and dates in my note-books, but for obvious reasons I omit them—a Chinese Viceroy ordered estimates for a complete set of rifle-making machinery from the United States. The total cost was (say) 500,000 dols. The Viceroy, supposing it was like a Chinese estimate, drew that sum from the Treasury, cut the estimate down to 400.000, and gave the money and the estimate to an official with orders to procure the machinery. He, in his turn, "squeezed" it a little more, and then made the estimate agree with the money that remained by striking his pencil through several important items. The machinery in due course arrived as ordered, and of course could not be set up.

I had a very interesting conversation with a foreigner acting as torpedo-instructor in the Chinese navy. He told me that Chinese officers receive pay for a certain number of men, and that they are in the habit of making up the total by putting all their relations and servants in uniform on inspection days, and drawing their pay all the rest of the time. When an admiral is appointed to a ship, he makes his brother-in-law the boatswain, and his cousin the cook. I asked this torpedo-instructor whether his pupils really acquired any comprehension of the art of torpedo warfare. He assured me that a considerable proportion of them really did. I asked him whether they would actually fight. He hesitated, and I added: "Would they not probably discharge all their torpedoes at once and then run away?" "I think they would," he answered. À propos of "squeezing," he told me that all his pupils had to give money, not being able to afford it, to the Viceroy before they could get the rewards that had been promised them by him when he inspected them. My informant himself, when he went to the Yamén to get his decoration, was stopped with a demand for

sixty taels by the Viceroy's head " boy," and finally beat him
down to forty dollars, without which it would have been impossible for him to get an audience. This system, he added, extends
through everything. All the " boys " at the Yamên actually
buy their posts, and only keep them by a regular subsidy to the
Viceroy himself. A Chinese official who "squeezes" up to 20
per cent. is regarded as honest; more than that the Chinese
consider grasping.

As an example of Chinese naval procedure, I may repeat a
story told me by the agent of one of the great European naval
contractors. The Chinese sent an Armstrong cruiser to carry
troops along the coast of Formosa, a very costly and complicated
vessel, instead of chartering a common merchant steamer. Her
captain ran her promptly upon a rock and stove in her lower
bottom; then he steamed down to Hongkong and had her
examined, the double bottom being full of water. To escape the
consequences of their mishap, the admiral and commander
determined to pay for the repairs themselves; so they told the
dock company that if the vessel could be put right for 15,000
dols. she might go into dock. But the company replied that so
far as they could judge from their divers' reports, the cost would
be at least 40,000 dols. So the vessel steamed away to Tientsin
just as she was, and was docked at Port Arthur. "But the
dock," continued my informant, "was so built that when the
water was let in, the pumping-house was submerged, and they
could not get the water out again, so there the ship lay and
rusted for I don't know how long."

While the French fleet was off Tamsui, the 27-centimetre
Krupp guns in one of the shore batteries had been trained upon
the *Gallissonnière* at 1,000 yards range for several days. At the
first French shot all the Chinese artillerymen fled, except one,
who succeeded in discharging three guns before a shot struck
him and blew his head off. One of the shells he fired pierced
the ship, and remained imbedded in the wood-work, failing to
explode. The vessel went to Hongkong, where with infinite

precautions the shell was removed and opened. It had been manufactured at the Foochow Arsenal, and contained—charcoal! The maker had, of course, been paid for gunpowder and had pocketed the difference.

The Japanese were blamed in many quarters for threatening to withdraw their promise to treat Shanghai as a neutral port, if the Kiangnan Arsenal did not cease its operations. The Chinese replied that the arsenal was only a very small affair, and its output unimportant. This is not the case. It consists of an engine department, capable of turning out marine engines up to 3,000 h.p.; an iron ship and boiler yard, containing a slip upon which has been built an iron cruiser of 2,000 tons, with a speed of 14 knots; a small-arms factory, manufacturing Remington rifles, the production of which is given by the Chinese at 200 per week, though under efficient superintendence this figure could be raised to 1,000; an iron and brass foundry, which has turned out castings up to 80 tons each; a projectile department, under a superintendent from Elswick, with capabilities of 5 tons a day, ranging from the 6-pounder shell for field guns up to the 800-pound shell for the Krupps; an ordnance department, capable of turning out guns up to 40 tons, with boring and turning lathes by a dozen different European makers; a steam hammer which strikes a blow of 135 foot-tons; and a furnace which will admit work 100 feet long. When I visited this arsenal there was an 8-inch gun of 12½ tons and 35 calibres, mounted on a hydro-pneumatic disappearing carriage, which had been entirely constructed at Kiangnan, and eight similar ones were in course of manufacture. The superintendent of this department, an Englishman of great skill and administrative talent—Mr. N. E. Cornish, from Elswick—had turned out in two years twenty-two 8-inch guns, eight 6-inch guns, and one 9-inch gun. Not far away are powder-works and cartridge factories, under native superintendence, with capacities respectively of one ton and 10,000 cartridges per day; but the quality of the output had fallen off so seriously since the foreign employees had been dismissed, that grave doubts were expressed as to whether it would be of any use at all. I give these details not only as an example of the falsehoods that the Chinese put forward and which find acceptance among foreigners, but also as a striking proof of the fact that the ability to produce all the implements of warfare has not prevented the Chinese from experiencing a humiliating defeat, on the first occasion that they have been seriously attacked during the last twenty-five years. Unless the character of the Chinese Government can be vitally changed, all the guns and ships in the world will not save them.

The Canton River can now be blocked against the most powerful fleet at a few hours' notice, and the story of how this came to be done is a curious one. The British Consul went one day to a former Viceroy of the province to protest against the partial barrier which then existed, as a great obstacle to trade. "Moreover," he said, "it is not of the least real use to keep out an enemy, as a foreign fleet could destroy it without the least difficulty." The Viceroy listened with interest, promised to give the matter his best consideration, and the moment the Consul had left his Yamên he issued instructions to his foreign naval instructor to replace the old barrier by one which could not be destroyed. Accordingly a number of huge iron piles were driven in, and these when filled with stones in war-time would constitute an impenetrable obstacle. The river, too, is very strongly defended by forts of the latest pattern, heavily armed. As a matter of fact, however, all these precautions are useless, because no enemy would think of attempting to force the entrance to the river in face of them. A strong force would be landed, would advance overland, occupy Canton, re-establish peace there, collect the duties of the richest city in China, and with this revenue to pay all military and naval expenses, war with China could be carried on for ever at a profit.

To Captain Lang, R.N., as I have said, is due almost all that there is of good in the Chinese navy of to-day, and if the Japanese war had taken place immediately after his retirement, the Chinese ships would undoubtedly have given a much better account of themselves. The universal testimony of people in China is that since Captain Lang left, the Chinese fleet has gone to the dogs as fast as possible. He was, as every conscientious British officer under the same circumstances would have been, too much of a *détailliste* for the Chinese. He probably made a mistake in accepting an executive position—no foreign officer should do that with the Chinese. He should have been merely adviser, with more or less power to get his advice insisted upon. "Captain Lang," said a Chinese commander, "is quite right to tell me about my ships and my guns, but he need not come and look at my water-closets." An arrangement under which an experienced officer of the British navy, and Ting Ju-ch'ang, who, on passing a Chinese literary examination, was made a cavalry officer and thence promoted to command the Northern Squadron, were placed nominally upon an equal footing as "Admirals," was destined to break down sooner or later. The strain which finally destroyed it came when the fleet was in harbour somewhere in Northern China. Admiral Ting went away as usual, whereupon the senior Chinese commodore hoisted his flag. Captain Lang immediately sent him orders to haul it down. He refused to do so, and Captain Lang thereupon telegraphed to the Viceroy, who replied ambiguously through the commodore. Captain Lang then went ashore with all his belongings, and sent in his resignation, which was instantly accepted. It is understood that the Admiralty refused permission for any British officer to replace him. Indeed they could not do otherwise; and the fate of Captain Lang should make it clear that no foreigner who is not prepared to pocket the indignities along with the salary should accept a post in the Chinese navy.

It may be supposed that the utter collapse of the Chinese navy in the war with Japan came as a surprise to the Chinese, and particularly to the Chinaman who has had the chief influence in creating it. On the contrary, I have had in my hand a

detailed and most crushing indictment of the Chinese navy,
written less than five years ago, which was handed personally
to Li Hung-chang by one of his highest foreign advisers. In
order to strike his imagination, this was drawn up in the form of
an imaginary account of what had happened to the Chinese in
a naval war—a species of Chinese "Battle of Dorking," in fact.
The Chinese ships, it said, were entirely urprovided with stores,
such as oil and patent packing, and these could not be obtained
nearer than Shanghai. When a merchant ship arrives bringing
them, it has to go to Port Arthur, at that time the only defended
Chinese port where any of the Pei-yang Squadron, except gunboats, could go. But Port Arthur is not large enough to accom-
modate the whole squadron, so that while the cruisers are taking
on board coal and stores, the ironclads must remain outside.
Then the enemy blockades Niuchwang and Taku, because there
are no torpedo boats there. The Chinese officers are so nervous
under fire, from having had no torpedo practice at night, that
they fire torpedoes at eight hundred yards. But the squadron
has no reserve of either good men, coal, stores, or provisions,
and on the outbreak of war it is too late to procure them. The
Chinese engineers are afraid of using forced draught, and when
they try to do so the boiler-tubes leak. The *Chao Yang* is
rammed, because her turning circle is so great and her manœuvring power so small. (This prophecy was strikingly fulfilled,
as the *Chao Yang* ran on shore while manœuvring in the battle
of the Yalu.) The enemy land a large force to the eastward of
Talien-wan Bay, entrench themselves strongly, and cut off all
supplies from Port Arthur, which ought to be provisioned for a
year but is not, and starve it out in two months. Finally, said
this report, an enemy with a smaller or even an equal naval
force, would thrash China, and take Port Arthur and keep it.
This report was written primarily to procure for the navy the
money to buy stores and supplies. It had, however, no appreciable effect, and a disastrous war has been needed to demonstrate
how well-founded were the criticisms it embodied.

The war has confirmed more than the severest critic has ever said of the *personnel* of the Chinese army. An eye-witness has described how the "picked troops" embarked at Tientsin on board the *Kowshing* were dressed in blouses, wore "thigh-pads," carried old rifles, and were provided with an executioner to each regiment! The discipline of these troops was such that they promptly mutinied as soon as they thought themselves in danger, and the first time they used their rifles was upon their own comrades who were saving themselves by swimming. Of desertions and consequent beheadings we have already heard more than enough. Both before and after being defeated, the Chinese troops outraged and plundered the peasantry of the districts to which they were despatched, until the Japanese were welcomed as deliverers in Manchuria, while in China the refugees asked the nearest way to a foreign settlement, knowing that there alone would they be safe. The Rev. John Ross, a well-known missionary and author, has stated that on the way to Mukden "every part traversed by the Chinese army has been stripped of its vegetation, and resembles fields over which locusts have passed, so complete is its devastation." When the last mail arrived from the Far East the first batches of Chinese prisoners were reaching Japan. The *Kobe Herald* says of four hundred of them: "If these are samples of the Chinese regular troops we must admit that they are a poor, miserable crowd, being without exception as ragged, dirty, and puny a collection of human beings as it has ever been our lot to inspect." And the Tokyo correspondent of the *Times* writes of seven hundred that arrived there: "It would be difficult to conceive a dirtier, less formidable-looking lot of men. They appear to have been collected from the highways and byways without any regard to age—some are in their teens, others in their fifties—or any thought of physical capacity." The Chinese have taken very few prisoners, but those they have treated according to their usual habit. At the beginning of the war I warned foreign corres- pondents that they must on no account be taken alive by the

Chinese, and Marshal Yamagata afterwards gave the same advice
to his troops. After impressing upon them that only those
Chinese who bore arms were the enemies of Japan, and that
mercy to the conquered and kindness to prisoners must be absolutely shown under all circumstances, he proceeds: " The
Chinese have, from ancient times, ever been endowed with the
cruellest and most merciless dispositions; therefore, if during a
battle a warrior by any chance falls into their hands, he is sure
to suffer the most pitiless treatment by them, to which death is
far more preferable; in the end even he will be put to death
with savage ferocity. It follows that in whatsoever circumstances a soldier should avoid being taken alive, and should
rather in such a case die gallantly, manifesting by such a death
the warrior spirit of Japan and perfecting the fame of our
heroic ancestry." His warning has been justified by events.
The first thing that the Japanese found inside Port Arthur was
a number of headless and mutilated bodies of their comrades,
and the correspondent of the *Times* whom I have already
quoted, writes: " The Chinese take no prisoners. From dead,
wounded, and vanquished alike they shear off the heads,
mutilate them in various ways, and string them together by
a rope passed through the mouth and gullet. The Japanese
troops have seen these ghastly remnants of their comrades. A
barrel full of them was found after the fight at Ping-Yang, and
among the horrible trophies was the head of a young officer
who had fallen wounded in a fort evacuated by General
Oshima's men."

Having been thoroughly beaten, the Chinese have decided to
" reform" the organisation of their army, and how have they
set about it? At the head of the organisation of reform they
have placed Chang Chih-tung, the notorious foreigner-hater, the
instigator of the murders of missionaries, the Viceroy who was
recently disgraced for defying Imperial orders from Peking.
Better than this, however, they have associated with Captain
von Hanneken, who is to be the chief foreign adviser, with the

rank of General, a certain Hanlin scholar named Hu Ching-kuei. That is, a man who represents above all things the old Chinese literary culture—an official of the Hanlin Yuan, or "Imperial Academy," which is the most conservative institution in China, and attaches more importance to the propriety of an ideograph than to all the Western knowledge in the world. The farce of Chinese "reform" could not be better illustrated.

To conclude, the truth is that like almost everything else in China, her offensive and defensive power is a sham. The offspring of corruption and bombast is inefficiency. The Viceroy Li said to me that along the thousands of miles of the frontier between China and Russia, the former was strong and the latter was weak. Yet a considerable proportion of the troops in Northern China is armed with flint-locks, gingals, and bows and arrows, and skill with the bow is still considered a most desirable military art. Gordon, with his habitual frankness, told Li that for China to think of fighting Russia was "sheer madness." And even Captain Lang, in the interview from which I have already quoted, declared that "when under arms, one-half of the Chinese army is made up of savages." A force made up half of coolies, torn from their homes, afraid of their weapons, clamouring for their pay, driven forward by the lash, punished by the headsman's knife; and half of uncontrollable savages, defiers of their own officers, insulters of foreigners, plunderers of peasantry, torturers of prisoners, murderers of missionaries, outragers of women, mutilators of the dead, is not the kind of army with which Englishmen should desire to stand shoulder to shoulder, and the sooner we learn to look for our Eastern alliance elsewhere than in China, the better.

CHAPTER XIX.

CONCERNING THE PEOPLE OF CHINA.

THE more one learns about China, the less confident become one's opinions about it. The first result of experience and study of this extraordinary people and this vast land is to teach that any sweeping generalisation is almost necessarily untrue. Every individual Chinaman is a mass of contradictions; the gulf between the theory of Chinese government and its practical administration is not to be bridged; the geographical differences of the country are greater even than those of the United States; the variations of race are almost equal to those of India; to the Chinaman of the south the Chinaman of the north is a foreigner, a person speaking a different language, and usually an enemy; to the Chinaman of the far west the central authority of the east is an alien and an incomprehensible dominion; at any moment an army could be raised in one part of China to operate against another part; public feeling or community of sentiment is unknown. In fact, there is no such thing as "China."

The wisest remark ever made by a foreigner setting out to write about things Chinese, was, in my opinion, that which Mr. George Wingrove Cooke, the special correspondent of the *Times* with Lord Elgin's mission, prefixed to the reprint of his letters. He said:—

I have, in these letters, introduced no elaborate essay upon Chinese character. It is a great omission. . . . The truth is, that I have written several very fine characters for the whole Chinese race, but having the misfortune to have the

people under my eye at the same time with my essay, they were always saying something or doing something which rubbed so rudely against my hypothesis, that in the
interest of truth I burnt several successive letters. I may add that I have often
talked over this matter with the most eminent and candid sinologues, and have
always found them ready to agree with me as to the impossibility of a Western
mind forming a conception of Chinese character as a whole. These difficulties,
however, occur only to those who know the Chinese practically: a smart writer,
entirely ignorant of his subject, might readily strike off a brilliant and antithetical
analysis, which should leave nothing to be desired but Truth. *

This book is old, long out of print, and forgotten, but between
the soiled and antique covers of my copy I find more common
sense about China, and more appreciation of what should be the
attitude of Europeans towards it, than in almost all the works—
with the exception of Professor Douglas's volume just published—
that have been written since. And if I may say so without
being misunderstood, I would add that to learn what China is
not, and what should not be our relations with it, one has but
to look at contemporary European opinion, and to examine the
actions of the British Foreign Office for the last ten years. In
writing of the people of China I shall certainly not attempt the
foolish task of including them all within the limits of any
definition, or laying down any rule about Chinese character
without exceptions. But there are so many mistakes prevalent
concerning China, and so many errors in dealing with her have
been made, that it is both easy and imperative for any one who
has seen under the least corner of the veil which conceals her,
to point out some of these as vigorously as he may.

By way of breaking ground for what is to follow, I may pause
for a moment to give an illustration or two of the difference
between Chinese and Western views upon a single point, and the
consequent extreme difficulty in the way of our comprehension
of this people. Take, for instance, the subject of human life.
A foreign resident of Peking who speaks Chinese well was riding
along one day and came to an excited crowd. Drawing near, he
discovered a circle of people quietly watching a man desperately

* George Wingrove Cooke, " China : being *The Times* Special Correspondence
from China in the years 1857–58," London, 1858, p. vii.

attempting to commit suicide by dashing his head against a
wall. He dismounted, restrained the man, harangued the
bystanders, and learned that this was a coolie who claimed that
his payment for a certain porter's job was short by ten cash—
less than a penny—and as the employer refused to pay more he
was proceeding to take revenge by killing himself on the spot,
knowing that by so doing he would get the other into considerable trouble. On another occasion a man threw himself into the
canal, but was dragged out. So he simply sat down on the edge
and starved himself to death, to be revenged against somebody
who had cheated him. Again, one day a man was found
murdered on a bridge near the British Legation. The law
of China prescribes that a murdered body must not be removed
till the murderer is caught. Therefore it was covered with a
mat and left. Days passed and a month and still the rotting
body lay there, till at last the Minister, who had to pass it every
day, vigorously protested, and it was taken off the bridge and
placed a little further away. And a Chinese newspaper is
responsible for this story, which indeed has nothing whatever
incredible about it. One day a sow belonging to a Mrs. Fêng
happening to knock down and slightly injure the front door of a
Mrs. Wang, the latter at once proceeded to claim damages, which
were refused. Whereupon a fierce altercation ensued, which
terminated in Mrs. Wang's threatening to take her own life.
Mrs. Fêng, upon hearing of this direful threat, resolved at once
to take time by the forelock, and steal a march upon her enemy
by taking her own life, and thus turn the tables upon her.
She accordingly threw herself into the canal.

This merely by way of illustration. First of all, as I said of
the Grand Secretary Li, most foreigners are wofully wrong in
regard to the feelings of all Chinese towards peoples of other
nations. So far from the Chinese growing more sympathetic
in consequence of greater commercial intimacy, they are
undoubtedly growing more hostile. "The ruling and influential
classes still only tolerate our presence in the country; and I

firmly believe they would hail the day when they could see (were such a thing possible) the last foreign factory razed to the ground and the last ship dismissed the coast, in spite of the loss to the national revenue and the ruin of the districts dependent on our trade that would certainly ensue." * This was written twelve years ago, but it is absolutely true to-day. I have said that the sights of Peking are not nearly so accessible to foreigners to-day as they were a few years ago. And it is the testimony of most of the foreign residents that their treatment by the Chinese grows worse each year, and that they are less safe in the streets. The closing of the top of the wall to pedestrians is the last act of petty unpleasantness. There was no reason whatever for this except to deprive the foreigners of their only decent walk. Another example is that the Marchioness Tsêng, when first she returned from Europe, used to have an afternoon "at home" once a week, like European ladies. This gave, however, such deep offence in all Chinese quarters that she was compelled to cease. A Chinese lady, again, who had been in Europe, called upon two European ladies who were visiting Peking. Next day, desiring to be polite, they returned her call. Immediately afterwards they received a message from her begging them never to come to her house again. So, too, if you begin to study Chinese with a teacher in Peking and you happen to meet him in the street, do not expect the least sign of recognition. He will cut you dead, and then come next morning to apologise and explain that it would be very unpleasant for his family if he were seen bowing to a foreigner. He will teach you and take your dollars : he will not greet you. And the Abbé Favier, the finest specimen of a priest I have ever met, a *beau sabreur* of the church, who wears Chinese dress and his hair in a queue, who speaks Chinese perfectly, who has even been decorated with a sapphire button by the Emperor, told me that he had just received the most remarkable honour and recognition of his whole life in China. He met the Governor

* Medhurst, "The Foreigner in Far Cathay," 1872, p. 177.

of the city in his official chair, and the great man positively
bowed to him, to the stupefaction of the lookers-on. "Il
m'a salué, Monsieur—comme ça!" And while I was in Peking,
H.R.H. Prince Henry of Bourbon (Comte de Bardi) desired very
much to see the Temple of Heaven, which had been closed to
foreigners for several years. Accordingly the German Minister
(he was travelling, of course, with an Austrian passport) applied
to the Tsungli Yamên for special permission for his distinguished
guest. After some delay it was granted, as some say only after
the Marquis Tsêng had carried the request to the Empress
herself, and an appointment was made. The Prince and his
party, accompanied by the Secretary of the German Legation,
rode out to the gates of the Temple and only succeeded in
passing the outer one after long discussion and altercation.
The next gate was still more difficult, and after an hour's parley
the keepers agreed to let the men of the party in, if the Princess
would go back into the street and wait for them. This was too
much, and the whole party naturally left in indignation. The
German Minister sent a formal and vigorous complaint to the
Tsungli Yamên, and after a while he received a sort of apology
and expression of regret at the misunderstanding. But the
exclusion was undoubtedly deliberate and according to orders
received. The Ministers could not well meet the request with
a flat refusal, but they took care that the permission should
have no value.

"As for any moral influence that foreigners may exercise by
their presence in the country, it may be regarded as simply
nil." I believe this to be absolutely true. The reader may
naturally be inclined to reply that in the face of many years
of devoted missionary work and the large sums of money that
are yearly subscribed in England to support this, such a statement is incredible. My answer is, that from the missionaries
themselves come some of the strongest testimonies in support
of the assertion of declining foreign influence. I once asked a
Roman Catholic priest whom I met in China, and of whose

knowledge and character I formed the highest opinion, if he believed that the result of missionary enterprise would result, even in the fulness of time, in anything that could be remotely described as the Christianising of China. "Jamais!" he replied, emphatically. "Then," said I, "why are you here?" "I am here," he replied, "simply in obedience to the command to preach the Gospel to all peoples. Like the soldiers in the ranks I obey the orders of my commander, without understanding in the least what good is to come of them." Yet no missionary who has been in China for conturies has achieved such extraordinary victories or has a position of so much power as this man. To pass from Roman Catholic to Protestant testimony, in September, 1888, the Rev. A. Williamson, D.D., read a paper at Chefoo on "Missionary Organisation in China." He said: "The startling, though it is not the most serious, aspect of the question is that not only is heathenism extending, but immorality is increasing in all directions. . . . Those of us who have lived long in China see the evil spreading before our eyes, especially in and around our great emporiums, with an ever-widening area every year. The Chinese are learning evil faster than they are learning good. They are adding foreign vices to their own, aping foreign free-living and habits, often in the most powerful manner; and the fact is, that in and around our centres of commerce they are less honest, less moral, and less susceptible to the preaching of Divine Truth than formerly by a long way." And again: "Further, we are not rising in the respect or esteem of the Chinese as we expected. A few years ago there was a general sense of satisfaction among us at the attitude shown towards us by many, both officials, wealthy civilians, and literary men. Now a change is perceptible in all directions. They respect us less than they used to do, receive our visits less readily. We find it more difficult to rent or buy houses, and so on." Another Protestant missionary—the Rev. William Ashmore, D.D., of the American Baptist Mission—in an article in the *New York Examiner*, wrote as follows: "Already the revulsion from the old, kindly feeling towards America has begun. Now they are learning to *hate* us. It is passing from mouth to mouth, from village to village, from province to province, from ruler to ruler, from prince to prince, from beggar to beggar, until we can contemplate the possibility of an epidemic of ill-will extending over a fourth part of the whole human race." After these witnesses I shall hardly be accused of prejudice in making the same assertions. I will add, however, one weighty piece of official testimony recently given on this characteristic of contemporary China. In his review of the volume of Customs Reports for last year the British Minister to China forwards, and therefore approves, a report written by one of his subordinates which concludes with these striking words : "I hardly venture to make any comments of my own upon the pages which I have reviewed ; but in one word I consider that the conclusion of the whole matter inevitably is that the trade conducted by foreigners in China has made but little progress during the ten years 1882–91 ; that it does not promise any immediate or considerable advance ; and that foreign interests and influence therein have decreased and deteriorated to an appreciable extent." *

The character of Chinese officialdom is probably more familiar to European readers than the diverse characteristics of the Chinese people, and therefore less need be said about it. Every Chinese official, with the possible exception of one in a thousand, is a liar, a thief, and a tyrant. This may be doubted in Europe, but it is recognised as an almost inevitable fact by every Chinaman, and volumes could easily be filled with examples of it. It is well known, for instance, that the larger part of the sums subscribed in England on one occasion for the relief of the famine districts in China found its way into

* Mr. Beauclerk's report upon the volume of "Decennial Reports," 1882–91, published by the Chinese Imperial Maritime Customs, forwarded to the Foreign Office by Mr. O'Conor, H.B.M. Minister to China. F. O., 1894, Misc. Series, No. 333, p. 38.

the pockets of the army of Chinese officials. I learned of one
instance of this which would be vastly amusing if it were
concerned with a less painful subject.   Some time ago the
turbulent Chinese of Canton attacked the foreign settlement
of Shameen and plundered and destroyed the houses of the
resident foreigners.   For this the Chinese Government was, of
course, compelled to pay an indemnity.   At the time, however,
the London Mansion House Famine Relief Fund had oppor-
tunely been collected and forwarded to China, and this sum
was in large part devoted to paying the Shameen indemnity!
One of my illustrations, by-the-way, shows instructively the
conditions upon which foreigners reside in safety in certain
parts of China.   Shameen is separated by a species of moat
from the native city of Canton, and access to it can only be had
across a bridge which is barred by iron gates and held by a
posse of Chinese soldiers.   My two friends who were good
enough to stand before my camera on this bridge, with the
Chinese soldiers by their side and the Cantonese mob held back,
like wild beasts, behind the bars, furnish a typical example of
the relations of Chinese and foreigners at the present day.   But
to return to the subject of Chinese officialdom.   One relief fund
was so carefully safeguarded by Europeans that the officials
were thwarted in their efforts to obtain it, and the Administrator
(Mr. Bruce) wrote: "In a country where corruption and bribery
are indispensable in all business—where in the case of distributing charity it is a large proportion for one-third of the
original contributions to reach those for whom they are designed
—the practically complete absence of 'squeezing' in this relief,
would seem to the natives to be a marvel."   By order of the
Emperor certain districts stricken by famine were to be
exempted from taxation, and proclamations announcing this
were to be posted up.   An Imperial decree, however, published
some time afterwards, declares the Emperor's abhorrence of
what he had learned of the way his orders had been carried out,
since "the lists of the districts for which exemption from the

tax is claimed are too often falsified, and what is worse, the officials take care not to post the Imperial proclamation until they have collected the tax in full. The revenue is lost to the state and goes into the pockets of the hangers-on about the yaméns." To the common people, adds the *Hongkong Daily Press*, from which I take the above, "lekin stations are 'squeeze stations' pure and simple, and yaméns are places to be avoided by every possible means. That the mandarins should practise extortion is looked upon as quite a natural circumstance, quite as natural, in fact, as that the people should evade payment of legal dues when opportunity offers. On both sides common honesty is held in more or less contempt, and a man who does not take advantage of his opportunities is regarded as a fool." As a matter of fact, in spite of the Emperor's pious indignation, it was a common occurrence for the tax-gatherer to follow the distributor of relief and seize upon the money as soon as it had been given. The subscriptions to relieve the starving Chinese were, unfortunately, but another example of mistaken foreign benevolence. From three of the distressed provinces grain was actually being exported while foreign relief was being given, and the foreigners' money merely caused the return of thousands of natives to a district wholly incapable of supporting them. The Rev. Mr. Candlin wrote that there was room for the refugees in other districts, where they could always get food and generally work, while they were worse than useless when they returned and hung about the famine region, subsisting on the missionaries' doles. Mr. Consul Allen, in a report written a few years ago, gave some striking instances of the failure of promising Chinese commercial undertakings, simply because of their connection with officials. Referring to the China Merchants' Steam Navigation Company, he says: "This is a powerful organisation enough, with a large fleet of river and sea-going steamers, and it might be supposed that the China Merchants' Company was a most flourishing concern. No doubt it is, but its connection with

the Government is felt by the trading class to be an effectual
bar to its ever becoming the lucrative association that an unhampered and free trading company could be, and its scrip
shows this." A Chinese company was started to develop the
mines of Yünnan, and the prospectus declared that the enterprise promised fabulous riches. An official of high rank was
to be placed in charge of the operations, and shareholders were
promised a minimum dividend of 6 per cent., with various
bonuses. But, says Mr. Allen, "the shares in the company
are not eagerly taken up. The Chinese distrust all official
connection with mercantile enterprise, alleging that all the
profits earned go into the pockets of the mandarins, while the
man who has no claims to official rank is left out in the cold.
Europeans, of course, will not touch such a speculation. The
risk is altogether too great."

The *Hupao*, a vernacular Chinese newspaper in which there
is often much frank information about China, mingled with
superstition and ignorance, reproduced once a proclamation
from the Provincial Treasurer of Kwangtung, in which he said
that the priest in charge of the Temple at Canton pays as much
as from 7,000 taels to 10,000 taels for the post, recouping himself afterwards for his original outlay by all manner of extortions
from the worshippers. Thus they are not allowed to bring in
their incense-sticks or candles, but must buy these from the
priest inside at ten times their value. They must also pay an
exorbitant hire for space on the mats on which they perform their
prostrations; and women are persuaded by the priest that a
night's sleep on the mats in the temple, for which they pay a
heavy hotel bill to the priest, will ensure them male progeny.
An amusing light is thrown upon Chinese ideas by a story told
me of Sir Harry Parkes. He once arrested several mandarins,
and kept them for a fortnight. All their friends were allowed
access to them, but they were not permitted to leave the house.
After a few days he sent to inquire how they were getting on.
"We cannot sleep at night," they said, "for the dreadful heavy

tread of the sentry round the Yamên. Our own watchmen come and clap, and then they go to sleep ; and we have waited night after night for yours to do the same, that we might get away. But he never stops! " So the sentry was told to stand still. A foreign mining engineer in charge of important Chinese mines, told me that he had eighty soldiers under him armed at first with percussion-cap guns, and afterwards with sniders. On one occasion he placed an armed sentry by the boiler to prevent the miners drying dynamite upon it, which they were constantly trying to do. The sentry went to sleep on the boiler ; a boy brought a box of dynamite and placed it there ; it exploded and blew up the whole place, including the sentry. Occasionally his soldiers were all allowed to drill, when the officers sat in their quarters half a mile away, with their red flags in front of them, and looked on. This expert foreigner—he was not an Englishman—added : " If you could take away from the English artisan his present character, and substitute for it the Chinese character, in six months English industries would be at a standstill, and in ten years the accumulated wealth of England would have disappeared." A correspondent of the *Times* recently told a capital and thoroughly characteristic story of Chinese officialdom, to the effect that about ten years ago some of our politicals had a meeting on the Sikkim frontier with some of the officials from Thibet. In the course of conversation some reference was made to our last war with China, ending in the occupation of Peking and the destruction of the Summer Palace. " Yes," said the Thibetan officials, laughing, " we know you said you went there, and we read with much amusement your gazettes giving your account of it all. They were very cleverly written, and we daresay deceived your own subjects into a belief that you actually went to Peking. We often do the same thing."

The most illuminating of my examples, however, of the natural mind of the official Chinaman came from my own personal experience. When in Peking I visited the Tungwen College, an institution where Chinese students are instructed in foreign

languages, literature, and science, by foreign masters, a small
monthly allowance being given them by the Chinese Government
for regular attendance. I was shown a class of young Chinese
engaged in writing essays in French upon the subject of "Protection and Free Trade." As a specimen of their work, the
composition of one named Tok-kun was taken from his desk and
handed to me. It was wholly an original production, and I venture
to think that the following passage, which I copied exactly, throws a
vivid light upon the point of view of the would-be Chinese official
after a number of years of foreign teaching : "Ce qu'il y a de
mauvais et de terrible à l'Etranger, c'est que le peuple forme des
partis qui se mêlent de politique, je suis enchanté de l'ignorance
des affaires d'Etat des Chinois, qui, s'ils s'y entendaient seraient
certainement libre échangistes, car nous achetons beaucoup plus
que nous ne vendons. Notre Gouvernement, profitant de cette
ignorance du peuple, peut augmenter les droits de douane à sa
fantaisie, cela ne fait aucun tort aux commerçants, mais beaucoup aux acheteurs, qui ne comprennent pourquoi. Les mar-
chandises venant de l'Etranger, augmentent de prix tous les
jours, et ne cherchent pas du tout à comprendre pourquoi. Ils
paient sans se plaindre du Gouvernement, c'est heureux pour la
Chine."

Dirt, falsehood, corruption, and cruelty are some of the least
objectionable of Chinese vices. Of the last-named I have drawn
a moderate picture in a previous chapter, but the following
description of what the Abbè Huc saw when travelling once in
the Interior may be added :—" Le chariot avança, et nous vîmes,
en frissonnant d'horreur, une cinquantaine de cages, grossière-
ment fabriquées avec des barreaux de bambou et renfermant des
têtes humaines. Presque toutes étaient en putréfaction et
faisaient des grimaces affreuses. Plusieurs cages s'étant dis-
loquées et disjointes, quelques têtes pendaient accrochées aux
barreaux par la barbe ou les cheveux, d'autres étaient tombées à
terre, et on les voyait encore au pied des arbres. Nos yeux ne
purent soutenir longtemps ce hideux et dégoûtant spectacle."

The Taotai of Ningpo recently issued a proclamation to agriculturists which contained the following admirable sentiments :—
" Frogs are produced in the middle of your fields ; although they are little things they are little human beings in form. They cherish a life-long attachment to their native soil, and at night they melodiously sing in concert with clear voices. Moreover they protect your crops by eating locusts, thus deserving the gratitude of the people. Why go after dark with lanterns, scheming to capture the harmless and useful things ? Although they may be nice flavouring for your rice, it is heartless to flay them. Henceforward it is forbidden to buy or sell them, and those who do so will be severely punished." The cruelty of the Chinese to animals is indescribably great ; hence the necessity for the inculcation of such sentiments. A friend with whom I rode a good deal in Peking told me that one day, hearing screams of laughter from his stable, he went to investigate. There he discovered that his groom and " boy " had caught a big rat, nailed its front paws to a board, soaked it in kerosine, set fire to it, and were enjoying the spectacle. But this is not so bad as one of the tricks of the professional kidnapper, who will catch a child in the street, carry it off to another town, blind it, and then sell it for a professional beggar. Their cruelty, moreover, is by no means confined to foreigners and dumb animals : they are cruel under almost all circumstances. A steam launch, built at Hongkong, blew up on her trial trip, and amongst others the wife of the editor of a Hongkong paper was thrown into the water. Some Chinese in a sampan paddled up, and positively refused to take her on board until she had promised them fifty dollars. Another member of the same party had to promise five hundred dollars before a boatman would undertake to convey several of the survivors to Hongkong. An eye-witness related to me how a junk upset off Macao, and the seven men of its crew were all drowned, though there were a dozen Chinese boats round them. While I was in Hongkong a Chinaman was terribly injured in an accident at Kowloon. His fellow-

workmen simply laid him in the gutter, and afterwards even refused to carry him to a steam launch sent to take him to the hospital. At one of the "dragon races" in the Canton River, 150 men were upset out of two of the long canoes, amidst a thousand other people afloat, and every one of them was drowned. One of the latest papers from China tells how a boat, paddled by two men, carrying rice from Shanghai to Pootung, capsized in the midst of a number of fishing-boats. The fishermen immediately seized upon the rice and property belonging to the capsized boat, but took not the slightest notice of the drowning men, whose bodies had so far not been found.

Foot-binding, which is practised in most of the provinces of China, and of which one of my illustrations shows the results, is a sufficient example of widespread cruelty; but the practice of infanticide is infinitely worse. Attempts have been made to deny the existence of this practice to any large extent, but proofs could be adduced by the thousand. One of the most thoughtful and instructive newspapers ever issued in China was the *Chinese Times* of Tientsin, conducted by Mr. Alexander Michie, who possessed a remarkable knowledge of Chinese life and a profound acquaintance with the Chinese mind. This paper, unfortunately, came to an end for want of foreign support a few years ago. In its columns I found the following account of infanticide in the province of Shansi. One man, who had been in the employ of a foreigner for two years and had received good wages, put his little girl to death because, as he said, he could not afford to feed her. A woman, without solicitation, told one of the foreign ladies that she had killed five children in order to go out as a nurse, and that her husband compelled her to do it. "Yes, it was a great sin," she said, "but I could not help it." A man, who passes for a gentleman, volunteered the information that he had allowed two of his girls to die for want of care. "Only a small matter. We just wrapped them up in bed-clothes and very soon they were gone. I am a poor man; girls are a great expense and earn no money, and as we already had two we con-

cluded we could not keep any more." The testimony of a
Chinese teacher is as follows :—"Infanticide is very common
among the poor, and even people in pretty easy circumstances.
There is hardly a family where at least one child has not been
destroyed, and in some families four or five are disposed of.
Nothing can be done. As soon as the little ones are born they
are laid aside and left to perish. Girls are more often destroyed,
but boys also are very often killed. The officials know it, but say
it is something they cannot control." Another man, who
is now a member of the Christian Church, says that in his
village there is hardly a family that has not destroyed two or
three children. And once more, "a woman said that 'it was
very common for poor people to go into rich families as wet-
nurses because they received good wages, and in fact they often
destroyed their babies that they might do so.' Such a state of
things is terrible in the extreme, and the worst feature about it
is that there seems to be no public or individual conscience
against it: even well-informed and otherwise respectable people
look upon it as a matter of course." A lady contributor to the
North China Daily News furnished the following statistics :—" I
find that 160 Chinese women, all over fifty years of age, had
borne 631 sons, and 538 daughters. Of the sons, 366, or nearly
60 per cent., had lived more than ten years; while of the
daughters only 205, or 38 per cent., had lived ten years. The
160 women, according to their own statements, had destroyed
158 of their daughters ; but none had ever destroyed a boy. As
only four women had reared more than three girls, the probability is that the number of infanticides confessed to is considerably below the truth. I have occasionally been told by a
woman that she had forgotten just how many girls she had had,
more than she wanted. The greatest number of infanticides
owned to by any one woman is eleven." Wife-selling and
child-selling are also common, and during the last famine a
party of beggars were actually observed in the streets of Tientsin
with baskets, loudly crying, *Mai nü*—"Girls for sale!" in one

of the baskets being four baby girls with pinched faces and wizened limbs.

The subject of Chinese medicine reflects the Chinese mind in a very instructive manner, but it is too large to be dealt with here. I will only say that when Sir Robert Hart recently instructed the Customs officials to prepare lists of the substances used in Chinese medicine, amongst the 1,575 entries appeared dried toads, toadspittle cake, dried snakes, liquid manure preserved for years, and various other preparations of human excrement, the genitals of different animals, deer foetus, the human placenta, centipedes, and the dung of different animals. Dr. Mackay of Tamsui, in Formosa, recently prepared a catalogue of Chinese prescriptions which had come under his notice, and he points out that the most repulsive and disgusting "medicines" are given to the unfortunate children. Among the remedies prescribed for diseases of children are the following:— For cough, bat's dung—name given in drug-shop, "night clear thread." For worms and yellowish face, grubs from filth washed and dried—name in drug-shop "grain sprouts." Also rabbit's dung, called "the worm-killer." For thrush, cockroach's dung—name in drug-shop "worm pearls." For bad stomach, earth-worms swallowed alive after being rolled in honey. Fever, dog's dung-prepared—the dog being first fed on rice. Eruptions, boil on upper lip, fowl's dung. If a child is frightened from any cause, prepared centipedes are given. Dr. Mackay adds that "for different diseases there are a number of worthless and filthy preparations, some of them scarcely mentionable." Some of the medicines prescribed for adults are not much better. Thus a man suffering from enlarged spleen would be ordered to take "grass of deer's stomach dried and cut in slices, skins of silkworms, lining of hen's gizzard, salted scorpions"; while another seized with colic might be asked to swallow a preparation made from horse-manure or, as an alternative, sow's excrement. I once procured from a Chinese drug-shop a typical prescription, consisting of about thirty different drugs mixed together to be taken as a dose, and the Protector of Chinese in Hongkong asked a Chinese physician, who had been educated in Europe, to translate it for me. He returned it, however, with most of the ingredients marked, "Substance unknown."

The greatest obstacle of all to any improvement of the masses of China is their profoundly ingrained superstition; this is common alike to officials and people, to the educated and the ignorant. The Viceroy of Nankin, Liu Kun-yi, recently declared that he had suddenly recovered his health in consequence of a vow to pay for ten days' theatricals to be performed on a stage before the shrine of Prince Siang-ting, a deified prince of the seventh century. When the Viceroy Chang's new iron-works were opened at Wuchang, the Chief Commissioner went through a ceremony of sacrificial worship before the various workshops, to ward off any evil influences. There is a wind- and water-compelling dragon known as Ta Wang, and he has a temple behind the Viceroy's yamên at Tientsin called the *Ta Wang-miao*. When a boat conveying a prefect and his family was nearly overwhelmed by a sudden storm, it was evident that the boatman with his long pole had inadvertently disturbed Ta Wang. On search being made a small snake was discovered near the railway bridge, and prostrations and apologies were at once made before it, and it was conveyed with great solemnity to the temple aforesaid. This occurred on August 11, 1890. It might be thought that intimacy with foreigners would destroy such beliefs; this, however, is far from being the case. The Chinaman born and bred in Hongkong or Singapore is every bit as superstitious as the Chinaman of the mainland. As an example of this I may tell the following story. One of the oldest inhabitants and most intelligent Chinamen in Hongkong had set his heart upon having two houses in a certain terrace to live in. At last his chance came and he bought them. Then he went to his lawyer and exclaimed in delight: "I would have given three times the sum for them!" "But why, there are plenty of better houses?" "Don't you know that house has the best *fêng-shui* of all Hongkong!" *Fêng-shui* means literally "wind and water," and refers to the geomantic or occult topographical influences. Even birth and half a lifetime under the British flag is not enough to eradicate the gross beliefs of the Chinaman. For instance, when an extensive reclamation of land at Singapore was begun by the Government, a colonial official had occasion one night to send his head-servant—a British subject and an old resident in the colony—on an errand into the town. He refused point-blank, and when asked his reason explained that no Chinaman would go down town at night for the next three nights because, as the Government were beginning their reclamation, they wanted a hundred Chinese heads to put at the bottom, and were on the look-out to catch Chinamen down-town and take their heads. During the recent plague at Hongkong placards were posted all over the city of Canton warning the people not to go to Hongkong, since their wives and children would run the risk of being chopped up by foreign doctors to make medicine out of their bones and eyes. This plague has had the effect of exhibiting the views of the Chinese mind with regard to foreigners and their ways perhaps more clearly than has ever occurred before. Mr. Sydney B. J. Skertchly, late of H. M. Geological Survey, has borne very remarkable testimony to this, and his words deserve the widest circulation and the closest attention. He says:—

"The sad fact has to be faced that some 200,000 Chinese are living voluntarily among us for the sake of the facilities the colony offers, and that they hate us, despise us, and fear us at the same time. Fifty years of British rule has taught them that we protect their lives and property better than their own countrymen, that wages and profits are better among us than in China proper, that we do not squeeze them, that our officials are not corrupt. In fine, that Hongkong is a temporary paradise where they are allowed to live as they like, to follow all their own customs, and where dollars are almost as easily earned as cash at home. They know, too, that we will educate them gratis, so that they can earn the high wages of the European clerk, and above all that when the loved dollar is netted no hungry mandarin will clamour for his share.

"In spite of all this they hate us and fear us. They acknowledge our skill as mechanics, they see our medical men and women daily minister to their wants unselfishly; but they dread the doctor more than the plague. They are firmly convinced that we destroy pregnant women, and cut out children's eyes to make our medicines, and they are taught this by their so-called educated classes. The Chinese mind is steeped in the most soul-destroying superstition. The dread *fêng shui*, the spirits of their ancestors, the myriads of demons that throng the air, are to them active principles, and as virulent as they are active. They know every European can cast spells over them, can, with an outward show of benefit, destroy their health, and they are sure we have deliberately caused this plague, for they see it passes the European by and slays the Chinaman. No African savage is more ground down by fetish than is the Chinaman by his superstitions. The way we designed this plague is to the Chinaman proof of our diabolic powers; we made a tramway up to the Peak! This interfered with the *fêng shui* by stopping the flow of benign influences from the south and causing the evil influences to stagnate in the island. Is not this proof positive? Were not the Chinese warned of the coming evil? Was not the sun eclipsed? Did not the bamboo flower this year? Is it not an established fact that all Englishmen can see the hidden treasures in the earth? Not one in a thousand has any doubts on these subjects. . . . Then we woke up and cleared out the filth, disclosing scenes of horror that no pen can describe. We pulled down the partitions in the rooms, we removed the people from the stricken haunts, we started hospitals, we nursed the sick, we buried the dead.

"And how did the Chinamen take it all? The answer is visible as I write, in the gunboat anchored off the China town, for they threatened to fire the city. They posted placards ascribing untellable atrocities to the doctors; they hid their sick from us; they refused to go to our hospitals, they threatened to poison the water supply. The viceroy of the province allowed Canton to be placarded with atrocious libels and threats against the European settlement, and he has stated to the governor of Hongkong that he will not guarantee the safety of the foreigners living in the country, though they have a right, under treaty, to be there. They nearly killed a lady doctor last week, who was attending to a sick coolie." *

Finally, the most important because the most fundamental fact to remember about the Chinese mind, is that theory and practice bear no relation whatever to each other. Chinese literature inculcates all the virtues: Chinese life exhibits all the vices. Chinese professions—and this is the point where foreign diplomatists have so often gone astray—are everything that is desirable: Chinese practices are everything that is most convenient. "The life and state papers of a Chinese statesman," wrote Mr. George Wingrove Cooke, "like the Confessions of Rousseau, abound in the finest sentiments and the foulest deeds. He cuts off ten thousand heads, and cites a passage from Mencius about the sanctity of human life. He pockets the money given him to repair an embankment, and thus inundates a province;

* *The Times.* Letter to the Editor. August 26, 1894.

and he deplores the land lost to the cultivator of the soil. He makes a treaty which he secretly declares to be only a deception for the moment, and he exclaims against the crime of perjury." One of the chief living authorities upon China has just declared the same truth, in those words:—" There is no country in the world where practice and profession are more widely separated than in China. The empire is pre-eminently one of make-believe. From the emperor to the meanest of his subjects a system of high-sounding pretension to lofty principles of morality holds sway; while the life of the nation is in direct contradiction to these assumptions. No imperial edict is complete, and no official proclamation finds currency, without pro-testations in favour of all the virtues. And yet few courts are more devoid of truth and uprightness, and no magistracy is more corrupt, than those of the celestial empire." * This con-trast was never more picturesquely shown than when the Emperor of China made his periodical procession with the sacred records. Here were documents of so sacred a character that hundreds of miles of roads were repaired for their passage; carried in shrines of Imperial yellow silk; escorted by high officials; preceded by the music of the Imperial band; and despatched on their journey by the Emperor in person—and yet the coolies who carried them actually jerked open the hangings of the shrines and threw in their indescribably filthy and vermin-haunted overcoats to be borne in state side by side with the boxes containing the precious records.†

My object in this chapter has been a simple one. I have at-tempted no complete analysis of any aspect of the Chinese character. Upon the virtues of the Chinese I have not even touched. But by describing a few of their views and vices I

* Professor Robert K. Douglas, "Society in China," London, 1894, p. iii. Professor Douglas's book tells the truth about China in so indisputable and enter-taining a manner, and he speaks with so much authority, that there is very little left for any one else, especially a much more superficial inquirer like myself, to say. I have omitted from this volume much of my material about China and my experi-ences there, simply because Professor Douglas's work appeared a few months ago and has covered the ground finally.   † *Chinese Times*, October 27, 1888.

have sought, first, to show how little likelihood there is of the reform of China coming, as Gordon believed it would ultimately come, from the inside ; and second, to make it clear that whatever change comes upon China from the outside, in consequence of recent events and the relations of foreign nations to one another, cannot be otherwise than a blessing to the Chinese people themselves.

CHAPTER XX.

THE FUTURE OF CHINA.

THERE is one building in Peking which every foreign visitor should be careful to see, not because it is in any sense a "sight," but because when its history and significance are understood it affords a great object-lesson on the relations of Chinese and foreigners. It is also necessarily the focus of any discussion of the future of China. This is the Tsungli Yamèn, the "Board of Foreign Affairs" for the Chinese Empire. My illustration shows its external appearance, and thereby hangs an instructive little tale. I desired permission to visit it and photograph it, and the Marquis Tsèng courteously endeavoured to procure this for me. This distinguished official, however, who was regarded by all Europe as one of the chief influences in modern China, who had negociated with half the Governments of Europe, who had set the world agog by a magazine article, and whose return to China was confidently expected to inaugurate a new era of sympathy with foreigners, was so destitute of authority in the capital of his own country and lay under so profound a suspicion of being permeated with the views of the "foreign devils," that he was actually unable to procure this small favour for me, and admitted the fact to me with his apologies. A friend thereupon applied on my behalf directly to Prince Ching, the Emperor's uncle and President of the Tsungli Yamèn, who instantly granted the permission and ordered several of the secretaries to make an appointment with me there. The buildings of the Tsungli Yamèn are not of a very imposing character, but they are superior to most Chinese public buildings in this respect, that they are in good repair. They consist of an external hall and a series of reception-rooms, leading finally to a small and trim Chinese garden. What they lack in appearance, however, is more than made up by the magnificence of the moral sentiments placarded upon them. The room in which I was received, and which serves, I was informed, as a reception-room for the Ministers of the foreign Powers, was a comparatively small one, containing a round table with a polished top, and a number of heavy black Chinese chairs. On one side of it were hung three scrolls, containing each a number of Chinese ideographs. The first of these reads, " When the tea is half [made] the fragrance arises." This I do not profess to interpret. Perhaps it is intended as an encouragement to persevere in the tortuous and interminable paths of Chinese diplomacy. The second declares, " To study is indeed excellent." The third, appearing where it does, can only be regarded in a humorous light. The most treacherous, untrustworthy, and unscrupulous set of diplomatists of modern times, of whom the united Ministers of foreign countries accredited to China have solemnly declared that no faith can be placed upon their assurances, meet their European colleagues beneath an inscription which reads, *Wei shan tsui lôh*—" To do good is the highest pleasure ! " In the large reception-room is the inscription, " May Heaven and Earth enjoy great peace "; while the inscription over the principal doorway, which is shown in my photograph and reproduced on the cover of this volume, is formed of the characters, *Chung wai ti fu*—literally " Centre, outside, peace, happiness "—China being the centre and the rest of the world the outside. The inscription thus means, " May China and foreign countries alike enjoy peace and happiness," an admirable sentiment, and one which the Tsungli Yamên has persistently done its best to falsify.

The future of China depends upon the relations of China and foreign countries—that is all that can be said of it with certainty.

A discussion of its future therefore amounts to a discussion of the history and prospects of its foreign relations. The Tsungli Yamèn, as I have said, is at the focus of those. It was founded by a remarkable man, Prince Kung, in 1861, after the war with China had come to a close and the Treaty of Tientsin was signed at the Board of Rites on October 25th, 1860, by Lord Elgin. By this treaty, foreign representatives were received at Peking, large indemnities were paid, the Roman Catholics were compensated for the destruction of their buildings, Chinese emigration was sanctioned, and Kowloon was added to Hongkong. A new era in the relations of the "centre" and the "outside" was thus inaugurated, and some new point of contact became essential. To meet this demand Prince Kung founded the Tsungli Yamèn, and remained at its head until 1884, when, after rendering very great services to China, and showing himself to be a man of great sense and power, he was suddenly disgraced for the second time, and deprived of all his offices. He was succeeded by Prince Ching, who died during the present year, when to the surprise of every one, Prince Kung, after ten years of degradation and inactivity, was again appointed by the same decree President of the Tsungli Yamèn, President of the Admiralty, and co-director with Li Hung-chang of the operations of war. The Tsungli Yamèn consists of the President, eight Ministers, six Chief Secretaries, two Assistant Secretaries, and thirty clerks of Department apportioned as follows:—English Department six, French Department seven, Russian Department six, United States Department seven, Maritime Defence Department four; and six superintendents of current business and the Manchu Registry Department. To "Their Excellencies His Imperial Highness the Prince of Kung and the Ministers of the Tsungli Yamèn" are addressed all communications from the foreign Ministers at the Court of China, and from it all Chinese representatives abroad receive their appointments and instructions. Theoretically the arrangement is an admirable one; practically, it has been an almost uninterrupted failure. If the

Chinese Ministers desired to promote foreign relations, the
organisation of the Tsungli Yamên would be perfectly suited to
their wish; as a matter of fact, they desire to obstruct foreign
relations and have moulded their institution accordingly. In the
first place, the Tsungli Yamên, while theoretically possessing
supreme political authority, has not possessed it practically.
The Emperor, and still more the Empress, have demanded a
considerable share of personal influence upon current politics,
and Li Hung-chang has always been the avowed rival of the
Tsungli Yamên, and with him most foreign arrangements have
been ultimately concluded. In the second place, the Tsungli
Yamên has never insisted upon its own authority for the defence
of foreign rights. Margary was treacherously murdered while
travelling with a special safe-conduct issued by this Board, and
beyond the money indemnity to his relatives, no punishment
was ever dealt out to his murderers. Missionaries have been
murdered on many occasions, in spite of the assurance of the
Tsungli Yamên that the strictest orders for their protection had
been issued. Chow Han, the well-known author of the vile
anti-foreign placards, is still unpunished. Rights assigned by
treaty have been deliberately suffocated under years of diplomatic
correspondence. In fact, so obstructive have the Ministers of
the Tsungli Yamên become of late that the foreign representatives regard it as a mere waste of time to enter upon the
discussion of any point with regard to which they are not prepared to insist upon an immediate settlement, by force of arms
if need be. Any Minister or Secretary of Legation who goes to
the Yamên is deliberately wearied out by needless talking,
ceaselessly recurring trivialities, an incredible fertility of puerile
argument—one of the reasons solemnly given for delaying the
treaty right of navigation of the Upper Yangtze was that the
monkeys on the banks were so mischievous that they would
throw stones on the deck of the steamers, and thus kill the
foreigners; and finally, by grudging promises made only to be
broken. Sir Harry Parkes declared that to get any definite

answer from the Tsungli Yamên was "like trying to draw water from a well, with a bottomless bucket." Whatever the Tsungli Yamên may have been created to do, it has served only to head off foreigners and postpone the satisfaction of their legitimate demands. It is to-day the great stronghold of Chinese procrastination.

Little or nothing, then, has been accomplished by this institution towards bringing China and Europe nearer together. In further support of this opinion, which will no doubt meet with much criticism, I will only refer back to the opinion of the present British Minister to China, as quoted in the preceding chapter, to the effect that foreign influence is not so great to-day as it was a few years ago. To see how small it is, take the recent example of the unprovoked murder of the two Swedish missionaries, Messrs. Wikholm and Johansson, at Sung-pu. In response to much pressure the Chinese promised to punish not only the murderers, but the officials and the Viceroy himself, all of whom were clearly among the instigators of the crime. The Swedish Consul foolishly accepted a small money indemnity, against which all his colleagues protested, and appealed to the Ministers of the Powers to make a united demand upon the Imperial Government for the execution of its promise. The Viceroy in question was Chang Chih-tung, whose offences against foreigners are legion. So far from being punished or disgraced in accordance with the undertaking given, Chang Chih-tung has received a series of distinguished honours, culminating with his appointment to the head of the scheme of Army reform. Except under direct pressure, or in an extremity of fear, the Chinese Government has never done anything to punish outrages upon foreigners. The Rev. Mr. Wylie was brutally murdered at Niuchwang by Chinese soldiers at the outbreak of the present war, and as the Chinese authorities naturally feared that any procrastination at that moment might bring the British as well as the Japanese down upon them, they promptly beheaded half-a-dozen privates and disgraced their officers. The same fear of

immediate foreign interference has just caused them to issue the
following edict in Peking :—

China is under obligation to exercise extra precaution for the protection of
(Christian) churches, missionaries, and other foreigners in the capital. We, as in
duty bound, give stringent orders to soldiers and people that they must, as hereto-
fore, behave amicably (towards foreigners). Let every one attend to his own
business and thus he will not wantonly listen to evil rumours or join in circulating
them. Should any dare to disobey orders let them instantly be seized and sent in
chains to this Yamên, where they will be severely punished, no leniency being
shown them. The American Missionary Headland and his wife were insulted and
reviled by local roughs outside the Chi-Hua Gate. We have already severely reprimanded the local officials, and the ruffian offender, Wang Yao-erh, has been taken,
and, as is right, will be severely punished by this Yamên. We further issue this
proclamation in the hope that there may be everlasting mutual amity (between
natives and foreigners). The local officials and police must honestly search out
offenders.

If our officials had properly insisted, this would have been done,
of course, years ago. So, too, the latest rumour is that the
Chinese Government is prepared to make foreign nations the
concession of opening two more ports to trade. They offer
two, of course, under the fear that twenty may be otherwise
demanded.

Now whose fault is this? The answer is easy. It is entirely
due to the supine attitude of foreign Governments with regard
to China, which, again, has sprung, so far as this country is
concerned, chiefly from the fantastic belief that China might be
a valuable ally in Asia and therefore must not be offended. The
one representative we have had in Peking who really understood
the Chinese and had his way with them, was Sir Harry Parkes.
Sir John Walsham introduced for the first time the manners of
the great world to the Court of China. With much personal
charm and dignity he conducted his diplomatic relations with
the Tsungli Yamên as he would have conducted them with the
Foreign Offices of Paris, Berlin, or Rome. The result was total
failure, unmitigated by the faintest redeeming success.

The history of the famous so-called "audience question"
points the same moral. The first Ambassadors to China were
required to perform the *Kotow*—knocking their heads nine times

against the ground in the Imperial presence. Lord Macartney, in 1793, refused to do this, and had an audience of the Emperor Kienlung, at which he merely bent the knee. Lord Amhurst refused to do it in 1816 to the Emperor Kia King, and had no audience. In 1873 the corps of Foreign Ministers refused either to perform the *Kotow* or to go down on one knee as Lord Macartney had done, and the Chinese Ministers accordingly arranged an interview at a place set apart for the reception of the Ambassadors of " tribute nations " like Korea. The foreign Ministers—to their disgrace be it said—fell into this trap and thus lowered the prestige of all Europeans for a generation. In 1891 " all the nations " were again received in the same place. In 1893 the British Minister was received with the same empty form, but in an Imperial temple; and during the present war he is said to have been received by the Emperor in person, within the enclosure of the Palace itself. It has thus taken a century and the dire extremity of a foreign war to enable a representative of Great Britain to be received by the Emperor of China as he would be received by any European Sovereign. As Professor Douglas says, " we have humbly implored, to use the Emperor's own words. to be admitted into the Imperial presence, and we have reaped our reward." Chinese representatives of all sorts have been accredited to the Court of St. James. They have often been men of no personal standing in their own country, but thought good enough to be foisted upon the outer barbarians. We have received them with the most elaborate honours, have accorded them the most formal and distinguished reception, and have even permitted them access, as a matter of right, into the personal presence of the Sovereign. All this time our own representatives have been snubbed, insulted, and deliberately humiliated in China, and have only been admitted into the Emperor's presence by an act of supreme condescension, accorded to them as an opportunity of laying the homage of the barbarians at the feet of the Son of Heaven. It is high time this ignoble farce came to an end.

In any consideration of the relation of Chinese and foreigners, the much-vexed Missionary Question cannot be passed over. I hold very strong opinions about this, but I will express them as briefly and as moderately as I can. I believe it to be strictly within the limits of truth to say that foreign missionary effort in China has been productive of far more harm than good. Instead of serving as a link between Chinese and foreigners, the missionaries have formed a growing obstacle. As travellers in the East well know, Oriental peoples are especially susceptible upon two points, of which their religion is the chief. We have forced the inculcation of an alien and a detested creed upon the Chinese, literally at the point of the bayonet. That very competent observer, Mr. Alexander Michie, whom I have previously quoted, sums up the results of missionary enterprise as having produced for the Chinese Government perpetual foreign coercion; for the Chinese nation, an incessant ferment of angry passions and a continuous education in ferocity against Christianity; for the foreign missionaries, pillage and massacre at intervals, followed by pecuniary indemnification—an indefinite struggle with the hatred of a whole nation, compensated by a certain number of genuine converts to their faith.* Of the truth of this, so far as concerns the attitude of the natives toward the missionary, a member of the China Inland Mission has just given striking evidence :—

> The Chi-nan-fu fop, dressed in silks and satins, flipping his sleeves in the face of a respectable foreign visitor met in the street; the middle-aged scholar, dressed as a gentleman, not thinking it beneath him to hiss out " foreign devil " or simply " devil "; young and old spitting on the ground in bitterness close to the visitor's feet, laughing right in his face, or on passing, turning sharply round and making a most hateful noise at his ear—these are some of the petty annoyances that the literati and gentry practise; underlings easily carry on the treatment to something more spiteful and serious than this.†

A careful distinction must be made, however, between Roman Catholic and Protestant missionaries. The former enjoy, on

* " Missionaries in China," by Alexander Michie, 1891, p. 71.
† China's Millions, September, 1894.

the whole, far more consideration from the natives, as well as from foreigners, and the result of their work is beyond question much greater. The Roman Catholic missionary goes to China once for all; he adopts native dress, lives on native food, inhabits a native house, supports himself upon the most meagre allowance from home, and is an example of the characteristics which are as essential to the eastern idea of priesthood as to the western—poverty, chastity, and obedience. To borrow the words of Sir W. Hunter, he has "cut himself off from the world by a solemn act." More than that, he meets native superstitions half-way by amalgamating the worship of ancestors, which is a vital part of every Chinaman's belief, to the worship of the Saints; and by teaching his native converts a prayer for the Emperor of China, which concludes with the petition, "de Le conserver jusqu'à une heureuse vieillesse, en prolongeant la prosperité de Son Empire, afin que nous puissions plûtard jouir *avec Lui* de la paix éternelle." He is also subject to one authority, and preaches and practises one doctrine. The two chief grounds of reproach against him are first, that in China as elsewhere he is nearly always a political agent; and second, that many a dangerous suspicion has been aroused by his habit of paying small sums for dying children, for the purpose of baptising them *in articulo mortis.*

To any one who has read my chapter on Manila, I need not explain that I am not prejudiced in favour of the Roman Catholic propaganda; yet I should not be honest if I did not add that for the personal character and the work of many a Roman Catholic missionary whom I have met in China, I have conceived a profound respect. The Protestant missionary, on the other hand, in a majority of cases, looks upon his work as a career like another; he proposes to devote a certain amount of his life to it, and then to return home with the halo of the Christian pioneer; he has, in most cases, his comfortable house, his wife, his children, his servants and his foreign food, and it is even stated that his stipend increases with each addition to his

family. For his doctrine he is virtually responsible to nobody but
himself. Whatever his own views upon the mysteries of Christianity happen to be, those he impresses upon his native hearers as
the one and only truth. He is jealous of his Protestant rivals,
between whom and himself there is a perpetual warfare of pious
intrigue to secure converts. So far as education goes, both men
and women among Protestant missionaries are often quite un-
fitted even to teach at home, where there would be little danger
of serious misunderstanding ; in their present sphere of work
they are often not too hardly described by the phrase which has
been applied to them—"ignorant declaimers in bad Chinese."
"The Protestant missionaries who enjoy the respect of their
compatriots," says one writer, "are the exception, not
the rule, and owe their reputation more to sinological ac-
complishments than to ecclesiastical prestige."[*] Protestant
missionary tracts are distributed bearing coarse illustrations
of such Biblical incidents as the swallowing of Jonah by
the whale, and the killing of Sisera by Jael. Moreover, up
to the present, the Protestant missionaries have circulated the
whole Bible in Chinese. They have recently seen their error,
and are now considering the advisability of following in the
steps of the more circumspect Roman Catholics, and withholding
certain parts obviously unfit for Oriental comprehension. Their
failure to do this hitherto has resulted in parodies of the most
vital doctrines of orthodox Protestantism being spread all over
China, of a brutality so revolting and ferocious as to be beyond
all possibility of mention. Again, they reproduce in China all
the petty sectarian divisions of their own country. I quote
a list of these from a missionary address. There are three
branches of the Episcopal Church, nine sects of Presbyterians,
six sects of Methodists, two sects of Congregationalists, two sects
of Baptists, besides several minor bodies. In Shanghai alone
there are seven missions—the London Mission, American
Presbyterian, the American Episcopal, the American Episcopal

* Balfour, "Waifs and Strays from the Far East," p. 118.

Methodists, the Church Missionary Society, the American Baptists, and the Seventh-Day Baptists. "Here, then," says the Rev. Dr. Williamson, "we have seven sets of foreign missionaries working seven different churches; seven sermons every Sunday, seven sets of prayer meetings, seven sets of communing services, seven sets of schools, two training agencies, seven sets of buildings, seven sets of expenses, four or five versions of the Bible, and seven different hymn-books at least." In the face of these facts, one is surely justified in saying that we have not yet reached a point of Christian unity which affords us any moral justification for thrusting our theological views by force of arms upon heathen nations.

I am well aware, of course, that to some missionaries the world is deeply indebted for its knowledge of the Chinese language and literature; and that among the Protestant missionaries of the present day there are some men of the highest character and devotion, upon whose careers no criticism can be passed. These, however, are a small minority. The Chinese themselves bracket missionaries and opium together as the twin curses of the country, and although it is true that among Christian converts have been men who have shown under persecution all the characteristics of the early Christian martyrs, it is equally true that the ordinary foreigner carefully avoids the employment of the native Christian in any subordinate capacity, having found by experience that in many cases he has only lost his native virtues to acquire foreign vices in their place. Conversion to Christianity is looked upon by many natives merely as a means of an easier livelihood. A friend of mine asked a Chinese servant whom he had previously known, what he was engaged in doing. He replied: "My have got that Jesus pidgin." He was no more intentionally irreverent in saying this than I am in quoting it; he merely meant that the profession of Christianity, with its comfortable concomitants, was his new occupation. Mr. Michie declares that were the alliance of the Christian nations with the military

Powers of the West to be brought to an end, a chief root of bitterness would be extracted from the Chinese mind. For my own part, I am convinced that if the subscribers to Chinese missions could only see for themselves the minute results of good and the considerable results of harm that their money produces, they would find in the vast opportunities for reformatory work at home a more attractive field for their charity. At any rate, in considering the future of China the missionary influence cannot be counted upon for any good.

The prospects of future reform in China may be estimated from the fate of her railway schemes. In 1876 the first railway in China was laid by a foreign firm from Shanghai to Wusung, where the notorious bar on the Shanghai River interrupts the traffic. It was well patronised, paid a dividend at once, and after running sixteen months was purchased by the Chinese authorities, who no sooner came into possession of it than they tore it up and shipped the materials over to Formosa. Under its energetic Governor, Liu Ming-chuan, now Commander-in-chief of the Chinese army, a railway was built in Formosa, and prospered for a time under foreign management; but the foreigners have almost all been dismissed—from 1886 to 1889 there were no fewer than six consulting "chief engineers" in succession in the Governor's service—and the working of the railway is now a farce. Six or seven years ago an Imperial edict was issued, declaring that "to make a country powerful, railways are essential," but the reactionaries at Court succeeded the progressives in their influence upon the Emperor, and a subsequent edict declared that "they must only be built with Chinese money." That is, they must be postponed indefinitely, for the Imperial Government in China is always poverty-stricken, and the wealthy Chinese would not dream of putting their money into a Chinese official scheme. But at this time foreigners were so confident that the era of railway construction in China had at last dawned, and that the consequent opening up of the vast Celestial Empire was about to begin in earnest, that long descriptions of the route of the first " Great Western Railway of China " were published; the Emperor called for reports from the leading provincial Viceroys; and the talk was of nothing but railways. The Imperial family, and Liu Ming-chuan, and a few others were strongly in favour of the introduction of railways, and against this powerful combination the conservative officials could not prevail directly. So they cunningly adopted the round-about method of declaring that not only must the railways be built with Chinese money, but that the ore must be mined and smelted, and the rails made, in China, since otherwise foreigners would acquire an influence so great as to be dangerous to the stability of the Throne, and would profit by enormous sums which ought to be spent in China. The result was that nothing whatever was done, and the subject has not been heard of for five years. The original proposals were to build one line from Liu-ko-chiao, near Peking, to either Hankow, the great port on the Yangtze, in Hupeh, or to Chinkiang, near the junction of the Grand Canal and the Yangtze, in Kiangsu. Another short line was to connect Tungchow, the village at which one leaves the Peiho River for Peking, with Tientsin, and thereby place the capital in communication with the coast; while a third, which would certainly prove an extremely prosperous undertaking and which British capitalists have long been eager to build, would connect Canton with British Kowloon, and thus bring the commercial metropolis of China into close relations with the great port of Hongkong. An American mining expert who had charge for a time of the largest silver mines in China, gave me this interesting explanation of the failure of the Chinese to take any steps with regard to railways. They desire, he said, to do the biggest thing at once. They reason thus: Great Britain, with 38,000,000 population, has 20,000 miles of railway; therefore China, with 350,000,000, ought to have x miles. They will not buy rails abroad: they insist upon making them; and they will not make iron rails, which they could easily do, and which would serve just as well for their light

traffic. They must have steel ones. But steel rails cannot be
made cheaply except on a very large scale, say the smelting of
250 tons of ore a day, and without long experience; and with
the Chinese habits such an output is utterly impossible, no
matter what the mines may be. They have already discovered
excellent iron mines, but as the phosphorus limit is exceeded,
steel cannot be made there, and they will not make iron. Moreover, they sent two Englishmen and two Germans to seek
for steel-making iron and coal throughout the provinces of
Southern China. This, again, was wrong—English and German
methods of work are entirely different, and the task should have
been assigned exclusively to one or the other.

One railway only have the Chinese—or, rather, has Li Hung-
chang—pushed towards completion. It was first laid from
Tientsin to the coal mines at Kaiping—80 miles. It is now
completed as far as Shan-hai-kwan, where the Great Wall
reaches the coast, a total distance of 180 miles, which a fast
train is supposed to cover in eight hours. It was next to be
extended to the Taling River, an addition of 128 miles—and
40 miles of earthworks at one end and 38 at the other have
been practically completed—whence one branch would run
south through Kinchow to Port Arthur, and another north to
Mukden and ultimately to the very important strategic city of
Kirin. The war has, of course, put a complete stop to this for
the present, but before the war broke out the birthday of the
Empress-Dowager came in sight, and the railway subsidy of
2,000,000 taels was promptly diverted to swell the funds for
celebrating the occasion. Foreigners have pointed out to the
Chinese authorities again and again, that without this railway
they could hold neither Port Arthur nor the sacred and rich
province of Manchuria, but no attention was paid to the
warnings, and now the inevitable result has come. Except as
the result of foreign pressure, China is as little likely to build
railways—except possibly for purely strategic and defensive
purposes—as she is to introduce any other feature of reform or
progress.

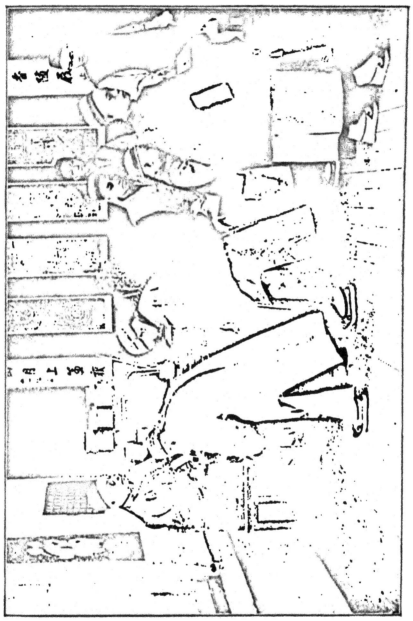

A CHINESE SCHOOL: VICTIMS OF CONFUCIUS.

police, competitors, doctors, cooks, tailors, and executioner, for
any offence within the sacred enclosure is punished by death—is
shut up irrevocably during the nine days that the examination
lasts. The strain is, of course, intense, and competitors frequently die from the close confinement and extremely insanitary
surroundings. As a specimen of the subjects of examinations,
the following passage from the Analects of Confucius was one of
the themes in the last competition at Nankin:—"Confucius
said, 'How majestic was the manner in which Shun and Yu
held possession of the empire, as if it were nothing to them.'
Confucius said, 'Great indeed was Yaou as a sovereign! How
majestic was he! It is only Heaven that is grand and only
Yaou corresponded to it! How vast was his virtue! The
people could find no name for it!'" The competitors, that is,
were simply invited to write an essay in the most extravagant
style of eulogy upon the wisdom of the sage as exhibited in this
passage. Three weeks after the examination, the names of the
hundred successful are published, and the happy ones are more
than repaid for what has often been a lifetime of study, by the
honours that await them. No actual reward of any kind is
conferred upon the "Promoted Scholar," but his position has
been compared with that of a victor in the Olympian Games,
and his fortunate family shares in his fame. He mounts a
larger gilt button upon his hat, places a tablet over his door,
erects a couple of flagstaffs before his house, and plunges into
study again for the third and final examination of the following
spring. "Though ordinarily not very devout, he now shows
himself peculiarly solicitous to secure the favour of the gods.
He burns incense and gives alms. If he sees a fish floundering
on the hooks, he pays its price and restores it to its native
element. He picks struggling ants out of the rivulet made by a
recent shower, distributes moral tracts, or better still, rescues
chance bits of printed paper from being trodden in the mire of
the streets." The final struggle takes place in Peking, and is,
of course, more difficult and even stricter than the preceding,

for success in it means public office — the offices being distributed among the successful by lot. Beyond this triumph, however, there is still a possible pinnacle of literary glory, namely, to be selected by the Emperor himself as the best of all the successful competitors in Peking, and to receive the title of *Chang-yüan*—say, " Poet Laureate "—the finest flower of the literary culture of the Celestial Empire. To have produced such a man is the highest honour to which any province can aspire ; the town of his birth is immortalised, and his happy parents are regarded as the greatest benefactors of the State.

As at present organised, this system of competitive examination has its excellent side. The Rev. Dr. Martin, who has written a luminous analysis of the system,* gives three great merits. First, the system serves the State as a safety-valve, providing a career for ambitious spirits who might otherwise foment disturbances. Second, it operates as a counterpoise to the power of an absolute monarch, since without it the great offices would be filled by hereditary nobles, and the minor ones by Imperial favourites. Every schoolboy is taught to repeat a line which declares that " the General and the Prime Minister are not born in office." It constitutes, in fact, the democratic element in the Chinese Constitution. Third, it gives the Government a hold on the educated gentry, and binds these to the support of existing institutions. " In districts where the people have distinguished themselves by zeal in the Imperial cause, the only recompense they crave is a slight addition to the numbers on the competitive prize list." On the other hand, the evils of the system are sufficiently obvious. Its sole effect, so far as education and the government of China are concerned, is to limit knowledge to the moral and intellectual level of the far past. As an example of the pitilessly mechanical character of the Chinese culture which this system promotes, the following

* " Hanlin Papers," by W. A. P. Martin, D.D., LL.D., Peking, 1880, p. 51.

sketch of the rise and fall of a Chinese literate is illuminating:—

"The provincial records have not been revised for many years, and thus are not available to determine what success Kwangsi has had in the examinations at Peking; but there are those who say that not for a century had a Kwangsi man taken first, second, third, or fourth place until 1889. In that year Chang Chien-hsün secured the highest honours. He was born in 1856 of a very poor family, of Hunan origin, living in Lin-kuei-hsien, Kuei-lin-fu. He became a *hsiu-tsai* at the age of 15, a *chü-jén* at 23, and *chuang-yüan* 10 years later. The story goes that in all the examinations before taking the *chü-jén* degree he was easily first, and his talents attracted the attention of Yang Chung-ya, appointed Governor of Kwangsi in 1876, who promised him his grand-daughter in marriage. We may suppose that from that time his poverty was not allowed to interfere with the prosecution of his studies. After Mr. Chang's success at Peking, he became, as is usual, a compiler in the Hanlin College. Unfortunately, the career which opened so well has received a sudden check. The report reached Kwangsi this summer that the *chuang-yüan* of 1889, in the course of tests upon the result of which depended appointment to the provincial literary offices, wrote another character of the same sound in the place of one he intended, as if, for example (the illustration is intended for readers unfamiliar with China), in writing of the position of the subject in the State, he had spoken of his *rites* and duties. The reader acquainted with Chinese feeling will understand how much worse than any moral delinquency was this error." *

The competitive system is the door beyond which lies the way to the civilisation of China. Upon that door is written the word Confucius; and unless this is erased and the word Truth substituted, China must remain the victim of more enlightened races, even until she be finally dismembered and disappear. If, however, any pressure could be found strong enough to provide for modern teaching in her provincial centres, and for the westernisation of her topics of competitive examination, with offices as rewards for those who distinguish themselves in the different branches of modern science, China might emerge from her slough of Confucian ignorance, prejudice, cruelty, and corruption. As Dr. Martin says, "If the examiners were scientific men, and if scientific subjects were made sufficiently prominent in these higher examinations, millions of aspiring students would soon become as earnest in the pursuit of modern science

* Chinese Imp. Maritime Customs, Decennial Reports, 1882-1891, Mr. G. G. Clarke's Report on Lungchow, p. 656.

as they now are in the study of their ancient classics." Nothing could have so great an effect in moulding the future of China as the modernisation of her best-preserved and most ancient institution.

War has once more given us our opportunity. Japan has pricked the bubble of the "awakening" of China, and has exhibited the Chinese Government as the imposture it really is. Without in the least exercising our power to dictate to Japan the terms she may make so far as regards herself—which we have not the faintest right to do—we must not fail to control the results of the peace so far as other nations are concerned. First of all, we must insist upon the opening of treaty ports wherever these may be required for foreign trade. It would, perhaps, be inadvisable to insist upon the opening of the whole of China at present, until the people of the remoter districts have had time to learn that we are only peaceful traders, and not barbarians, though if this should be possible, no scruples regarding extraterritoriality should be allowed to stand in the way for a moment. Second, we must insist upon foreign representatives being received by the Emperor himself at regular intervals, and under such circumstances as to make it clear that the honours of the audiences are divided; and the Ministers of the State must realise once for all that diplomacy and procrastination are not synonymous terms. Third, for the protection of our future interests in the Far East, we must secure by purchase, exchange, or otherwise, a naval base a thousand miles north of Hongkong. This is an absolute necessity, and there will not again be such an opportunity for acquiring it. Chusan at once suggests itself, if we do not want the responsibility of taking Formosa, which has no harbour. Chusan has been occupied by us before; it has an excellent harbour, which can be easily fortified and made impregnable; and it is at the mouth of the great trade route of China. But this is a point that our naval authorities must decide. Fourth, the literal fulfilment of our previous convention with China regarding Indian trade with Thibet must now be demanded. The Chinese will say that they cannot guarantee that the Thibetans will not oppose us by force. This is quite true—it is wholly out of the power of the Emperor of China to give any such guarantee. Our answer must be that in that case we will look after ourselves. The present moment is the turning-point in our relations with China, and it must not be allowed to pass. China, we must never forget, yields only to pressure. She has never been opened except by war, and will never admit reform except at the point of the bayonet or at the sight of the ironclad.

It may be said that I am calmly assigning the predominant role in the present situation to Great Britain, to the exclusion of other Powers. To this I unhesitatingly reply that the predominant role belongs to us, and that it is not our policy to exclude anybody, for, unlike other nations, whatever we get is thrown open to the whole world. Beside the commercial interests of England in China, those of all other nations are almost insignificant. This is an assertion which can be proved in a moment. Take the question of foreigners in China first. On December 31, 1891, a census was taken in all the treaty ports of China, including the two Customs stations of Lappa and Kowloon, by the Chinese Customs service. These were the results :—

	British.	American.	French.	German.	Portuguese.	Spanish.	Italian.
Residents ...	3,746	1,200	681	667	659	316	133
Firms ...	345	27	24	82	7	5	4

That is, in the Treaty Ports alone, there were 3,746 Britishers and 345 British firms, against 3,811 subjects and 161 firms of all the other European Powers and the United States put together. But to this must be added the British population and firms in Hongkong and Singapore trading with China, by far our most important representatives in the Far East. When this addition is made, it is clearly not too much to say that the interests of other nations are insignificant in comparison.

Second, take the question of trade. The figures furnish the following astonishing results :—

FOREIGN TRADE OF CHINA WITH EACH COUNTRY, 1898.

	Haikwan Taels.
Continent of Europe, except Russia 21,070,968	
United States 17,109,218	
Russia 10,307,748	48,507,944
Great Britain and British Possessions	195,710,240

That is—taking the Haikwan tael roughly at four shillings (it averaged 3s. 11¼d. in 1898)—the total trade of Great Britain and British possessions for 1898 amounted to £39,000,000, against £9,700,000 for the whole continent of Europe (except Turkey) and the United States. These are the figures given by the Customs, but a considerable reduction must be made from British trade in view of the fact that a good deal of the trade passing through Hongkong and Singapore is not British. It is impossible to calculate how much this is, but to show the overwhelming superiority of British trade, let us suppose that Hongkong and Singapore, our greatest trading centres with China, were wiped off the map, with all their trade. Even in that case British trade would still stand at 62,288,486 taels, or £12,400,000 against £9,700,000 for all our civilised competitors put together ! If under these circumstances we do not recognise that we are the predominant Power in all foreign relations with China, and act accordingly, then we are indeed unworthy of the heritage of good fortune that sturdier Englishmen have made and bequeathed to us.

In all the foregoing I have written upon the supposition that at the conclusion of the present war we may still have a united China to deal with. This, however, may well not be the case. The Abbé Huc, Cooke, and Gordon, all thought that the Chinese Empire would possibly one day collapse, and indeed the ties which hold it together are much weaker than is realised by most people. The victory of the Japanese, if carried beyond a certain point, would quite surely bring about the downfall of the present dynasty, seated as it is upon an insecure throne. If China, however, is torn asunder or falls to pieces, then a much vaster problem will face us. For in that case we shall find ourselves face to face with the momentous suggestion of Asia for the Asiatics. Upon this I shall have something to say in a later chapter.